PYRAMIDS
AND
FLESHPOTS

PYRAMIDS
AND
FLESHPOTS

The Egyptian, Senussi and
Eastern Mediterranean
Campaigns, 1914–16

S TUART H ADAWAY

To the memory of David Moscato
1951–2013
Who taught me all I know about horses, and much else besides.

First published 2014
by Spellmount, an imprint of

The History Press
The Mill, Brimscombe Port
Stroud, Gloucestershire, GL5 2QG
www.thehistorypress.co.uk

British Library Cataloguing in Publication Data.
A catalogue record for this book is available from the British Library.

ISBN 978 0 7524 9906 2

Typesetting and origination by Thomas Bohm, User design
Printed in Great Britain

CONTENTS

FOREWORD

I was delighted to be asked to write a brief foreword to this book, *Pyramids and Fleshpots*, as much of the content mirrors the experiences of officers and soldiers from my former regiment, The Queen's Own Warwickshire and Worcestershire Yeomanry which, prior to amalgamation in 1956, served in the First World War, in the Middle East as separate county yeomanry regiments, The Warwickshire Yeomanry and The Queen's Own Worcestershire Hussars. Their movements, over the four years of warfare and policing duties, can be traced in many of the chapters throughout this book.

Over the next four or five years, as we approach the one hundredth anniversary of The Great War, the British public will learn a great deal about the First World War through exposure to images and stories in the media. These images are most likely to feature the Western Front in France and Belgium as it dominated much of the news at the time.

However, on other fronts, namely Gallipoli and the Middle East, the British and Dominion Troops were fighting a very formidable enemy in the shape of the soldiers of the Ottoman Empire.

Into these theatres of war stepped cavalry and infantry regiments from Britain and overseas, many of these units formed from Territorial or Reserve soldiers who had no experience of fighting in battle except for those, relatively few in number, who volunteered to serve with the Imperial Yeomanry during the Boer War.

These untried and untested soldiers would play a crucial role at Gallipoli, being forced to trade their sabres and horses for bayonets and infantry backpacks and experiencing the horrors of trench warfare in the blazing heat of the peninsula. When the campaign in Gallipoli was brought to an end the much depleted regiments were withdrawn to Egypt to regroup, re-equip and take their places in the order of battle in the Sinai and Palestinian campaigns as part of the Egyptian Expeditionary Force (EEF). They would learn the tactics of desert warfare, some would learn to ride camels rather than the familiar mounts they had ridden at home and many would experience for the first time the intoxicating atmosphere of the Middle East, many taking a step outside their country, or indeed their county for the first time.

This book paints a fascinating and detailed picture of the preparations for the protection of the Suez Canal and how critical it was to the Allied war effort to maintain the flow of traffic through the Canal to ensure the passage of goods to and from the Empire.

This book would be a first-class read for those who make a study of the war in the Middle East; however, it also provides a fascinating glimpse, for the casual, interested reader, at the life of the soldier from Britain and the Empire, as well as Ottoman Turkey, who served in this theatre for four long, hot, dusty years, where the reliance was on your comrades and your horse.

Colonel (Ret'd) Stamford J. Cartwright MBE TD
Chairman Worcestershire Yeomanry Museum Trust
January 2014

NOTE ON NAMES, QUOTES, TERMINOLOGY AND FOOT/END NOTES

This book principally concerns two empires, each of which contained numerous nationalities and ethnic groups. As a rule, I have kept to the terms 'Ottoman' and 'British' to refer to the political entities of the opposing forces. The forces of the British Empire and its Allies in Egypt are generally referred to as 'the British', although they also included (among others) Australians, New Zealanders and Indians. Where particular nationalities were the majority of the forces involved, due credit has been given. The Ottoman Army mainly consisted of Turkish troops from Anatolia, although it also included Arab and Bedouin forces. Again, the term 'Ottoman' has been used as a cover-all, with particular sub-contingents credited where appropriate.

I have taken a few liberties with the official British Army nomenclature of First World War combats. The official system says that any engagement that involved less than a full division of British troops (roughly 18,000 men) was an 'Affair'. If it involved one or more complete divisions, it was an 'Action', and one or more complete army corps (each about 38,000–40,000 men) upgraded the fight to being a full 'Battle'. This system was drawn up by the Army Council in 1920 to standardise the terminology in the official histories and for battle honours, and was very much based on the standards of the Western Front. It was recognised that it was less than fair on some of the peripheral campaigns, where fewer troops were involved, and indeed by these standards the only true 'Battle' in the Egyptian theatre between 1914 and 1916 was Romani. However, considering that the defence of the Suez Canal in February 1915 involved, directly or as reserves, the whole of the British forces in Egypt, and took place over a front of 100 miles, I have unofficially promoted this to the status of 'Battle', too.

A certain amount of liberty has also been taken with Arab or Ottoman names, be they places or people. For places, I have largely stuck to the names used at the time (i.e. Constantinople instead of Istanbul and Cairo for al-Qāhirah) or the most common spelling. Arabic names get recorded in an entertainingly varied number of ways in Western sources, but I have taken the most common and, except in direct quotes, stuck with that. For the names of persons, given the difficulties of Anglicising Arab or Ottoman words, I have used my own judgement on which is the most acceptable translation.

It should also be noted that some of the words used in quotes are very much 'of their time' when it comes to opinions regarding the locals in Egypt. These have been left in as reflecting the honest views of those present, even if they are utterly unacceptable today.

I have used both footnotes and endnotes. As a rule, footnotes (at the bottom of the page) give additional information that is directly relevant to the matter at hand, but would clog up the text too much, i.e. the units that constituted various columns or forces. Generally I only do this for temporary formations put together for a particular action or campaign, and for the composition of permanent formations I recommend that you consult the Orders of Battles in the Appendices.

Endnotes are mostly references, citing where certain information came from or recommending where you can find out more. However, some do also give further information that is (to my mind) interesting, but not really vital to the overall story.

ACKNOWLEDGEMENTS

I would like to thank many people for their help while researching and writing this book. On the home front, I'd particularly like to acknowledge my debt to Nina for her constant support, understanding, advice and patience, and to my parents for their support. A special thank you goes to Marnie for her help on SW duties.

More professionally, as always David Buttery has been a great help, and I'd especially like to thank him for his work on the production of the excellent maps. My interest in this campaign was first sparked many years ago while working for the Museum of the Worcestershire Soldier (to which I recommend all readers as being well worth a visit), and I'd like to thank Colonel Stamford Cartwright MBE for his (and his regiment's) many kindnesses and support then and since. My bibliography would have been considerably thinner without the help of Chris Kellas, Caroline Chapman, David Kivlehan, and the staff of the Prince Consort's Library at Aldershot, and I owe them all my thanks. And, as ever, the staff at the Imperial War Museum have been very helpful.

For the production of this work, I'd like to thank (apart from Dave, again, for the maps, despite being busy with his own book) all of the staff at The History Press, particularly Jo de Vries, Sophie Bradshaw, Rebecca Newton and Paul Baillie Lane. I'd also like to thank the Trustees of the QOWH for their permission in the reproduction of some of the illustrations, and Lee Barton for his technical assistance with scanning.

Map 1: The Eastern Mediterranean Theatre 1914-1918

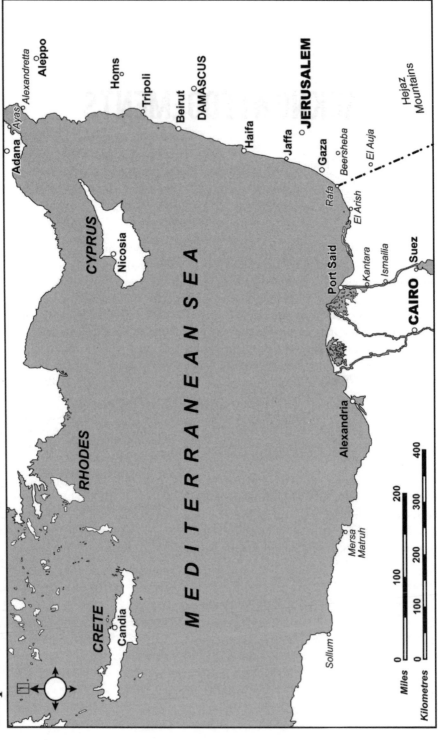

Map 2: Assault on the Suez Canal - February 1915

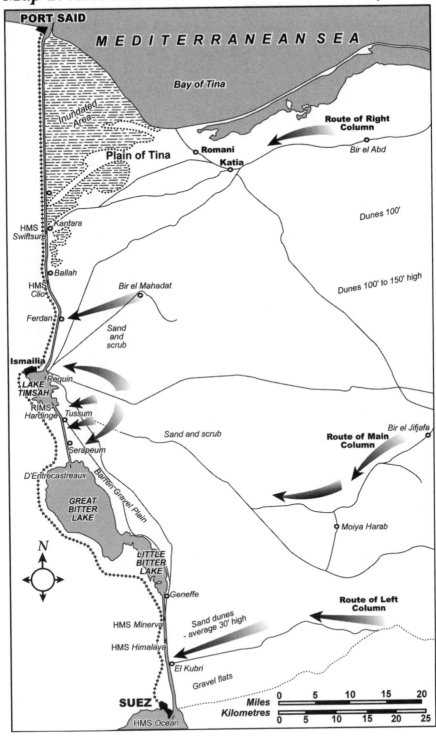

Map 3: The Sinai Desert

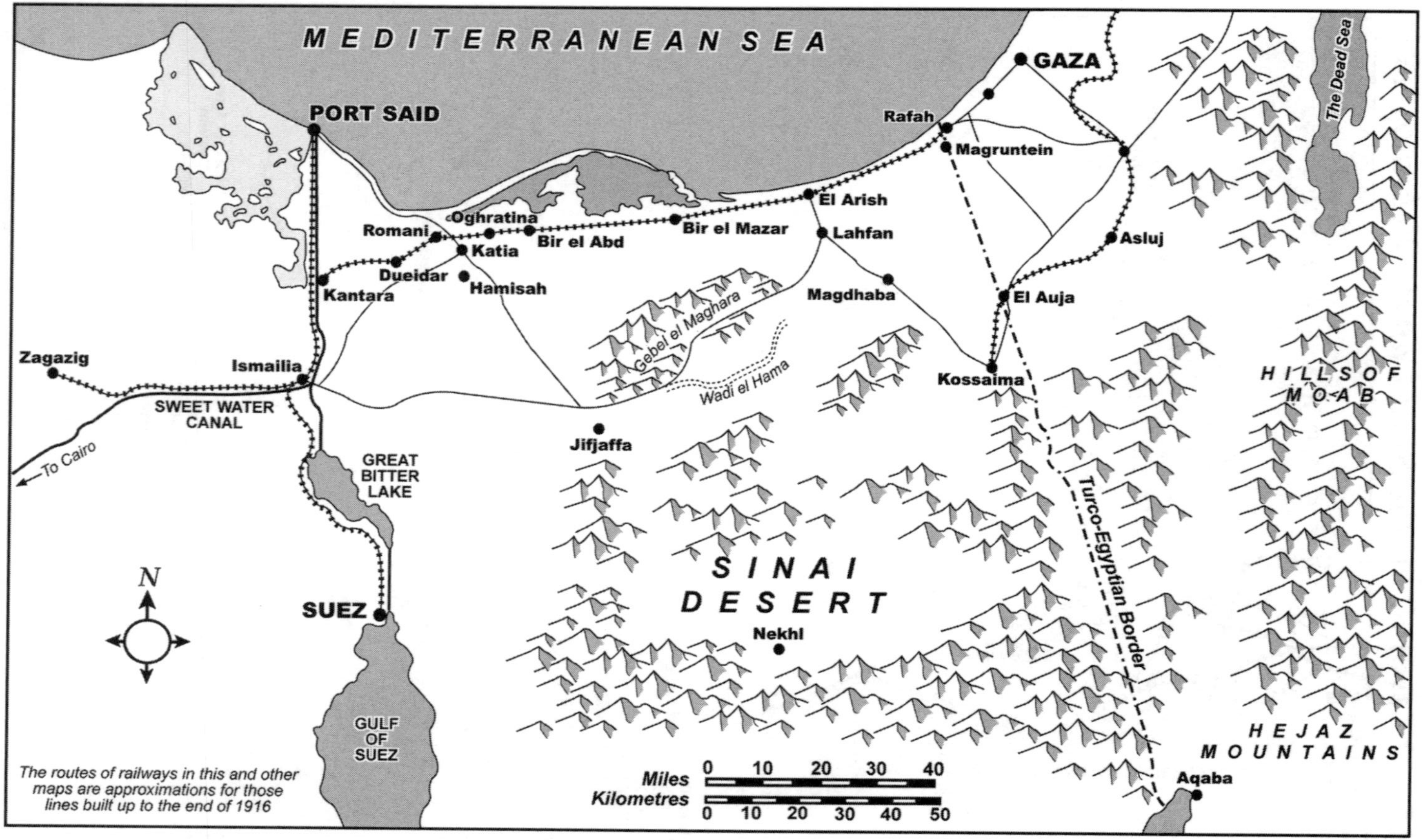

The routes of railways in this and other maps are approximations for those lines built up to the end of 1916

Map 4: The Western Desert

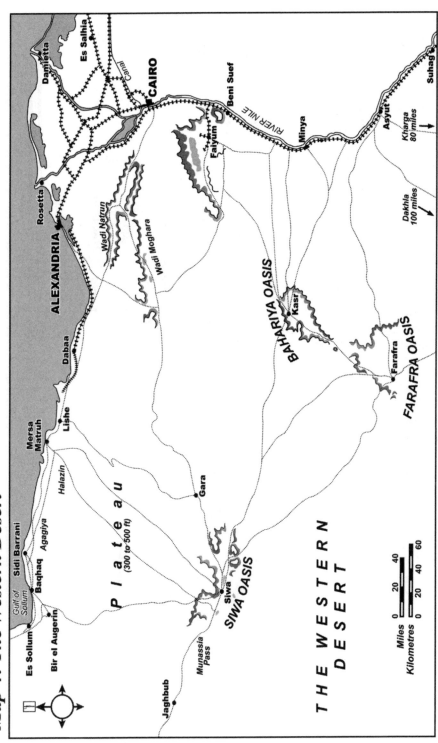

Map 5: The Battle of Romani – August 1916

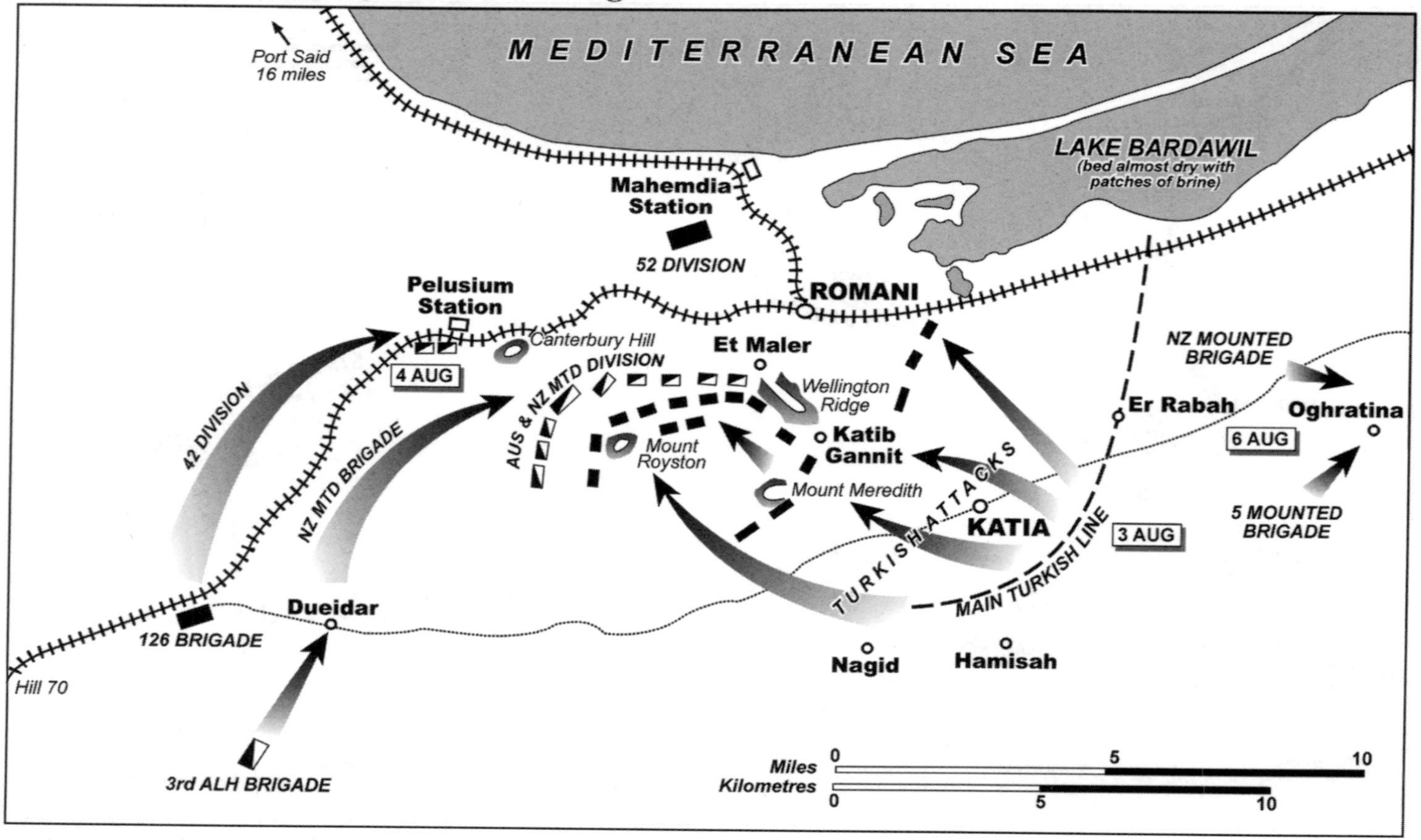

MEDITERRANEAN SEA

Port Said
16 miles

LAKE BARDAWIL
(bed almost dry with
patches of brine)

Mahemdia
Station

ROMANI

52 DIVISION

Et Maler

Wellington
Ridge

Katib
Gannit

Mount Meredith

KATIA

KATIA OASIS

NZ MOUNTED
BRIGADE

Er Rabah

6 AUG

3 AUG

Oghratina

5 MOUNTED
BRIGADE

MAIN TURKISH LINE

Hamisah

Nagid

Mount
Royston

Canterbury Hill

AUS & NZ MTD DIVISION

Pelusium
Station

4 AUG

NZ MTD BRIGADE

42 DIVISION

Dueidar

126 BRIGADE

3rd ALH BRIGADE

Hill 70

Miles

Kilometres

0   5   10

0   5   10

Map 6: The Action at Rafah - 9 January 1917

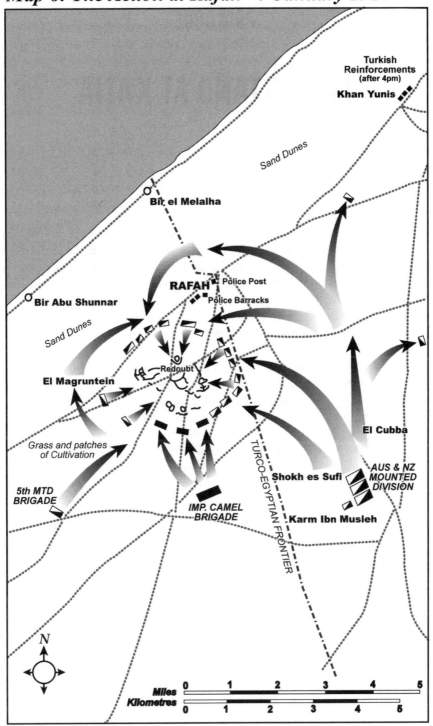

Turkish
Reinforcements
(after 4pm)

Khan Yunis

Sand Dunes

Bir el Melalha

RAFAH · Police Post

Police Barracks

Bir Abu Shunnar

Sand Dunes

Redoubt

El Magruntein

El Cubba

Grass and patches
of Cultivation

AUS & NZ
MOUNTED
DIVISION

Shokh es Sufi

5th MTD
BRIGADE

IMP. CAMEL
BRIGADE

Karm Ibn Musleh

TURCO-EGYPTIAN FRONTIER

N

Miles

Kilometres

0 1 2 3 4 5

0 1 2 3 4 5

PROLOGUE

LAST STAND AT KATIA

For Arthur Dabbs, a 28-year-old bank clerk from Birmingham, it was all over. His war, and probably everything else, was going to end at a desolate oasis in the Sinai Desert, 30 miles east of the Suez Canal, on this Easter Sunday, 23 April 1916. Outnumbered and surrounded, his troop of the Queen's Own Worcestershire Hussars (Yeomanry) had ridden all night, and then fought most of the day under the blazing sun, burrowing into the hot sand for cover. Now, at 3 p.m., with ammunition and water all but gone and no hope of help, the end had come:

> Suddenly I saw the right flank beginning to fall back and saw that the Turks were in amongst them. Then the Turks opposite us leapt up shouting 'Allah, Allah' and charged us. I stood up and fixed my bayonet and waited for the end, hoping it would come quickly. I felt miserable to think I had to die, especially in a hole in the desert like this and I wondered how my people would get to know of it and who would be alive to write and tell them. I wondered which of the advancing Turks would kill me and if I should be able to kill one or two before I was done in. We had almost stopped firing, and the Turks too and it was strangely quiet except for their shouting.
>
> Then the colonel said 'It's no good, boys, throw down your rifles.' Very gladly I obeyed though feeling very cheap and very much conquered as I held up my hands. I was astonished to see that the Turks who came up were holding out their hands and saying 'Ingleesi good'.[1]

Corporal Dabbs would be one of the 'lucky' ones, experiencing two and a half years as a prisoner of war in Turkey, kept on short rations and worked hard to build roads and railways. Many of his comrades would be left behind in the desert at Katia, and more still would die as a result of the harsh conditions of their captivity (*see* Appendix I).

Their sacrifice stalled an attempt by German-led Ottoman Turkish forces to establish positions where their artillery could dominate the Suez Canal. This sliver of water, connecting the Mediterranean to the Gulf of Suez and the Indian Ocean beyond, was Britain's lifeline to its Dominions and Colonies in India, the Far East and the Pacific. Millions of tons of vital war supplies and raw materials flowed through it to feed Britain, the Empire's industrial powerhouse, and tens of thousands of men to feed the insatiable demands of the Western Front. At the same time, the trade goods that helped fund the war effort flowed out to the Empire and neutral countries.

While these supplies could be sent around the southern tip of Africa, such a route would add days and weeks to the journey. Throughout the war, Britain suffered an acute shortage of shipping and walked a fine tightrope of having just enough ships carrying just enough supplies, arriving just in time. To divert Far Eastern traffic around the Cape would be a serious disruption.

The Suez Canal had been of increasing importance since it was first cut in the 1860s. After initial British disinterest, a growing realisation of its significance had led to the purchase of a controlling interest in the Canal in 1878, and an occupation of Egypt in 1882, even though the country remained nominally part of the Ottoman Empire. Allies for most of the nineteenth century, the early twentieth century saw friction between the two empires grow, coming, with the rest of the Europe, to a crisis point in the summer of 1914. The Ottomans held off against the demands of their German allies for as long as possible, but finally, in November 1914, war was declared. To preserve the safety of the Suez Canal, Britain immediately declared a protectorate over Egypt and would spend the next five years in fear of nationalist and Islamic unrest and revolt within the country. Externally, the great fear was of an Ottoman strike against the Canal.

The first such strike came in February 1915 and the resulting battle was fought and won on the banks of the Canal itself. Any attempts to prevent future attacks by dominating the Sinai Desert were forestalled by the Entente campaign in the Dardanelles, which sucked in all of the available troops and resources of both sides. However, when this misadventure finally ended in the first days of 1916, protection of the Canal again became the centre of attention. Control of the Sinai Peninsula now became the priority.

To move even a few divisions into the desert would require significant logistical effort. Water, in particular, would be a problem, and while railways and water pipelines were constructed from Kantara (El Qantarah) stretching out into the desert, water holes and oases along the way would also need to be exploited. In April 1916 parties of Royal Engineers, with strong cavalry escorts, began to locate and develop such sites.

Of particular importance were the wells around Katia (Qatia). Numerous wells covered a large area, and several of the main tracks across the desert met there. Throughout April, this area was swept by the Yeomanry units of the 5th Mounted Brigade, under Brigadier Edgar Wiggin. Consisting of the Queen's Own Worcestershire Hussars (QOWH), Royal Gloucestershire Hussars (RGH), and the Warwickshire Yeomanry (each of around 500 men), the brigade had served on foot at Gallipoli, and since January had been recovering in Egypt and readjusting to mounted operations. Through April they swept the Katia area, tangling on several occasions with long-range patrols of Ottomans and their Bedouin allies.[2]

By mid-April, the brigade had settled into a north–south line to cover the work of the Royal Engineers. Furthest north, the RGH was concentrated at Romani, where the railway, already well underway, was expected to run, with a single squadron of around 150 men detached to Katia to the south, in the centre of the line. Furthest south were the Warwickshires, with 'C' Squadron of QOWH, grouped around Hamisah. In front of the line, at Oghratina, 7 miles east of Katia, were the two remaining squadrons of the QOWH.[3]

On 19 April 1916 Brigadier Wiggin, then at Hamisah, received intelligence from patrols of the Royal Flying Corps (RFC) that a force of 200–300 Ottomans had been spotted at Mageibra, about 10 miles south of his position.[4] After conferring with his own commanding officer, he decided to make a reconnaissance in force, with the hope of catching and engaging the enemy.[5] On 22 April he led his entire force (two squadrons of Warwickshires and one of QOWH) in a night march to come upon the reported camp at dawn. His decision to take his whole force was later criticised by many of his men, although there is perhaps more than a touch of hindsight in these opinions. In the event, while only halfway there, Wiggin's scouts reported back to say that the camp at Mageibra was deserted. Wiggin decided to push on, but when he reached the camp at dawn on Sunday 23 April the campsite was indeed empty except for half a dozen Ottoman orderlies. These were captured, but more interesting was the clear evidence that a body of several hundred enemy troops had been there only the night before.

In fact, this Ottoman force was only one of several busy in the area that morning, albeit probably the smallest. Earlier that month a force of some 3,700 infantry, 1,000 irregular (Arab) camel troops, six artillery pieces and four machine guns had set out from Palestine under the command of the German Colonel Kress von Kressenstein. Their mission was to roll back the British forces in the Sinai, pinning them back behind the Canal to enable larger Ottoman forces (then being prepared) to follow up and establish strong points from where artillery could dominate the Canal, effectively cutting it. A secondary objective was to create such a threat that the movement to France of troops being withdrawn from Gallipoli would be stopped.

They crossed the Sinai Desert by a route judged by the British as impassable, and had arrived within a few miles of the British outposts without detection, despite warnings by the RFC that forces were gathering.[6] In the south, a small force had camped at Mageibra, but moved on the evening before Wiggin's arrival. This contingent would get the closest to the Canal, attacking a redoubt held by a single company of the 5th Royal Scots at Dueidar just after dawn. Despite artillery support, their repeated attacks failed, and the Ottomans were forced to withdraw in the early afternoon when reinforcements from the Australian Light Horse arrived.

The other, much larger, Ottoman forces met with greater success. In the early hours of 23 April 1916 they converged upon Oghratina, where 'A' and 'D' Squadrons of the QOWH, under Major Williams-Thomas, were protecting their party of Royal Engineers (RE). A thick fog, caused by moisture rolling in from the sea during the night and evaporating as the dawn broke, had covered the area around the oasis. Although three patrols were sent out to maintain a watch in the dawn, visibility remained minimal. Two patrols returned and reported no contact, but the third did not come back. No alarm was raised, even when one of the outposts reported hearing activity around some of the outlying wells to the west, towards the Canal. A small patrol under Captain E.S. Ward of 'D' Squadron was sent out to investigate, expecting to find the lost patrol. Instead they observed through a gap in the fog a small Ottoman patrol watering their animals. Returning to the main force, Ward collected the rest of his troop (about thirty men) and headed back to ambush them. Creeping up under cover, they managed to surprise the Ottomans, who fled with heavy casualties.[7] The Yeomen eagerly took up the chase, but this had only been a scouting party. Within moments, they ran into the advancing main body of Kress von Kressenstein's force, and, under heavy fire, it became the Yeomen's turn to retreat.

As Ward returned to the main position, Williams-Thomas faced a tough decision. Through the fog he could see sizable Ottoman forces closing in from the north and west. His orders had been clear: if faced by a major attack, he was to mount up and fall back. Unfortunately, this order did not take into account the REs in his care. Although the mounted Yeomen could retreat rapidly, the Engineers were on foot and would not be able to outrun the Ottomans.[8] Williams-Thomas decided that he could not abandon the men he was charged with protecting, and, after sending back mounted messengers as well as telephoning Katia, formed his men into a defensive circle on a slight hill, ready to receive the enemy.

The first hurried Ottoman attack, at around 4 a.m., was successfully repulsed. The soft sand of the hill impeded the sudden rush, slowing the attackers and leaving them open to the Yeomen's fire. Next, the Ottomans took a more methodical approach. They moved around to totally encircle the British position, cutting the telephone lines to Katia at around 4.30 a.m. An hour later they attacked from the north, south and west. This time machine guns gave covering fire and the infantry advanced in short rushes.

Overwhelming Ottoman numbers began to tell. Despite holding hard, at times fighting hand-to-hand, the Yeomen were pushed back all along their line, moving back up the slopes of the hill to where the REs had set up a second line of defensive positions. Again heavy fighting (with consequent heavy casualties) engulfed the Yeomen, and again the line was pushed back, this time to the very crest of the hill. The fog was now lifting, allowing the Ottomans to bring their artillery to bear, while machine guns were repositioned to enfilade the British positions. At the north-west (highest) end of the line, Lieutenant Sir John Jaffrey's troop caught the worst of the fire. Only a handful of men were left able to fight; many of those who had not been killed or wounded now found their weapons clogging up after continuous use in the soft, fine sand.[9]

At around 7.45 a.m. the final rush came. Despite a gallant and desperate fight against overwhelming odds, the two squadrons were overrun. The Ottomans 'seemed to pour in among us' recalled Sergeant Horace Mantle, 'a lot of us were knocked out while still in position'.[10] Of Jaffrey's troop, only two men were left alive.[11]

No one had time to escape; most of the survivors had been wounded and all were captured. They would face a long, harrowing march into captivity, and spend the rest of the war in appalling conditions. Many would die as prisoners.

The worst of the wounded, about half a dozen men, were simply left behind. The Ottomans dressed their wounds and abandoned them in the shelter of a few palm trees. One of the men, Saddler-Sergeant Joseph Pratt, was wounded in the hip and shoulder:

> There was an Engineer with me. A plucky little chap. I don't remember his name, but he was [a] Scot. He was badly wounded in the face. An old Arab woman … found us and brought us water from the well. One day she didn't come, but the Scotsman managed to drag himself to the well … A party of Bedouins, who are regular desert pirates and cut-throats, came across us, and wanted to put an end to our misery. They were only stopped by their leader. On the Thursday [fifth day] I saw a horseman on the sky-line. I lifted my helmet, waved it, and shouted as well as I could in my weak state. Sound carries in the desert. He heard me, and I heard him shout something about coming down. He was one of a troop of Australian Light Horse who happened on us accidentally. We were taken to hospital at Kantara and then to Cairo. My companion, I am sorry to say, died.[12]

Pratt was shipped back to England, but died of his wounds in December in a Manchester hospital.

Messengers from Oghratina had reached Brigadier Wiggin and his three Squadrons just before 7 a.m. His horses were tired and thirsty after their night march and unfit for any fast movement across the desert. Nevertheless, he turned his force back north.

With Oghratina overrun, the bulk of the Ottoman force moved on and at 9 a.m. began to attack 'A' Squadron RGH at Katia. German aircraft had plotted the positions of the defences and the horse lines, and as the Ottoman infantry deployed, their artillery began to fire against those lines to prevent a breakout. The garrison had already moved many of their horses in preparation to relieve Oghratina, but enough were left in the lines and were subsequently killed to present the commander, Captain Lloyd Baker, the same dilemma as had faced Major Williams-Thomas.[13] The mounted men could escape, but there was now a body of dismounted men who would not stand a chance. His decision, like Williams-Thomas, was to stand by his men, and a defensive perimeter was formed.

Closing in from the south, Brigadier Wiggin could not only hear the artillery, but see the shells bursting over Katia. After much pleading by his officers, he agreed to let Colonel the Hon. Charles Coventry, commander of the QOWH, take his 'C' Squadron and attempt to break through to Oghratina. As they got closer, though, Coventry reassessed the situation and decided that as the guns there had fallen silent, Oghratina was probably beyond help. Instead, he turned towards Katia and pushed his tired force onwards. Corporal Arthur Dabbs remembered that ride:

> The horses had done 36 miles during the night and were terribly thirsty – and so were we, having only the tepid water in our bottles to drink, and thinking longingly of the tea which we now should have no time to make.[14]

Off to the north at Romani, Lieutenant Colonel Ralph Yorke of the RGH had come to the same conclusion, and led his two remaining squadrons to Katia's aid.

By coincidence, both forces reached the area at about 10 a.m., albeit from opposite directions. As they pushed through the Ottoman flanking units, Yorke and Coventry independently came to the conclusion that Katia could not be held. As Corporal Dabbs recalled, new orders were given to ride in 'as fast as possible and hold the line while our men in camp saddled up and got away, afterwards following them as fast as we could'.[15]

However, Katia was now surrounded by heavy fighting so even this plan was impractical. The relief forces arrived at the gallop but could only get to within 400yd (360m) of the perimeter before getting pinned down. Dismounting, it took several hours of careful advancing before they could link up with the garrison.

Inside the perimeter, the remaining Yeomen were being assaulted on three sides, and those inside and out were thirsty, tired and taking heavy casualties. Colonel Coventry got an order back to Major William 'Bill' Wiggin (officer commanding 'C' Squadron and brother of the Brigadier) to bring the remaining horses forward to enable as many men as possible to mount up and escape. Although he received this order at about 1.30 p.m., Major Wiggin had suffered a bad shoulder wound and, on moving to the rear, fell unconscious from loss of blood. He lay for an hour before coming to and carrying on.[16] It was 3 p.m. before the horses were brought to the front.

Meanwhile Colonel Coventry had ordered a general retreat. Many men, mainly those furthest from Katia, fell back in a running fight and met Brigadier Wiggin as he came the other way. The Ottomans, seeing the British line break, surged forward to finish them.

Those who stayed, like Colonel Coventry and Corporal Dabbs, were captured, while those who tried to escape faced a desperate dash for freedom. Corporal Bob Eaton of the RGH had two horses shot from under him before catching another and making it to safety; he was one of only nine of the 106 men of his squadron to escape.[17] That evening the QOWH mustered just fifty-four NCOs and men.[18] During the roll call the single surviving officer, Major Wiggin, fell from his horse as he again passed out from loss of blood. While the RGH and Warwickshires fared slightly better, the brigade had, for the time being, been effectively wiped out.

However, Kress von Kressenstein too had received a setback and his force was in no condition to carry on towards the Canal. With the alarm raised, and his prisoners and wounded to care for, he pulled back into the desert. By the time his reinforcements arrived in July – a fighting strength of some 12,000 Gallipoli veterans – the British had also had time to prepare. They had established strong lines around Romani, supported by redoubts. A stubborn defence, coupled with effective use of cavalry (particularly the Australian Light Horse), saw the Ottomans turned back at the Battle of Romani in early August.

The action at Katia vividly highlights how the war in Egypt differed from the more widely known campaigns in France. Many of the traditional images of the First World War simply do not apply or are even drastically reversed. In complete contrast of the mud and trenches of France, this was an open war of movement fought across burning deserts, where manoeuvring was possible and front lines were frequently abstract markings on a map. Small units could wander far and wide, completely cut off from logistical or military support; if one got into trouble, help had to come from considerably further away than the reserve trenches.

Logistics were also a far more fundamental problem. In France, keeping the flow of food, munitions and water moving to front-line troops required a massive and complicated machine based on railway networks, shipping convoys and fleets of lorries. In Egypt, and later Palestine, the process was far more precarious. Keeping a force marching across barren desert suitably supplied left very little room for delay or error, and water supplies in particular would on several occasions form the margin between defeat and victory. Equally, rest was rare. Whereas units in France rotated through the front, support and rear areas every few days, men in Egypt, and later Palestine, could and often did remain at the front for weeks or months on end. Even when withdrawn for a 'rest', the principal blights on their lives – the heat, clogging sand, sores, and, always, the perpetual swarms of flies – were inescapable.

Troops in Egypt would often complain in their letters and journals, and later in memoirs, of the complete lack of appreciation they felt they received from the rest of the army in France or the civilians at home. The popular perception was that anyone who had not served in the Middle East believed that theirs was an easy war, spent enjoying, in the popular biblical misquote, the 'pyramids and fleshpots' of Egypt instead of fighting. This complaint even entered the annals of regimental histories, in this case that of the 5th Battalion, Highland Light Infantry:

> The Egyptian Expeditionary Force was associated in the minds of the average citizen with the idea of Pyramids and flesh pots. For the first, symbolic pictures were largely to blame. There never was a design representing 'Britain's far flung battle line' which did not show a comfortable man in a sun helmet with a Pyramid in the background. Pyramids are so easy to draw. The artists are beaten by the flesh pot – because they had no very clear conception of what a flesh pot looks like. But the old Biblical phrase rose irresistibly to the mind mingled perhaps with recollections of some globe-trotter's stories of the delights of shepherds. Both ideas are quite false. Our flesh pot was the Dixie [mess tin] – and there was a great deal less to put into it than there was on other, more canteen-blessed fronts – while many a man who joined us early in 1916 left for France in 1918 without ever having set eyes on a Pyramid.[19]

Yet the task they performed was critical. The Suez Canal was 'the most vital and most vulnerable link in the maritime communications between Europe and the East'.[20] In 1915 and 1916 alone, over 5,000 British ships totalling over 21m tons passed through the Canal, in addition to over 1,700 Entente or neutral ships totalling over 5m tons.[21] Even at the height of the submarine threat, the Suez and Mediterranean route was still preferred as being the quickest and most efficient way to deliver the men and material needed within the fastest possible time.

1

EGYPT IN 1914

In August 1914 Egypt was in a very difficult position. Diplomatically and legally speaking, the country was in a grey area, being at the same time part of the British and Ottoman Empires. Britain's interest in Egypt stretched back for over a century, straddling as it did one of the main (and the quickest) routes between Britain and the jewel of its Empire, India. Military expeditions had been sent to Egypt in the 1790s and 1800s, taking part in the disorder and confused fighting that followed the French invasion of 1798. After the French had been evicted, the country descended into a protracted civil war. Although Egypt had been part of the Ottoman Empire for centuries, the traditional ruling class had been destroyed by the French and control of the country was being fiercely contested. Over the following decade Britain intervened on the losing side, fought a brief and unsuccessful war with the Ottomans, had a small field army all but wiped out and eventually decided that its Egyptian policy was better conducted from a distance.

For most of the nineteenth century, the *Walis* (governors) of Egypt gradually moved away from Ottoman rule, even fighting their own wars with Constantinople, while expanding their influence into Libya and the Sudan. Progressive rulers (later designated *Khedives* – Viceroys) modernised the country, improving the bureaucracy, infrastructure, agriculture, industry and education systems, while also forging links with the European Great Powers. Unfortunately, the quality of the rulers was not consistent and in 1858 the then *Khedive* struck a very bad bargain with the French engineer Ferdinand de Lesseps and his Universal Suez Ship Canal Company (USSCC). The plan to build a canal from Port Said in the Mediterranean to Suez on the Red Sea should have brought the country great wealth but the terms of the deal led to rising international debt as unscrupulous European investors squeezed the country dry. Internal unrest followed and in 1875 the *Khedive* was forced to sell Egypt's shares in the Suez Canal. Britain, which had been initially sceptical about the Canal and had declined to invest, now leapt at the chance to buy them, effectively gaining a controlling interest. The money raised paid Egypt's debts for only one year and in 1876 the country was bankrupt. The Great Powers stepped in and took control of Egypt's finances and government.

The loss of independence was not popular in Egypt and a series of revolts followed, culminating in 1882. In that year an Anglo-French task force was sent to re-establish control, but at the last minute the French withdrew. The Royal Navy forged ahead alone to bombard Alexandria and land a British army. After fierce fighting, Britain emerged as de facto ruler of Egypt. A British Agency was established to control the country's finances and over time it inevitably spread into all government and public offices, the legal system, and the army. However, Egypt would officially remain, in the words of the British Foreign Office, 'a semi-independent tributary state to the Ottoman Empire'[22] and pay a yearly tribute to Constantinople, rather than being legally annexed into the British Empire.

The Ottomans, meanwhile, were in no real position to counter the British takeover. Egypt was a largely unprofitable backwater for the Empire, and given all the other problems besieging the 'sick man of Europe', it was far down the list of Ottoman priorities. Throughout the nineteenth century the Ottoman Empire was wracked by internal and external strife. Wars with Russia in the 1850s and 1870s were damaging, but it was internal uprisings that were almost crippling. Many of the subject peoples of the Empire were increasingly dissatisfied and rebellions were frequent. Most serious were the uprisings in the Balkans, particularly as when the Ottoman territories in Europe were torn away, so too was a significant part of the empire's population base and a very large part of its industrial capability.

Politically, the major change came in 1908 and 1909, when power was seized by the so-called 'Young Turks', who were determined to abandon the traditionally inclusive stance of the Ottoman Empire in favour of a pro-Turkish policy. Essentially, the 'Young Turks' meant the new ruling triumvirate, known as 'The Three Pashas': Mehmed Talaat as Minister of the Interior, Ismail Enver as Minister of War, and Ahmed Djemal as Minister of the Navy.[23] To them, 'Ottoman' meant everyone, whereas 'Turkish' meant a focus on the Muslim majorities of the Anatolian heartlands. The idea of Constantinople as the traditional protector of international Islam, with the Sultan of the Ottoman Empire as the *Caliph*, their spiritual leader, was reasserted, to the consternation of Britain and other European Powers. The concern that the *Caliph* had the loyalty of, and could call on military support from, the large Muslim populations in India and Africa would become a recurring nightmare for the Great Powers, who feared massed uprisings should they ever go to war with the Ottomans.

On two occasions direct conflict between the British in Egypt and the Ottoman Empire became a close possibility. The first was in 1904–6, when the Ottomans began to encroach on the traditional borders of Egypt on the eastern side of the Sinai Peninsula. Known as the Taba Crisis after one of the disputed settlements, it saw British troops pouring into Egypt, and the Royal Navy preparing to support a counter-invasion on the Syrian coast or to force the Dardanelles and bombard Constantinople. The Taba Crisis was eventually settled peacefully, although it made Britain take a long hard look at the defence of Egypt, and make plans that would prove useful a few years later.

The second crisis came in 1911, when Italy invaded the neighbouring Ottoman states of Tripolitania, Cyrenaica and Fezzan, collectively known as Libya. Legally, the Ottomans could have demanded free passage for their forces to pass through Egypt to counter the invasion, and that Egyptian forces themselves take part. Unable to be seen to be taking sides against Italy, Britain declared Egypt to be neutral, and closed its borders to anything but humanitarian aid. In actuality, the long Egyptian–Libyan border proved fairly porous and Ottoman military aid (including Enver Pasha himself to take command) slipped through either unseen or ignored. Indeed, Britain even took the opportunity to push the poorly-defined border slightly farther to the west. The already struggling Ottomans were unable to contest the British position, not least because, in the spring of 1912, the Italians opened further fronts in the war in the Dodecanese and eastern Mediterranean. In the autumn, matters became worse still when an alliance of Balkan states decided to take advantage of the situation to start another war with the Ottomans. Faced with protecting either their few remaining lucrative European lands or the vast deserts of Libya, the Ottomans made a quick peace with Italy in order to focus on the campaign closer at home. In Libya a strong resistance movement of Bedouin tribes, led by the Senussi religious sect, maintained a guerrilla war against the invaders.

Inside Egypt, British rule was tolerated by the majority. Reforms in education, agricultural methods (including land reclamation in the fertile Nile Delta), and investment in infrastructure did much to improve the lives of average Egyptians. Economic reforms certainly meant that they were better off under British rule, as the foreign debts and other government spending was bought under strict control; in the first twenty-five years of British rule, taxes fell by 25 per cent.[24]

Small groups continued to oppose British rule and campaigned for greater political independence and control over their own government. These nationalist groups were a thorn in Britain's side, and several of the British consuls general experimented with various forms of democracy at different levels. In truth the level of political freedom was no less and perhaps somewhat higher than the Egyptians had enjoyed under the direct rule of the *Khedives*. However, the new, more efficient governmental systems were not Egyptian, and resentment at having to adapt to foreign ways enforced by foreign officials, both of which often ignored local traditions, culture and even languages, rankled with many.

The legal system was a particular cause of resentment, in no small part because the British enjoyed what were known as the Capitulations. These had first been agreed with the Ottoman Empire and (among other things) gave British (and certain other European) subjects accused of crimes in Egypt the right to be tried by their own national, rather than local, courts. An extension to this system was made in 1895, when anyone suspected of committing crimes against the occupying British forces would face trial by a special tribunal, outside the usual legal system.[25] This led to several travesties of justice, such as the infamous Denshawai Affair of 1906, and a general feeling that the British were above and outside Egyptian law.

In 1912 a new British Consul General was appointed: the perhaps unlikely figure of Field Marshal The Right Honourable The Viscount Kitchener. A blunt military man, Kitchener knew the country from his time there during the 1880s and 1890s. Although his direct methods annoyed many political figures, in 1913 he introduced a new legislative assembly with elected members and real powers. He also showed genuine concern for the people, introducing reforms in agriculture and the cotton trade, and in the areas of banking and loans, as well as a series of urban improvement and land reclamation projects.[26] By 1914 the country was prospering and, for the most, part, settled.

As war erupted across Europe in July and August 1914 the Ottoman Empire appeared to be keeping neutral. Britain, however, was not, and the big question was how Egypt should react. Secret discussions within the British government in 1913 had addressed this issue.[27] Although a de facto British colony, Egypt was, in Kitchener's words, 'still technically and legally outside the British Empire'. The ramifications were almost endless. With the _Khedive_ still responsible for law and order, Britain would be unable to round up enemy aliens, including spies and saboteurs. Nor would she be able to stop Egypt from trading with countries at war with Britain, some of whom may be bound by trade agreements signed with the Ottomans, or stop them using the Canal. Perhaps most importantly, defence of the Canal would become almost impossible. The sure way to cut through this Gordian Knot of legal issues would be either to declare Egypt a protectorate, and thus a formal part of the British Empire, or to declare martial law, which was, legally, a step down from a full protectorate but would still send the very clear message to the world that Britain was in control of the country. From either of these actions there would be internal repercussions. The nationalist and anti-British portions of the country would likely receive a swell of support, possibly even sparking the much-feared Islamic uprising, and Britain would suddenly face internal as well as external threats. The issues were complicated and the weighing of them would have to be finely balanced. In the end, it was decided that the decision would have to be left to the man on the spot (with Foreign Office advice) as and when the time came.

When the time did come, however, it was the height of summer and many of the most senior officials were at home on leave. Lord Kitchener had left for England on 18 June 1914 and although he hurried to return to Egypt when war broke out, he was detained and appointed Secretary of War instead.[28] The _Khedive_, Abbas Hilmi, was also out of the country. He had been on a visit to the Sultan when, on 24 June, he had been the subject of an assassination attempt by an Egyptian student. Badly wounded, he was still recovering in Constantinople despite being desperate to leave, as he believed that the Young Turks were behind the attempt.[29] Meanwhile, the Legislative Assembly of Egypt was adjourned.[30]

With Kitchener definitely not coming back, Milne Cheetham, who had been left as the _chargé d'affaires_ at the British Agency in Kitchener's absence, was made tempo-rary Consul until he could be replaced by Sir Henry McMahon, who would arrive in early January 1915. On the Egyptian side, Hussein Rushdi Pasha, the President of the Council of Ministers, took charge and acted with a mixture of good sense, calm and more than a dash of resignation, to pull his country through this complicated interna-tional situation.[31] Between them, they steered the country through the rocky opening months of the war. The international status of Egypt was settled on 5 August, the day after Britain declared war on Germany. Rushdi issued a 'document which committed Egypt virtually to a declaration of war against the [British] King's enemies'.[32] In it, several wartime measures were detailed, such as forbidding Egyptian citizens from trading with Britain's enemies or giving them loans, which would realistically have only limited impact on the country while at the same time making it publically clear that they were supporting Britain.

The reaction across Egypt was surprisingly muted. Financial uncertainty struck the country, causing a drop in the market, but this was only to be expected when war is declared.[33] At other levels in the towns and cities, life appeared to go on very much as usual, with only the higher echelons of the British Agency showing signs of frantic, even chaotic, activity, as they worked to deal with the (real or perceived) political and military repercussions of war.[34] One serious area of worry that did reverberate down to the lower levels of society, especially in rural areas, was that of food supply. In 1913, around one-third (260,000 tons) of Egypt's wheat had to be imported, principally from Russia.[35] With the potentially hostile Ottomans controlling the Russian trade routes in and out of the Black Sea through the Dardanelles, this supply was effectively cut off. A few other foodstuffs were also imported and their supply also jeopardised. It was now just after the harvest, and so Egypt would not face any food shortages in the short term, but a knee-jerk reaction by the government saw regional food commissions spring up across the country, buying up all surplus stocks and banning all exports. There was little central co-ordination, and so the prices paid differed between regions, causing some discontent, and the system did little to calm the population.[36] Meanwhile, the amount of agricultural land was increased by instructing growers to decrease the amount of cotton cultivated. As foodstuffs were less profitable than cotton, this was not popular with farmers.[37]

Even with such a muted reaction, the British in Egypt remained on edge. Should the Ottomans declare support for Germany, it would raise the spectre of a potential Muslim uprising in Egypt, preventing the use of the Suez Canal, as well as possibly more serious problems in India. There was little anyone in Britain or Egypt could do but wait to see which way the Ottomans would jump.

2

OPENING SHOTS

The big question in August 1914 was which side the Ottomans would choose, if either. There was a general assumption, based on recent close relations, that the Ottomans would side with Germany and the Central Powers. This assumption perhaps explains the incident that sparked a chain of events that would, publically at least, justify their eventually joining Germany in November. There were two Ottoman dreadnought-type battleships currently sitting in British dockyards. The largest was the *Sultan Osman I*, which had been originally ordered for the Brazilian Navy until monetary problems had led to her sale to the Ottomans in 1913. With seven turrets mounting a total of fourteen 12in guns, she was the most heavily armed ship of her type ever built. The second was the *Reshadieh*, which was also formidably armed, mounting ten 13.5in guns, and had been paid for by a public-subscription scheme (although a considerable sum was still outstanding[38]). These powerful, modern ships were high-profile symbols of the status of the Ottoman Empire, and outcry followed when, on 31 July, First Lord of the Admiralty Winston Churchill ordered them to be seized for use by the Royal Navy. The Ottoman personnel who had already arrived to take delivery were bustled away and the next morning British sailors arrived to take possession. Although perfectly legal under the contracts signed with the Ottomans, the conversion of *Sultan Osman I* into HMS *Agincourt*, and *Reshadieh* into HMS *Erin*, stung Ottoman pride badly and the Germans took full advantage of the opportunity to show the British up.

The German presence in the Mediterranean in 1914 consisted of two warships: the battlecruiser SMS *Goeben*, and the light cruiser SMS *Breslau*, under the command of Rear Admiral Wilhelm Souchon. Both were fast (although *Goeben* suffered from persistent boiler problems[39]) and heavily armed. If war broke out, they could be a considerable threat. Although it was unlikely they would remain for long in the Mediterranean, where they could be cornered by superior forces, the French were deeply concerned about them. In the event of war, the primary initial function of the French Navy would be to carry XIX Corps, the Army of Africa, from Algeria back to mainland France. Two heavily armed, fast warships could wreak havoc among the lumbering troopships and seriously upset French plans. For the British, the fear was that the *Goeben* and *Breslau* would break out of the Mediterranean, raiding merchant shipping in the North and South Atlantics. The attention of both countries would be directed at the western end of the Mediterranean, ready to react to the first sign of German ships.

The Germans, however, knew this too, and knew that any attempt to break through the western Mediterranean would probably end in disaster. Instead, they decided to present the two modern warships to the Ottomans as a sign of friendship: a grand gesture that would not only win political favour with the Ottomans but also avoid the negative publicity of losing their ships to British and French guns. On the back of this, and the resulting Entente annoyance at having former-German warships blocking communications with the Russians through the Dardanelles, the Ottomans would be drawn into the war on Germany's side.

That, at least, is the popular version of events, but the actual facts are far more complicated. For one thing, the Ottomans and the Germans had already signed a secret treaty. In July 1914 the Ottomans had canvassed not only Germany but Britain and France for an alliance, and had been rejected by them all.[40] However, a sudden enthusiasm by the Kaiser led to Germany returning to the Ottomans with their own proposals only days after rejecting them. In particular, the Germans were keen to have the Ottomans as an ally on the southern flank of Russia. After several days of frantic negotiations (during which time the *Sultan Osman I* and *Reshadieh* were seized), a secret treaty was signed on 2 August 1914. It committed the Ottomans to attack Russia, which they were still loathe to do, and in the rush to sign they managed to word the treaty so that this obligation only came into effect if Russia declared war on Germany. In fact, the previous day, it had been Germany who had declared war on Russia.[41]

While the Ottomans continued to dither and attempt to avoid entering actual hostilities with anyone, the Germans scrambled for ways around the treaty. They desperately wanted the Ottomans to divert at least some of Russia's strength onto her southern, Caucasian border, and they also wanted Ottoman spiritual help. Extensive plans had been made, under the guidance of the eccentric orientalist Max von Oppenheim,[42] to use the Sultan's position as *Caliph* to declare a *jihad*, a holy war that would spark Islamic uprisings across the British, Russian and French empires. After all, the British Empire alone contained more Muslims than the Ottoman Empire did.[43] Extensive German preparations were made, spreading propaganda[44] and sending envoys into Russia and the northern borderlands of British India, hoping to raise rebellion in the name of Islam.[45]

The concept of a *jihad* was at the time, as now, greatly misunderstood by many people. Europeans in particular viewed it with fear. For the Germans it was a magic bullet that could knock their enemies out of the war at one stroke, and for Britain it was a nightmare scenario. Religion, and the Sultan's status as *Caliph*, had haunted British plans in Egypt for decades, perhaps because, even sixty years on, the scars of the (at least partly) religiously motivated uprising in India in 1857 were still vivid and raw. The Ottoman view was somewhat different and distinctly more muted.[46] *Jihad* (literally, 'striving') was not clearly defined in the Koran and could mean anything from holy war to the search for inner peace, with hundreds of interpretations in between. The Ottomans had called for a *jihad* in some of their previous conflicts but equally had not in many more, and it appears to have been seen within the Sublime Porte as little more than rhetoric. While a *jihad* was eventually called in November 1914 it was as much as anything a sop to placate their new German allies.[47]

But first, the Ottomans had to be enticed into actually declaring their allegiances. The delivery of the *Goeben* and the *Breslau* into the Dardanelles was going to be the spark that ignited what the Germans hoped would be a powder barrel of religious discontent. To do this, they had to run the gauntlet of the Royal Navy.

The Royal Navy (RN), though, was weak in the Mediterranean. For a hundred years the ability of Britain to dominate this sea had been a clear and present reminder to the rest of Europe of her reach and military might. The RN had been used to interfere in countless wars, diplomatic disputes and political decisions in the region, but as the twentieth century dawned, RN ships had increasingly been needed elsewhere. As the arms race with Germany escalated, Britain could no longer guarantee domination of the North Sea without stripping other areas of their assets, and an agreement with France had made this possible. After the ancient enemies had signed the Entente Cordiale in 1904, further agreements for mutual protection had followed. In 1912 this had included an arrangement whereby each took responsibility for a different sea. The RN had bases in Scotland and the middle of the English Channel, far enough from Germany to be safe from surprise attack and yet perfectly poised to bottle up any German attempt to break out, and so they took responsibility for the North Sea. The French Navy, fearful that a surprise attack on the Channel ports could destroy its fleet piecemeal, and preoccupied with moving troops home from Africa in case of emergency, took the Mediterranean.[48]

Gradually the RN stripped back its Mediterranean assets, although a sizable force was still needed. After all, the sea was still teeming with British traders and merchantmen, and the threat from Italy and Austro-Hungary also loomed large. These two nominal allies were both modernising their fleets, albeit in an arms race with each other, and it was feared that a combined Italian-Austrian fleet would be able to overwhelm the French.[49] In late July the RN Mediterranean Fleet, under the command of Admiral Sir Berkeley Milne RN, consisted of three battlecruisers, four cruisers and four light cruisers, plus a number of destroyers (*see* Appendix A). For all that one midshipman, on being posted to HMS *Defence* in early 1914, would state 'I knew little or nothing about foreign policy, beyond the fact that the Mediterranean belonged to us',[50] this was a weak force. It would stand little chance against Italian or Austro-Hungarian dreadnoughts, and individually even the battlecruisers were likely to be outclassed by the *Goeben*.

The British fleet began to gather at its main base at Malta on 27 July.[51] For the cruiser HMS *Defence* and the destroyer HMS *Grampus*, this meant leaving the small multinational flotilla off Albania, where they had been ensuring the independence of that new country.[52] Here, HMS *Defence's* crew had mounted landing parties next to sailors from SMS *Breslau*, and subsequently enjoying dinner in the mess of the German light cruiser. At Malta, rapid resupply was undertaken, particularly of coal. Fifty years before, warships had been dependant on the wind for their speed and direction of travel, but could stay at sea for months at a time. The modern, steam-driven fleet could move with virtual impunity but required frequent recoaling, either at a port or by rendezvousing with coaling ships, although oil was beginning to see increased use as ship fuel as well.[53] This limitation on freedom of movement would be a major factor in the debacle that would follow.

Once in harbour, preparations for fitting the RN ships for war began. Although, for now, they would remain at a lower, peacetime crew strength, the ships themselves had to be prepared for combat:

> We were told to prepare for war. This included throwing over the side all unneces-sary furniture, chairs, tables, etc., and anything flammable. This also included the removal of layers of enamel on the quarter deck bulkhead and after turrets. This had to be done by chipping and was undertaken by the PMO, the Purser and the Chaplain. After trial and error, they found the best way to do it was to hammer it off with the end of a golf club.[54]

On 30 July 1914, Milne received orders to assist the French in guarding the ships which should even now be transporting thousands of troops from Algeria, although his orders stated that his forces were not to engage any enemy ships unless they were already exchanging fire with the French.[55] By 31 July Milne's entire force was ready and HMS *Chatham* had been despatched to watch for the *Breslau* and *Goeben* in the Straits of Messina between Italy and Sicily. On 1 August, the Royal Navy received orders for a general mobilisation for war, and on 2 August Rear Admiral Ernest Troubridge RN was despatched with the 1st Cruiser Squadron to take up watch at the mouth of the Adriatic. The rest of the fleet, meanwhile, remained at Malta, although Milne at last received permission from the Admiralty to contact the French commander, Admiral De Lapeyrère, to liaise. Attempts to raise him by wireless failed.[56] Finally, after the Admiralty informed Milne that they believed the *Breslau* and *Goeben* would make for the Straits of Gibraltar and the open Atlantic, Milne ordered his main force to sea, to patrol between Malta and Sicily.[57]

But the German warships were already past Malta. On 1 August Souchon had taken his ships down to Brindisi, on the heel of Italy, for recoaling. They had been turned away by the Italians, a sign that perhaps Italy was not going to join the war on the side of Germany and Austro-Hungary after all, and had instead sailed for Messina. After illegally refuelling there on 2 August, the ships slipped north in the night and were already well clear of the British patrol areas by the time Milne's ships were fully deployed.[58] The *Breslau* and *Goeben* were now loose in the western Mediterranean, and at liberty to attack the French troop convoys at will.

These convoys, meanwhile, were in chaos. De Lapeyrère had managed to confuse what was an urgent situation by countermanding orders from Paris, changing exist-ing plans, and moving with excruciatingly slow speed.[59] The delivery of XIX Corps to France was delayed by days, tying up the French war fleet to a relatively narrow corridor, and preventing any co-ordinated hunt for the German ships. Instead it was left to Milne, who on 3 August received confirmation that Souchon had already left

Messina heading west, to send forces in pursuit. After detaching units to watch the mouth of the Adriatic, the bulk of Milne's ships (at sea, that is; a reserve was held at Malta) were ordered west.[60]

Their quarry had now split up, and were sweeping south onto the Algerian coast. Souchon ordered his ships to attack two ports on the coastline – *Goeben* to Philippeville and the *Breslau* to Bône – in order to disrupt the French troop movements.[61] In the early hours of 4 August, as they bore down on their target, Souchon received orders from Berlin to turn his ships and head for the Dardanelles. Unwilling to abandon his bombardment scheme after coming so far, Souchon pushed his ships ahead. At just after 4 a.m., *Breslau* began a nineteen-minute bombardment of Bône, firing nearly 200 rounds at shipping, shore installations and a signals station. An hour later, the *Goeben*'s attack began, firing thirty-six rounds from her secondary 5.9in guns at various targets onshore.[62] Damage was limited, although some railway and other installations were hit and a magazine at Philippeville exploded.[63] Souchon turned his ships back towards the eastern Mediterranean, although with *Goeben* now low on coal he decided to sail via Messina. This decision would bring his ships into range of the guns of the Royal Navy for the first time.

At around 10.30 a.m. on 4 August, 50 miles south of the island of Galita, two British warships were sighted heading almost directly towards Souchon's ships. These were HMS *Indomitable* (under Captain Francis Kennedy RN, the senior officer present) and HMS *Indefatigable* (Captain Charles Sowerby RN). Both forces cleared for action, going to battle stations and loading their guns. As the ships neared, Souchon ordered *Breslau*, too small to take on either of the British ships, to make off to the north-west, and ordered *Goeben* to turn slightly to port, making a relative course that would bring her closer to the British ships, and possibly even across their bows. Kennedy ordered his own ships to follow the move, causing Souchon to steer further that way himself. As the distance closed, the tension heightened. While *Goeben*'s guns remained in their fore-and-aft rest positions, Kennedy's force kept their main armament trained on the German ship.

However, Britain and Germany were at peace. Although events in Belgium and France were pushing them to the brink of war, it had not been declared. Usually in peacetime, warships would be expected to render passing honours in this situation, saluting each other. Now, though, neither side dared make a signal in case it was misinterpreted, and the battlecruisers passed each other at a distance of 10,000yd (9,000m), well within accurate gunnery range. Once past, Kennedy ordered his ships about to give chase. At 2 p.m., the light cruiser HMS *Dublin* joined the British force, just as the *Breslau* rejoined *Goeben*. At the same time news came that an ultimatum had been sent to Germany demanding the withdrawal of their troops from Belgium. The deadline of the ultimatum was midnight.

By early afternoon, Kennedy's ships were beginning to lag seriously behind the Germans. The British ships' slower design speed and understrength crews served to allow the Germans to slip away, although not without considerable effort. The entire crew of the *Goeben* rotated through the engine room, working shifts in between their usual duties. Goerg Kopp recalled:

Two hours in that hell below was all a man could stand. Smarting and irritating, the fine coaldust in the bunkers penetrated the nose and clogged the throat. Lungs laboured heavily as men struggled at their work ... The stokers stuck to their work – half-naked, in nothing but their trousers, they served the fires, tearing open the furnace doors, trimming the coal, drawing out the ash and putting the fresh coal ready. The sweat ran in streams down their gleaming torsos. The searing heat steamed from the furnaces, burning the skin and singeing the hair.[64]

Shortly after 3.30 p.m., *Indomitable* and then *Indefatigable* lost contact. Two hours later the *Dublin* also lost sight of the soon-to-be-enemy. It had been a deeply disappointing first round for the Royal Navy.[65]

At midnight, the ultimatum passed and Britain declared war on Germany.

With the general location and probable destination of the enemy known, Milne ordered his ships to sweep in and blockade Messina. At 6 p.m., news arrived that the Italians had formally declared themselves neutral, which meant that no warships would be allowed to enter within 6 miles of her coasts. As the Straits of Messina, between Italy and Sicily, were narrower than 12 miles, this must surely mean that *Goeben* and *Breslau* would have to turn back to the west, in order to sail back around Sicily. Deployments were made on this assumption, but the German ships forged ahead into Messina anyway, where they refilled their almost empty coal bunkers. Many of Milne's ships were also low, and were despatched either to Malta or Bizerta in Tunisia to recoal.[66] A single light cruiser, HMS *Gloucester* (Captain Howard Kelly RN) was left watching the southern entrance of the Straits of Messina.

On the afternoon of 6 August, as Milne's forces still patrolled north and west of Sicily, Souchon put out of Messina with his ships widely separated, heading east. Their progress was immediately spotted by HMS *Gloucester* and Kelly signalled Milne before giving pursuit. Souchon's plan was to head towards, and if need be into, the mouth of the Adriatic, before doubling back after dark to slip around Greece and into the Aegean.[67] At the mouth of the Adriatic, Rear Admiral Troubridge RN, with the 1st Cruiser Squadron, was still on patrol. On picking up *Gloucester*'s signal, and despite his destroyers being low on coal, Troubridge immediately led his force north, although daylight was fading. Once the last light was gone, Souchon turned south, but his move was spotted by Kelly, only 3,000–4,000yd (2,750–3,650m) away, and the change of course was broadcast to the fleet. Unfortunately, Troubridge thought this was a feint, and ordered his force to carry on regardless, an action which he would have to later answer for at a court martial. He did, however, order the light cruiser HMS *Dublin* (Captain John Kelly RN, brother of HMS *Gloucester*'s captain), which was coming up from Malta with two destroyers, to investigate.[68]

HMS *Dublin* came across *Breslau* in the early hours, and only then did Troubridge change course. Based on the course and speed data supplied by the Captains Kelly, he now planned to intercept *Goeben* (still widely separated from *Breslau*) before dawn, although it would be a close-run thing considering the distances involved. However, given the advantages that the *Goeben* enjoyed over Troubridge's heaviest ships (27 knots of speed to 19 knots, and 14,000yd (12,800m) gunnery range to 8,000yd

(7,300m) range) it was an understandable precaution. The cloak of darkness might be the only way the British ships could intercept the Germans without being blown out of the water before they could get into effective range.[69]

By two hours before dawn, it was clear that no intercept would be possible before first light. HMS *Dublin* had lost contact and Troubridge had no accurate information on where the enemy was. Torn between the conflicting sides of his duty – either to press on regardless and engage a vastly superior enemy in daylight, in the finest traditions of the service, or to preserve the lives of his men and ships (which were a significant proportion of the Mediterranean Fleet) from being lost in a futile action – Troubridge, with tears in his eyes, ordered his force to give up the chase.[70]

The only British ship still in the game now was the *Gloucester*, under the command of the younger Kelly. Ignoring Troubridge's order to disengage, Kelly remained resolutely in pursuit of the *Goeben*, despite the obvious and massive discrepancy in firepower. Even when the *Breslau* reappeared, Kelly hung on. At 1 p.m. on 7 August, *Breslau* began to fall back from her position in formation with the *Goeben*, clearly attempting to push HMS *Gloucester* away. Undeterred, at 1.35 p.m., and at a range of 11,500yd (10,500m), Kelly ordered his forward 6in gun to open fire. *Breslau* responded immediately with two ranging shots, followed by full salvos of her main armament. Still undeterred, Kelly closed to 10,000yd (9,100m) and began to return the broadsides. The *Goeben* fell back as well, as if to enter the engagement, but then both German ships drew away, and out of range of the *Gloucester*. The *Breslau* had taken a single hit, which dented her side armour, but, despite excellent shooting, had not managed to hit *Gloucester*.[71] HMS *Gloucester* was now short on coal but had at least confirmed that the Germans were heading for the Aegean. When a second order to disengage arrived from Troubridge, Kelly obeyed.[72]

It took several days for both fleets to recover. For the *Goeben* and *Breslau*, it took until 10 August to reach the Dardanelles, and several more days spent in talks to convince the reluctant Ottomans to accept this gift.[73] Milne, meanwhile, was busy restocking his ships with coal, before leading them into the Aegean, also on 10 August. By 15 August, Milne was commanding a blockading force at the entrance to the Dardanelles, guarding against the reappearance of Souchon, although his force was in a constant state of flux.[74] With Austro-Hungary now in the war, ships had to be despatched to assist the French in blockading the Aegean, while French ships arrived to support Milne. More units were detached to clear German merchant shipping out of the region, to patrol the Suez Canal, and monitor the sea lanes across the Mediterranean. During the course of the reorganisations, the centre of gravity in the Mediterranean for the Entente powers (as officially overall command in the sea was given to the French) shifted so much to the northern blockades of the Aegean and Adriatic, that the Red Sea, Suez Canal and Syrian coast passed from Milne's control into the remit of the Commander-in-Chief East Indies, Rear Admiral Richard Peirse RN.[75]

The arrival of the *Goeben* and the *Breslau* certainly increased tension in the region, but it did not immediately lead to war. The *Goeben* was renamed the *Yavuz Sultan Selim*, and the *Breslau* the *Midilli*. Their commanders and crews remained the same, although they now donned the fez of Christians serving in the Ottoman Navy. Not until dawn on 29 October 1914 would the issue come to a head. The Ottoman government finally succumbed to German pressure and a strong internal pro-war party, and the *Yavuz Sultan Selim* and the *Midilli* appeared off the Crimea and began a series of bombardments against Sevastopol and several other Russian ports. The surprise attack would, finally, launch the Ottoman Empire into the First World War. On 2 November Russia declared war on the Ottomans and the rest of the Entente powers were bound to follow. The same day, martial law was declared in Egypt.

The reaction to martial law was more muted than many had expected. A proclamation was circulated, signed by Lieutenant General Sir John Maxwell (the British military commander in Egypt), stating that, under the terms of the agreement signed by the Egyptian government on 5 August, he was now taking charge of all matters, military and otherwise, for the defence of Egypt. Private citizens would suffer 'no interference' in their own business as long as they complied with the new rules.[76]

An equally matter-of-fact response followed the declaration on 18 December that Egypt was now a British protectorate. Those who had always been vocal in their opposition to the British presence continued to be, while the supporters continued to support. The majority of the population meanwhile carried on with the same dogged resolve they had always shown in trying to make a living in this hard country.[77] At the top level of government this change meant that the British Consul now became the High Commissioner (or, rather, Cheetham became acting High Commissioner), and that the anti-British Abbas Hilmi, even now still in Constantinople, could not remain *Khedive*. On 19 December, his pro-British uncle Hussein Kamel was appointed as his replacement, with the title of Sultan, and a telegram was sent to Abbas Hilmi to inform him of the change.[78]

One interesting facet of the declaration of martial law was that Maxwell used it to publically waive the usual right of shipping caught in an enemy port when war was declared. Theoretically, any enemy ships should be given a period of grace to depart in peace, as long as they had entered before hostilities were announced or in genuine ignorance afterwards. In those circumstances, under Article II of Convention VI of the Hague Conference of 1907, they could not legally be seized, but only detained for the duration of hostilities (although the impounding power could purchase the ship from the legal owners). Perhaps this formality was considered inappropriate, given the recent tensions and the fact that the British had already been blockading the Ottomans for two months. Equally, it could have simply been part of the recent pattern of Britain not letting even international legislation get in the way of protecting the Suez Canal.

Under the 1888 Constantinople Convention, the Canal was open for use by all international shipping.[79] Neither Britain nor Egypt had the right to deny its use to anyone, but regardless, on 5 August 1914 the Egyptian government did just that.[80] A number of German and Austrian ships were lodged at different points in the Canal. Some had simply been caught in the Canal on the outbreak of war, while others had put in to seek sanctuary from the Royal Navy. Either way, they were congesting the docking areas, and possibly represented a threat to the Canal's safety. Using a ship already in the Canal to block it, by laying mines or scuttling themselves across it, was a possibility, and some enemy ships had wireless sets and could transmit information on shipping movements and defences.[81] Now all of these ships were ordered to leave, while guarantees were given that they would not be molested or boarded while within the Canal or the 3-mile limits at either end. Even so, many were snatched up just outside the limit by the British and French navies, and brought to the prize courts established at Alexandria.[82] This traditional system whereby captured ships and their cargoes were purchased by the government from the RN ships involved was slightly modified in 1914 and all 'prize money' from this source was instead paid into a central fund, to be distributed between the whole RN at the end of hostilities.

Within days, patrols were being mounted up and down the Canal. Destroyers were transferred from Malta and, with locally procured gunboats, they swept the Canal regularly looking for mines or signs of sabotage.[83] A valuable addition to this force were the small boats of the Suez Canal Company, which had placed its entire resources at the disposal of the Egyptian government, free of charge, for the duration of the war.[84]

Larger warships also passed through the Canal. Once the *Goeben* and *Breslau* were safely blockaded into the Dardanelles, the cruisers HMS *Black Prince* and HMS *Duke of Edinburgh*, and the light cruiser HMS *Chatham*, were sent to the Red Sea to protect the convoys of Indian, Australian and New Zealand troops that were expected soon. Two other German warships, the *Königsberg* and *Emden*, were loose off Africa and in the Indian Ocean, threatening the Canal from the south, and could easily intercept the incoming troops. Only after the *Emden* was sunk by Australian warships in November off the Cocos Islands, and the *Königsberg* had been blockaded into the Rufji river, was the Indian Ocean considered safe, and these forces transferred back to the Mediterranean.[85] On its way back, HMS *Black Prince* joined the cruiser HMS *Warrior* in rounding up fourteen large and two small German and Austrian steamers from the vicinity of the Canal, sending them back to Alexandria with prize crews on board.[86]

Such actions were being carried out across the eastern Mediterranean, with German and Austrian shipping being winkled out and captured. An electrician on HMS *Chatham*, V.E. Denby, recorded the frantic activity in his diary for August:

13th Orders to proceed to Port Said at full speed. Called at Crete on the way. 8pm sighted a large steamer, put searchlight on her found her to be Austrian Lloyd steamer Marinbad trying to make Trieste. We boarded her having two officers on board & destroying wireless, gave orders to follow us, we altered course of [*sic*] Alexandria.

15th Arrived at Port Said. Coaled ship 960 tons. Harbour full of German ships.

17th Left Port Said & proceeded through the Suez Canal. Four p.m. arrived Suez, more German ships here also 2 ships captured by the *Black Prince*. We sent prize crews aboard each to take them through the Canal.

British mastery of the seas also began to be used to watch the enemy. Egyptian forces had already been withdrawn from the Sinai Peninsula, and so the cruisers HMS *Doris* was despatched to the coast off El Arish to monitor troop movements, and HMS *Minerva* to do the same off Aqaba.[87] After the bombardment by British and French ships of the fortifications at the mouth of the Dardanelles on 3 November,[88] thought was given to bombarding other areas, too. Isolated Ottoman positions in Arabia were considered but discounted for fear that it would cause political problems among the Arabs, whom it was hoped would come into the war on the Entente's side,[89] although HMS *Minerva* was allowed to fire upon Ottoman patrols, even mounting small landing parties.[90]

When Admiral Peirse was ordered to mount a reconnaissance along the Syrian coast in December, he allowed his captains to attack targets of opportunity on the way. The Russian warship *Askold* and the light cruiser HMS *Doris* (under Captain Frank Larken RN) were despatched north. Larken threw himself into his task with gusto.

Starting on the 14 December he began several days of cruising along the coast of Palestine and Syria. A French seaplane was carried, and each day it was lowered over the side to take off and fly inland, survey defences and troop movements. While waiting for the aircraft, with its French pilot and British observer, to return, Larken conducted his own reconnaissances along the coast, intercepting neutral ships to question the crews, bombarding earthworks and putting landing parties ashore to gather intelligence. On 18 December, having cleared the action with Admiral Peirse by wireless, Larken landed parties under Commander K. Brounger RN, 4 miles south of Sidon. Two miles of telegraph poles and wires were cut down, seriously disrupting communications between the Ottoman forces in Palestine and those further north. That night, parties under Lieutenant Hulme Goodier RN were landed 2 miles north of Bab-i-Yunis, where they cut the telegraph lines again and also sabotaged the railway line. Evading Ottoman patrols, the landing parties returned to their boats safely, and in time to see a train derailed. After dawn a second train was shelled and destroyed, as was a railway bridge. On 20 December 1914 'H.M. Ship was bought to an anchor, and the day being Sunday, Divine Service was read.'[91]

On 21 December Larken requested and received permission from Peirse to enter Alexandretta harbour. Here he delivered a note, as required under international law, explaining that unless the town surrendered its railway locomotives and military stores, it would be shelled. Having exchanged threats with officials ashore, Larken left them to consider their options and sailed off north. He landed more parties, destroying more stretches of rails and telegraphs, a railway bridge, and even a railway station. Interestingly, three Armenian staff members from the railway helped with the destruction, then requested to be evacuated with the landing parties, and were allowed to leave with the *Doris*. At 9 a.m. on 22 December, Larken sailed back into Alexandretta to see whether a decision had been reached. He was met by the US Consul, who informed him that, on the orders of Djemal Pasha, the former Ottoman Minister of the Navy and now governor of the Syrian province, all British nationals in Syria were being rounded up and imprisoned, and would be executed should any further bombardments occur.[92] Larken, aided by his officers, drafted a reply stating that should this scheme, 'contrary to the usages of all civilised warfare',[93] be carried out, then a clause would be entered into any future peace treaty demanding that Djemal be handed over for trial under the Hague Convention.

Having delivered his reply, Larken again took his ship out to look for suitable targets while the Ottomans considered their position. When he returned the next morning, either his threats or the entreaties of both the US and the German ambassadors had changed Djemal's mind, perhaps showing a weakness that confirmed a pre-war British diplomat's view that he was a 'reed painted to look like iron'.[94] War materiel was gathered and prepared for demolition.

According to the *Official History*, a sticking point was caused because honour would not allow the Ottomans to let anyone but one of their own destroy the gathered locomotives and stores (which was their right under international law). For his part, Larken would not allow the Ottomans loose with the amounts of explosive that would be needed for the demolition to be completed. In the end, one of HMS *Doris's* officers was given a temporary commission in the Ottoman Army, to allow him to place and set off the charges without the local authorities losing face. However, in his final report Larken does not mention this incident, nor does it appear in personal accounts of officers on board.[95]

This extraordinary episode completed, Larken turned back south, bombarding a shore battery at Ayas Bay, before returning to Port Said.[96] Because of the exchange with Djemal Pasha, Larken's report was forwarded all the way up to Cabinet level for examination. Based on this, the Foreign Office advised the Admiralty that, while anxious that British and French civilians should not be put at risk, they would rather not interfere in military operations or appear to yield to Ottoman threats. With this ambiguous missive delivered, and the buck nicely passed, it was left to Peirse to call off any further shore bombardments for the time being. However, HMS *Doris* and HMS *Philomel* (plus the French ships *Requin* and *D'Entrecasteaux*) continued to patrol the region through January and February 1915, sending ashore landing parties, questioning neutral shipping, and landing agents on the Syrian coast.[97] As a result the Ottomans formed three new infantry divisions to protect the coastal regions of Syria and southern Turkey from such attacks or the larger landings it was feared may follow. Although these remained greatly understrength, given that the average strength of the Ottoman Army through the war was just forty-five divisions, this was a highly satisfactory return on the RN's investment.[98]

For now, Entente naval dominance of the eastern Mediterranean was assured. Meanwhile, steps were being taken to secure the land borders too. In the opening weeks of the war the British had withdrawn their troops from the Sinai back to the natural defence line of the Canal, and had been busy preparing for the attack ever since. It was known that the Bedouin were surveying the areas in front of the Canal for the Ottomans, but while some Bedu were busy working for the Ottomans, others were busy selling information to the British on movements and developments in the desert. Indeed, many of the Ottoman informants and the British informants were probably one and the same individuals. Much of the intelligence passed to the British was unreliable, but it is unclear whether it was deliberate misinformation, exaggeration based on inexperience, or simply passing on made-up reports for the money.[99] But other information clearly pointed to growing Ottoman activity in the Sinai and in November hard evidence of this was obtained.

A patrol of the Bikaner Camel Corps of one officer and twenty *sowars* (Indian troopers), under the command of Captain A.H.J. Chope, attached from the 2nd Gurkha Rifles, had encountered an Arab group on 20 November 1914 near Bir El-Nuss, about 10 miles east of Kantara. There had been some confusion due to at least a few of the Bedouin riding the distinctive white camels, and possibly wearing the uniforms, of the Egyptian Coastguard, but when an attempt was made to meet under a white flag shots were fired. The patrol escaped the 200-strong party of Bedouin, but at the loss of the Indian officer, *Subedar* Abdul Khan, and twelve other ranks killed and three of the *sowars* wounded.[100]

3

PYRAMIDS AND FLESHPOTS

It was immediately apparent in August 1914 that more troops were needed in Egypt. Not only was the peacetime garrison of around 5,000 men[101] far too small effectively to maintain internal and external security under war conditions, but these trained and experienced regular troops were desperately needed to reinforce the British Expeditionary Force being sent to France. Initially it was decided to reinforce Egypt from the closest available pool of troops. Two Indian infantry divisions, an independent infantry brigade and the Bikaner Camel Corps were being mustered in India to be sent to France, via the Suez Canal, and it was decided that at least some of these would be diverted to Egypt.[102] Debate raged over who and how many should be diverted. Amar Singh was an officer of the staff of General Brunker, commander of the 9th (Sihind) Brigade and temporarily in command of the 3rd (Lahore) Division, but even though:

> I went on the Divisional Staff as far as Suez ... all this time, we knew nothing as to what was going to happen to us or where we were going to be sent.[103]

The military commander in Egypt, Major General the Honourable John Byng, was eventually given the powers to delay a single infantry brigade if he felt it was needed. At the same time, he was informed that he was to lead the existing British garrison to France in person, and that he would be replaced by Lieutenant General Sir John Maxwell.[104] By the end of August, a further change ordered the Bikaner Camel Corps, perhaps logically, to remain in Egypt.

The first actual troops started to arrive on 8 September 1914 when the lead elements of the 3rd (Lahore) Division landed at Suez. Maxwell arrived on the same day, and sent orders to retain the 9th (Sihind) Brigade and 3rd Mountain Artillery Brigade for defence of the Canal. The rest of the division immediately moved on to France. The next arrivals were from the UK. The East Lancashire Division (Territorial Forces), soon to be renumbered as the 42nd (East Lancs) Division arrived from 27 September, although with well below their usual complement of artillery.[105] The 42nd Division were part-time soldiers whose training levels were below the level required for service in France. This particular division was sent to Egypt to undertake intensive training as well as guard duties because, it was said, Lord Kitchener thought it only fitting that, as so much Egyptian cotton ended up in Lancashire factories, the Lancashire lads should see where it came from. With replacement troops arriving, the existing garrison departed to France on 30 September, and took with them a considerable portion of the military stores in the country.[106]

This still left Egypt horribly vulnerable, with only a single brigade of trained troops available. Further reinforcements were arranged from India, but over half of these were Imperial Service Troops: units raised and trained by local Indian rulers, albeit under British supervision, whose training and equipment was also below par, and only now converting to the latest types of rifle. They began to arrive in late November, releasing the 9th (Sihind) Brigade to move to France,[107] and were organised into the 10th and 11th Indian Divisions. On 3 December, the first of tens of thousands of the volunteers who would come to make up the Australian and New Zealand Army Corps (ANZAC) began to arrive, and within days set up camp just outside Cairo, at the foot of the Pyramids. Although impressive in numbers and enthusiasm, the standard of training of the ANZACs, many of whom had only been in the army for a couple of months, was below that even of their British and Indian comrades, and they would not be deemed as coherent and battle-ready formations for several months. The Australian official historian, C.E.W. Bean, would recall that, although the raw materials were there:

> They were no more a division than a set of wheels, pistons, nuts, cranks, and cylinders, stowed in a merchant-shop and labelled for overseas, would be a railway-engine.[108]

In fact, it would take until the following spring for the ANZACs, Indians and British soldiers to forge themselves into a fighting force. Apart from the eight regular Indian Army battalions, all of the forces in Egypt had a lot to learn, while the ANZACs needed to build themselves from section level up, learning to work in the small teams of men who would place their lives in each other's hands in combat. Even the British Territorials and the Indian Imperial Service troops would have had little experience in operating together, in the field, as full battalions, let alone as brigades or divisions. Each would need to learn and develop the skills needed for tens of thousands of men to act in unison in the chaos of battle. Infantry, cavalry and artillery would need to learn how to co-operate effectively, and with all of the support services – the signallers who passed orders and reports, the personnel who brought up the ammunition and, just as vital, water to front-line units when needed, and the medical staff who would recover and treat the wounded – they had to be brought together into a coherent, battle-winning whole. Senior and staff officers, too, had to learn their trade at a higher level than most would ever have experienced before. Most of the military staff in the country were stripped out for use in France along with the garrison. Just when large numbers of new units, whose own officers were woefully undertrained, were arriving, those who could guide them through the procedures for obtaining military stores, camp equipment, and rations, and who would know how to establish camps, divide up safe water supplies, and organise logistical support, were all leaving. Within three weeks of arriving, General Maxwell had to inform Lord Kitchener that: 'I cannot spare more Staff Officers … The inexperience of the Territorials will add to the work and all departments are shorthanded.'[109] But at last there were now sufficient troops in the country to make it at least nominally secure.

The Australians and New Zealanders took over a month to sail to Egypt, including several stops along the way, and even from Britain the journey involved a 10- to 15-day[110] voyage on a troopship. Some of these were pre-war, purpose-built troopships, with well-ventilated decks and the sanitary and messing facilities to take on large numbers of troops. There were too few of these to cope with the demands of war, though, and so civilian liners were requisitioned en masse, and even freighters were converted for the purpose. The newly seized troopships were often woefully inadequate in their facilities for taking on so many people at once, and conditions could be grim. Anthony Bluett of the Honourable Artillery Company sailed out in early 1915 in:

> A troopship packed to three or four times its normal peace-time capacity; where men slept on the floors, on mess-tables, and in hammocks so closely slung that once you were in it was literally impossible to get out until the whole row was ready to move; and where we were given food (!) cooked and served under conditions so revolting as to turn the stomach at the bare sight of it.[111]

The routine on board could be monotonous, with few recreational facilities, although some found the experience itself invigorating. Private William Lindsay of the Royal Scots recalled the daily experience in a letter, as well as attempts to educate the passengers on their destination, albeit by resorting to racial stereotypes:

> Reveille 5, hammocks stowed 6. Breakfast 6.45. Parade 10–11. Dinner 11.45. 2–2.30 parade. 4.45 tea. 9 bed. There are two orderlies for each table. They draw the food, wash the dishes and clean up … The men are all in the best of spirits and time does not hang heavily on our hands for there is usually something strange to see … Yesterday we had a lecture about the climate and inhabitants of the place we expect to go to but it was applicable to the East in general. It seems we will have to be very careful about our food and will have to regard one class [of locals] as thieves and another class as liable to attacks of fanaticism. But of course only a senseless person will give offence to any of them.[112]

In some ways the occupants of troopships had it easy. As well as men, thousands of horses needed to be moved to Egypt. These were not only for use by the cavalry, but the guns and ammunition of the artillery, ambulances, and the baggage and stores of infantry units were all moved by horsepower. Hundreds would be jammed tightly onto converted merchantmen, with usually only a small detachment of men to care for them. Trooper S.F. Hatton of the Middlesex Yeomanry was selected to take part in such a move:

The whole of the top, first, second and third decks were fitted up with narrow stalls, 3ft 6in wide at the most; the passage-ways were very narrow, and the sloping gang-ways from one deck to another very steep … There was, of course, no grooming to be done, as the horses were packed so tightly together; but every horse had to be watered separately, feed had to be prepared, and hay packed into hay-nets … so that by the time the whole shipload had been watered, fed and hayed-up, it was time to start feeding again.[113]

Conditions could be deeply insanitary, and the move of the 42nd Division suffered from particularly high rates of sickness. Across five ships, 125 horses died, while more were so sick that they were of little use when they arrived in Egypt. An enquiry was ordered, which found that a combination of existing sickness (which spread quickly in the cramped stalls) with lack of water, poor ventilation, and shortages of both veterinarians and veterinary supplies were to blame, all exasperated by the inexperience of the soldiers detailed to look after ten horses each.[114] Even after reforms were introduced, mortality remained high. In Hatton's convoy, 32 out of 600 horses died:

Another difficult task, and a hateful one, as may very well be imagined, was the disposal of the bodies of the dead horses. There was hardly room for a horse to fall down in its stall as it died, and working in the cramped space it called for great strength to heave the carcasses into the passage-ways. If possible we turned the body on its back, for the more easily manoeuvring along the gangway to the hatchways, through which the derrick chains could reach it for slinging overboard … The frequent sea-burials were a melancholy sight, as men who understand know that horses have their characters as well as humans, and some of our very best pals were dumped into the waters of the Mediterranean.[115]

Arriving in Egypt, at Port Said or Alexandria, was both a relief and an adventure. This was an age when the vast majority of the Britons or ANZACs would never have been abroad. To be heading to the exotic East would have been an incredible experience, and many fill their letters and diaries with vivid descriptions of the sights, smells and sounds of Egypt and its people. Many reacted as modern tourists do, marvelling at their surroundings, although others also acted as the archetypal 'Englishman abroad'. One young Lancashire Fusilier wrote home that:

It's a lovely place here but they are dirty Black people and you can't understand what they say and you can't understand their money so well.[116]

At least some of the troops were warned about the dangers of foreign food, although of course their main subsistence came from army rations. These, however, were barely adequate in the opening weeks of the war, as the massive influx of men stretched the existing stores and logistical systems. Private John Taberner of the Manchester Regiment would write to his parents in late September to describe their food:

I will tell you what we had for dinner today. A bit of boiled meat, one potato & half a teaspoonful of dry beans. For breakfast we have sometimes dry bread & canned fish & tea. There is a little bit of butter served out but not much. We get a quarter of a loaf each & we have to save half our breakfast for tea time because nothing is served out for tea.[117]

Another more immediate problem was the heat, even relatively late on in the year. On landing at Alexandria on 24 September 1914 Taberner and his comrades had had to carry all of their kit to their new post, Mustapha Barracks:

You have no idea how much work there is to march with full pack on from the boat including the army Great Coat which is enough for any man by itself ... The sun was scorching & we had to march to the fort without a stop. Sweat was running off our faces & hands in a continual stream ... We are still in the same heavy uniform we had in England which is worse than cruelty to animals although we are expecting new thin uniforms any moment ... The army shirts are thick woollen & the socks are of that coarse wool & are too thick for this climate.[118]

It would be a week until they were to receive thin, khaki drill uniforms and sun helmets. This would be a persistent problem for troops arriving in Egypt. With the unprecedented expansion of the army in 1914 and early 1915, demand outstripped supply in almost every area. Many troops even well into 1915 would have to wait weeks or months after arriving in Egypt to receive appropriate uniforms, making an already uncomfortable transition all the harder.

Accommodation was a major issue for the arriving troops. The Indian troops were distributed along the Canal, and began preparing defences (and exchanging loud greetings with the boatloads of passing ANZACs). The 42nd Division was mostly placed into existing garrisons, forts and barracks. The ANZACs were directed to set up at Mena Camp at the edge of Cairo, at the foot of the Great Pyramids. Further Territorial and Yeomanry (the cavalry arm of the Territorials) units were placed in camps such as Chatby, on the beach at Alexandria, and wherever else room could be found. The logistical strain of so many troops arriving at once was considerable, and most camps would take days or even weeks to locate and unpack their luggage, erect tents and be properly laid out. Many men's first nights in Egypt were spent sleeping on the surprisingly uncomfortable sand under the stars.

Cramming men in wherever there was room also caused problems when it came to training. The troops garrisoned in the cities, or on the edges of them, had to be rotated through camps in the desert for acclimatisation, to be taught how to survive in the desert, how to manoeuvre in large bodies, and to receive musketry training. Going from the comfortable camps out into the remote desert could be a rude awakening. While in both locations the days tended to start early – 4 or 5 a.m., or earlier if there were also horses to care for – to get as much done before the heat of the day as possible, the days in the desert went on much longer into the night. In the camps near

Alexandria or Cairo there was generally less training that could be done due to space and location, and so there was usually much more time off.

In these off-duty hours, men could visit the cities. Although passes were needed, these were usually freely given despite the frequent trouble that occurred. In the early months of the war, several factors came together that led to severe disciplinary problems, particularly (and famously) in Cairo. Inexperienced officers were less able to control their men or keep them fully occupied. This was most notoriously an issue with the Australians, who are often demonised for their misbehaviour in Cairo. There had been problems with troop discipline in Australia, and on the troopships to Egypt, and the trend continued once they arrived.[119] Bean, the Australian official historian, gives several explanations: the essentially civilian attitudes of most Australians, the fact that these young men had just spent two months cooped up in troopships, that it was often their first time away from home, and that the whole expedition was suffused with an air of adventure.[120] Other factors can also be applied. Australia was a more egalitarian society where the average person was more independently minded, and unlike Britain or India there could be said to be no natural officer class, or indeed ranker class, with the result that men were less willing to fall in with military discipline.[121] The Australians were also paid more than their British counterparts, which not only meant they had more money to spend on entertainments that could get out of hand, but also gave a ready source of resentment with other troops.[122] Certainly the records bear out the problems with the Australians. The 1st Battalion, Australian Imperial Forces (AIF), recorded 220 soldiers committing offences in the first three weeks that the unit was in Egypt.[123] Most of these were leave violations, which were probably exasperated by the proximity of their camp to Cairo.

Drunkenness was also a major problem for the army. Strong drink was cheap and widely available in Cairo, particularly in the flourishing red-light districts. A common complaint was that the drink was regularly 'spiked', having a disproportionate effect on the drinker and lowering their inhibitions dangerously.[124] In fact, this was generally the side effect of the poor quality of the alcohol. Even supposedly 'branded' spirits and beers were usually brewed locally and sold under forged labels. The brewing process was often unhygienic and slap-dash, leading to high alcohol content and potentially dangerous impurities.[125]

In these vibrant slums, where prostitutes would line the balconies over clubs and music halls in which drink flowed and exotic dancers performed, it was extremely easy to go astray and succumb to temptation, regardless of nationality. Few of these young men would have ever seen such flagrant displays of freely (or at least cheaply) available drink and sex, and it was only human nature that many would give in to their baser desires. Poor quality alcohol lowered inhibitions and led to increased business for prostitutes, while equally, Trooper Hatton recalled, 'no man in his sane mind could enter a brothel stone-cold sober'.[126] It is perhaps true to say that the Australians, with more money, found it easier to go further. Even Major General William Birdwood, commander of the ANZAC forces and often praised for his understanding of the antipodean soldier,[127] wrote to Kitchener on Christmas Day 1914 that:

the men are perfectly without discipline, and Cairo has been perfect pandemonium ... [they are] coming in droves every evening and large numbers [are] constantly rolling about in the streets drunk.[128]

It would take several months, some extreme measures, and a lot of small, practical changes to crack down on the disciplinary problems in Cairo. In February 1915 Birdwood sent 131 of the worst offenders home to Australia,[129] which served to concentrate the minds of many, for no one could deny the genuine enthusiasm to serve of the average ANZAC. Colonel Harold 'Pompey' Elliott, later a legendary brigade commander in France, was well known as a strict disciplinarian. He sympathised with his men over their reactions to Egypt and the Egyptians, but was all for making an example of the worst offenders by returning them home in disgrace, feeling that:

It is just scandalous the way a few men are going on getting us a very bad name with everybody. They get on the drink and go with the women and get disease and cheat the nigger cabdrivers ... I am out of all patience with them.[130]

Better regulation of leave passes was also instigated for all nationalities, and there was a sudden growth in the number of military police employed around the camps and in the city itself. Perhaps most importantly, experience began to kick in. The results of getting drunk and the frequently associated visit to a brothel, which could lead to the extremely painful treatment of certain unsocial diseases, began to outweigh the novelty.

Military factors also began to tell. The rates of venereal disease became excessive and could put a serious dent in the fighting strength of a unit. No figures exist for the first sixteen months of the war, but even in 1916 over 14,000 troops were hospitalised with VD in Egypt, or approximately 7.5 per cent of the army (compared to approximately 1.8 per cent of the army in France).[131] More military police patrols and stricter punishments for those diagnosed with VD were imposed to help reduce numbers. Officers, non-commissioned officers and men all became more accustomed to discipline and military order. An increase in the tempo of training also helped, as Chaplain-Captain Guy Thornton of the New Zealand forces, and an ardent anti-drink and anti-brothel campaigner, put it:

They found by experience that a soldier's life is no sinecure. It was drill, drill, drill from morning to night. Fatigue duties demanded their daily quota of victims. Guards always had to be kept. Manoeuvres taxed their strength to the utmost. Route marches made them desire to go to bed early, and made sleep sweet.[132]

Another significant development was recreational facilities in the camps themselves. These were slow to build-up, but by the spring of 1915 organisations such as the YMCA, the Salvation Army and other religious groups had made significant inroads into providing centres where soldiers could gather to socialise without having to enter the city, or could attend series of concerts and lectures, as well as more spiritual activities.

The trouble did not entirely go away, and drunks in particular would continue to cause a headache to the various military police forces, and the brothels would continue to sap the fighting strength of many units. In fact, probably the worst incident in Cairo did not occur until 2 April 1915. In the so-called 'First Battle of Wazza' (after the street on which it occurred) a group of Australian and New Zealand troops attacked and then torched a brothel they felt had been cheating them. Other buildings also caught fire and further crowds gathered at the scene. An Australian provost patrol attempted to disperse the crowd, but they were themselves attacked. When the fire brigade arrived, these too were attacked, and then the British Military Police arrived and fired warning shots over the rioters, which managed to wound three Australians and a New Zealander. The crowd, by now numbering in the thousands, responded badly and the MPs were forced to withdraw. Only after troops from 42nd Division were called out was the riot dispersed.[133] The Second Battle of Wazza was a smaller affair on 31 July, shortly before massive reinforcements for Gallipoli left Egypt. The causes and size of the riot was much the same, although the military policing authorities managed to deal with it more effectively.[134]

While many soldiers dabbled in the more sordid sides of Cairo and Alexandria, and a few became hardened frequenters of low establishments, higher-brow culture was also prevalent. Often immediately, or perhaps after getting the novelty of the delights of wine, women and song out of their systems, most soldiers also visited the bazaars, museums and ancient sights of Egypt. From the fleshpots, almost every soldier passing through Egypt at this time seems to have made time to 'gaze at the Sphinx, to marvel at the Pyramids, and, of course, to ride on a camel – everyone does that'.[135] At this time, visitors were free to explore these incredible monuments in their entirety, climbing to the summits (where at least some carved their names or initials) and descending into the tunnels that honeycombed the structures. Corporal Victor Godrich of the QOWH voiced a fairly common opinion of the site:

> The first impression is a huge mountain of stone, consisting of little steps up which it looks possible to run, but when you get near to them; you find that they are five feet high ... As a contrast to the age of the old Pyramids, I was surprised to see a wireless aerial suspended between a high mast and the top of the Great Pyramid ... It is so big you cannot persuade yourself that it was built by human hands.[136]

The museums of Cairo were also considered 'well worth a visit'[137] by thousands of troops who came to marvel at the ancient artefacts, and particularly the mummies preserved there. These were sites and names known from school and from church. In 1914, the average soldier was far better versed in the Bible than most people are today, and in Egypt (and even more so in Palestine in 1917–18) many diarists and correspondents would avidly record the various ancient and biblical sites that they had visited. In Cairo Museum, for Corporal Godrich, this meant:

> the Mummy of Ptolemy the Great. One can look at the actual features of the man who scowled on the Jews and ordered that they be cleared out of Egypt thousands of years ago.[138]

Along with enjoying the sights, sounds, and experiences of Cairo and Alexandria, serious business was also undertaken. As training proceeded, more British and ANZAC troops were detailed to aid with the defences on the Canal. The Indian and Gurkha troops who had been posted there since September had already constructed systems of trenches and redoubts, but more digging in was always needed. This was no easy matter in the loose, shifting sand, where even a narrow trench required a hole several times the size of the finished article to be dug first, and then solid walls or 'revetts' built to hold the sand back:

> This meant six hours' digging almost every day for almost every man, divided into a morning and an afternoon shift. Now sand is admittedly nice stuff to dig in, you do not need a pick, and can fill your shovel without exertion. But to trench in sand is not the faintest use unless it is revetted. Our revetting material was matting on wooden frames, and these had to be anchored back on stakes driven in deep down, six feet clear of the parapet … so that to produce a trench you had to take out six feet of sand extra on either side, hammer in your stakes and attach your anchoring wires to the matting and then fill in the whole again. Traverses had to be dug right out and then filled in again when the wall of matting was in position and secure.[139]

At least, for the first troops and the first defensive works, there was the advantage of it being winter. True, it was still much hotter than those from the UK had ever experienced (although not such a change for the ANZACs and Indians), but this was still a far easier environment to adapt to and work in than summer heat. The transition into the full force of summer would be gradual, but even so come May or June:

> The heat was almost unendurable, and flies, mosquitoes, and midges contributed their quota to the already sufficiently hardships of the life. People at home, who have never experienced the flies of Egypt, cannot realize what a persistent and exasperating curse they can be, clustering in black clouds over everything, hardly deigning to leave the food one is eating even as it is swallowed.[140]

The heat (up to 120°F/45–50° C in the shade at the height of summer, if shade could be found) and the flies were a constant and irritating feature of everyone's life. The lack of water was also an inevitable fact of life, and the initial training of all arriving in the country included an element of acclimatising the men to thirst:

> The water ration was most precious, this consisting of but one waterbottle per man per day. This was the sole issue of fresh water, which could only be supplemented for ablution purposes at times by a trickle of the bitter brackish desert water, often collected most laboriously over long hours … In the great heat of the blazing desert the temptation to drink freely was well-nigh irresistible, but every man had to exercise the greatest care, and no more than sip at his water-bottle. Water supplies were uncertain, no one knowing definitely how long it would be before more was available on these desert adventures.[141]

Food was an almost equal preoccupation. In the camps and fixed defences, fresh meat, bread, vegetables and fruit were often available, but in the desert basic rations usually had to suffice: the army's standard-issue bully beef and biscuit. The tins of beef, heavily salted and stodgy, were hardly ideal for desert conditions, while the hard, dry biscuits could be just as difficult to swallow. It was not just the lack of calories, but the lack of nutrition that was a problem. Between the diet and the insanitary conditions of desert life (complicated by the lack of water for basic hygiene purposes), disease and illness was rife. The worst afflictions in 1916 were venereal diseases (as we have seen) at 7.5 per cent of the army admitted to hospital, diarrhoea and dysentery at around 3 per cent of soldiers each, and enteric fever at 1.6 per cent.[142] The problems of keeping the army healthy were serious issues. In 1916 alone, the equivalent of 75 per cent of the strength of the army was hospitalised,[143] and at any one time some 7.2 per cent of British and Dominion and 3.5 per cent of Indian troops were in hospital.[144] These are just the figures for those who were hospitalised; many others, perhaps milder cases, opted to stay with their units. Sores, for example, were also common, as sand was ground into already course uniforms, and these then rubbed against the skin. Without plentiful fresh water, infection was a certainty. So many men suffered from such lesions that only the worst cases were hospitalised, the rest simply putting up with the pain and discomfort for the months that it could take for them to heal. With a stoic practicality that would in many ways characterise the coming campaigns, the vast majority of men would put up with personal discomforts that would have horrified those at home:

> I cannot describe to an ordinary clean person the most revolting sensation that a fellow undergoes when first he discovers that he has become the prey of body-lice. I think I was more inclined to be sick at their first appearance than at anything I saw or smelt during the whole War. After a time one got quite used to the little pests, and entered into the sport of the daily 'louse' with glee.[145]

De-lousing clothes by hand became a regular, and even a social, event, although some old hands who had served in the Boer War or with the Regular Army in India soon spread the tip that if lousy clothes were draped over an ant-hill, the ants would swarm up to eat the lice and their eggs, although a good shake was then needed to get rid of the ants.

Severe medical complaints, and wounds received in battle, meant evacuation to the rear areas. Each battalion or cavalry regiment had its own doctor, medical staff and small field hospital. Here, wounds would receive very basic treatment, and pills and potions could be dispensed to the sick. Wounds and any illness likely to incapacitate for more than a few days would require the patient to be carried back to a Casualty Clearing Station. Motorised transport was extremely rare in Egypt, especially in front areas where there were very few metalled roads, and so the journey was likely to be by either a horse-drawn ambulance (with wheels or, more so later in the war, skids) or on a camel. Either means would be uncomfortable in the extreme, especially in cacelots (or cachelots). These were coffin-like boxes which would be slung one either side of a camel's hump, in which wounded men would sit or lay. The rocking motion of the camel's walk was both nauseating and jarring, inflicting great pain on the passengers. Once at a Casualty Clearing Station, wounds would be treated more thoroughly, and from there, with any luck, the comparative luxury of a train would be able to remove the soldier to the hospitals of the rear areas.

All of the training, suffering and sweating endured by the men would soon pay off. In late January 1915 the Ottomans began their first serious test of the Canal defences.

4

THE BATTLE OF THE SUEZ CANAL, FEBRUARY 1915

There were several reasons why the Ottoman Empire had been reluctant to enter the war straight away, and one of them was the length of the army's mobilisation period. None of the other main players had suffered such comprehensive military upheaval as the Ottomans had in the previous two years. The Balkans Wars had cost the Ottoman Army 250,000 casualties, and forty-three entire divisions had been removed from their order of battle.[146] On top of this, a significant amount of land had been lost. This territory, from their European lands, was among the most populous and industrially advanced of the entire Empire. Not only were large recruiting grounds lost, but also huge amounts of military stores and the manufacturing capacity to replace it.[147]

To adapt to the new reality, a widespread reorganisation of the army was instigated under Ahmed Izzat Pasha, at the end of 1913. The army was based on regional recruiting grounds, with particular areas supporting designated divisions. With the loss of so much land in Europe, these needed to be significantly redrawn to compensate. A whole new method of organising the army followed, as all distinct reserve units were abolished. Instead, front-line units were held at a peacetime strength of about 40 per cent.[148] In time of war, reservists were channelled out to regular units to bring them up to full establishment. On the one hand, unlike for example in the British, French and German armies, where entire divisions were made up of reservists, this meant that each division had at least a backbone of experienced officers and non-commissioned officers (although these were in very short supply after the Balkans Wars[149]), theoretically increasing combat effectiveness. On the other hand, the posting of large numbers of stray reservists to distant corners of the Empire upon mobilisation would tax the organisational, and even more so the lamentable transportation, resources of the Ottomans to breaking point.

Ahmed Izzat Pasha was replaced by Enver Pasha in January 1914 but reforms continued along the already established line.[150] Training, mobilisation plans, war plans and the organisation of units were all comprehensively reviewed. Much of the credit for these reforms, which greatly modernised the Ottoman Army, are often laid at the door of German advisers, who arrived in the country in early 1914 under the command of Liman von Sanders.[151] How much use these officers really were is still open to much debate. While the Ottomans clearly acted under some German influence in their practices and tactics, this had been the case for many years before von Sanders had arrived and perhaps was no more than the way most armies had copied Prussian ideas after their successful campaigns in the 1860s and 1870s.[152] Previous German military missions, from the 1880s onwards, had led to a number of Ottoman officers attending German training colleges, and so German influence already pervaded through the higher levels of the Ottoman establishment. On the other hand, Sanders' team were rather restricted in what they could hope to achieve. The language barrier was considerable, while the newcomers were also entirely unfamiliar with Ottoman practices and systems.[153] Many were still trying to find their own feet when war began to loom. And, although German staff officers were posted to numerous headquarters at different levels to offer advice and guidance, none were posted to training units where they could influence the tactics and procedures learned by Ottoman soldiers at the most basic level.[154] Indeed, one Ottoman recruit recalled that the new systems caused considerable confusion with training staff:

> These instructors had a hard time of it; the German military system, which had only recently been introduced, was too much for them. They kept mixing up the old and the new methods of training, with the result that it was often hopeless to try and make out their orders.[155]

For their part, one British diplomat in Constantinople remembered:

> All the time I was in Turkey, members of the German military mission took the line that their task was impossible; they said they disliked the Turks, and thought them stupid and unteachable, and despaired of any results.[156]

Given the time frame and the myriad problems caused by the defeats of 1912, it is not surprising that the Ottoman Army entered the First World War with some significant deficiencies. Artillery, rifles and in particular machine guns, were all in very short supply. Many of the support arms were almost non-existent, including medical facilities and transport.[157] On the other hand, the organisational framework of the army was in relatively good shape, with the new 'triangular' structure (later adopted by most of the Western powers) proving flexible and efficient.[158] Under this system, each army corps commanded three infantry divisions (plus an artillery regiment and a cavalry regiment), each of which consisted of three infantry regiments (plus an artillery regiment). Regiments, and as far as possible divisions, were organised along ethnic lines, partly as a result of the regional recruiting policies but also to simplify language issues. Although some mixing took place, a general character was maintained, for example of Anatolian Turks or of Arabs, each of which was reckoned to have its own strengths and weaknesses.[159] Alexander Aaronsohn, for example, a Palestinian Jew who was conscripted in the opening weeks of the war, thought that Anatolians were 'splendid fighting material', whereas Arabs were 'very inferior troops … once stupid and cunning: fierce when victory is on his side, but unreliable when things go against him.'[160] He had been called up as part of a predominantly Arab intake but felt that the handful of Christians or Jews 'were the best-disciplined troops of the lot'.[161]

The recruiting of non-Muslims into the army was a relatively new thing, introduced in 1909. Until then, Jews and Christians (around 20 per cent of the population) had simply paid higher taxes for the privilege of being exempt from the draft, and even after 1909 the rules were only loosely imposed. As a rule, non-Muslims were placed in labour battalions rather than fighting units, and strict limits were imposed on how high they could be promoted.[162] Muslims, too, could pay to be exempt, although there were cheaper ways to get out of serving. Of the 100,000 or so recruits called up every year, at the age of 19 or 20, around 25 per cent would be discarded as medically unfit.[163] The Arabs in particular, whose way of life made the discipline of the army an anathema, would attempt to wrangle medical discharges through various means, although in wartime the rules were significantly tightened. Aaronsohn recalled:

> To these wild people the protracted discipline of military training is simply a purgatory, and for weeks before the recruiting officers are due, they dose themselves with powerful herbs and physics and fast, and nurse sores into being, until they are in a really deplorable condition. Some of them go so far as to cut off a finger or two. The officers, however, have learned to see beyond these little tricks, and few Arabs succeed in wriggling through their drag-net. I have watched dozens of Arabs being brought in to the recruiting office on camels or horses, so weak were they, and welcomed into the service with a severe beating—the sick and the shammers sharing the same fate. Thus it often happens that some of the new recruits die after their first day of garrison life.[164]

The rest of the recruiting process was equally harsh. Aaronsohn recalled that no food was issued during the four-day march to the training depot, so that recruits had either to buy or often steal their own. At the depot, only old and second-hand uniforms were issued unless bribes were placed, accommodation was extremely basic, and physical punishment of the recruits was common.

Throughout the war, the lot of a *Mehmetçik* (literally, 'Mehmet', the equivalent of Britain's 'Tommy' or Australia's 'Digger') would be a hard one. Problems would persist regarding lack of uniforms and (particularly) boots, and long delays in pay.[165] Food was a constant problem. Ottoman food production fell by 40 per cent during the war, and what was available had to be transported across increasingly inadequate communications networks. Fresh fruit and vegetables were always in short supply, leading to a widespread problem with scurvy, and the full ration of meat and bread was seldom reached.[166] The poor diet led to increased rates of sickness and disease, even if these were usually treated (if such a word can be used regarding the woefully inadequate Ottoman medical services) at unit level rather than at hospitals.

The Entente powers had entered the war with scarcely concealed contempt for the Ottoman Army, based largely on their poor showing in the recent Balkans Wars as well as conflicts going back to the Crimean War of 1854–56. However, 'Johnny Turk', as *Mehmetçik* were usually known to their enemies, soon won the grudging respect of the soldiers fighting them. They were dogged in defence and fierce in attack. Despite all of the logistical, health and equipment problems faced by the average *Mehmetçik*, their tenacity and dedication allowed the Ottomans to fight against vastly superior forces (both in numbers and usually equipment) simultaneously on fronts as widely separated as the Balkans, Mesopotamia, the Caucasus, and the Sinai, and inflict some humiliating defeats along the way.

In Egypt, though, the war would start badly for the Ottomans. In mid-November, Djemal Pasha, the former Naval Minister and member of the ruling triumvirate of the CUP, was despatched to take over their forces in Syria and Palestine. On leaving Constantinople, he was hailed as the 'saviour of Egypt' and, it is claimed, promised not to return until Cairo was again Ottoman.[167] A late shuffle saw the Second (Ottoman Turk) Army, less VIII (OT) Corps, move from Syria back to Constantinople, and the new Fourth (OT) Army was formed to take its place.[168] While Djemal Pasha undertook a torturous journey across the poor roads and incomplete railways to take up his new command, XII (OT) Corps moved across from Mesopotamia to join VIII (OT) Corps. As these formations gathered, and received the required reservists to bring themselves up to strength, the timetables for mobilisation slipped; VIII Corps would take thirty-six days (as opposed to the twenty-six days planned) and XII Corps thirty-one days (against twenty-three days planned) to become officially ready for wartime operations.[169]

Djemal, meanwhile, formed his plans. He had been ordered by Enver Pasha to launch an attack on the Suez Canal, to cut it and to stir up a rebellion in Egypt. However, this would be a major undertaking, meaning as it did a crossing of the Sinai Desert. The Chief of Staff of VIII Corps, the German Colonel Kress von Kressenstein, was already working on various studies, but, even Djemal admitted, they were severely inhibited by the lack of proper support services with the army.[170] Not least, the perennial problem of transport reared its head. Any attacking force would need to carry all of its food and most of its water with it, and for that they would need camels. The number of camels of course depended on the number of troops, and by a process of compromises it was decided that the attacking force would consist of approximately 25,000 men. Even by restricting rations to 1kg of biscuit, dates and olives and one gourd of water per man per day, the army was still short of at least 11,000 camels.[171] Supplies of camels from the nomadic Arab tribes was drying up due to political unrest, and the Ottomans had to resort to requisitioning animals from across Palestine and Syria, along with civilians to tend them. Although the required numbers would be met, there would still be a very strict limit on how long the army could hope to remain in the desert.

The first echelon of the attacking force was mustered at Beersheba, and consisted of the 25th (OT) Infantry Division, augmented by an additional infantry regiment from each of the 23rd and 27th (OT) Infantry Divisions, five batteries of field artillery and two of mountain artillery, a 15cm howitzer battery, a cavalry regiment, four squadrons of the Camel Corps, 1,500 Arab volunteers, six companies of engineers (with pontoons for crossing the Canal), a telegraph section and various medical units.[172] In all, 12,642 men, 968 horses, 12,000 camels and 328 oxen were gathered, and even supplying such a force in camp near an established town proved difficult. Aaronsohn, who by now had taken advantage of the widespread corruption in the army to purchase his discharge, witnessed the scene:

> Beersheba was swarming with troops. They filled the town and overflowed on to the sands outside, where a great tent-city grew up. And everywhere that the Turkish soldiers went, disorganization and inefficiency followed them. From all over the country the finest camels had been 'requisitioned' and sent down to Beersheba until, at the time I was there, thousands and thousands of them were collected in the neighbourhood. Through the laziness and stupidity of the Turkish commissariat officers... no adequate provision was made for feeding them, and incredible numbers succumbed to starvation and neglect. Their great carcasses dotted the sand in all directions; it was only the wonderful antiseptic power of the Eastern sun that held pestilence in check.[173]

The second echelon, consisting of the 10th (OT) Infantry Division, with supporting units, was concentrated further north, at Zahle in the Lebanon, ready to follow at a decent interval. Now, time began to be of the essence. The rainy season, such as it is, for the Sinai is from December to January, and full advantage of this would need to be taken. On 14 January 1915 the forces began to move.[174] The first echelon broke into two long columns, each spread over several days' march to ease the strain on the wells along the way. The smaller right wing marched out to El Arish before turning west, marching along the ancient route through Katia at around 6–8 miles from the coast, and stopping short of Kantara. The larger, left wing column, marched down to Aqaba before turning into the desert, marching via Kalat-ul-Nahl, deep in the desert, before also stopping some 6 or 7 miles short of the Canal on 31 January. The march had taken around twenty days, the last week or so with the force moving only at night in an attempt to avoid detection.[175]

It had been a considerable feat of endurance for the Ottoman troops, although an unusually wet rainy season had allowed greater use of desert wells and cisterns so that apparently not a man or beast had been lost,[176] but now the final objective was in sight. Having said that, accounts vary as to what the final objective was. Djemal claimed in hindsight that he knew that cutting the Canal was impossible, and that his goals were to gain intelligence and provoke an Egyptian uprising.[177] Kress von Kressenstein claimed to have been more dubious about an uprising but hoped that even seizing the Canal for a few days would allow them to do enough damage to at least temporarily block it.[178] Aaronsohn, speaking to the troops gathered at Beersheba, recorded that their general belief was that they were going to sweep across the Canal and throw the British out of Egypt.[179] All three of these sources should be taken with a pinch of salt but it does perhaps show that, once the initial assault on the Canal had been made, there was some confusion on what should happen next.

What is clear is that the British were fully expecting the attack to come. Apart from old-fashioned human intelligence from Bedouin informants, aerial reconnaissance also kept them informed. French seaplanes began to push inland from the

Sinai and southern Palestine coasts, managing patrols as far as Beersheba and El Auja. Operating with French pilots and British observers, these were flown principally from HMS *Doris* and two converted captured German steamers, the *Aenne Rickers* (later HMS *Anne*) and the *Rabenfels* (later HMS *Raven II*).[180]

Within a few weeks of the declaration of war on the Ottomans, the Royal Flying Corps also began operations in Egypt. On 4 November 1914 Captain S.D. Massy (on secondment from the 29th Punjabis and formerly commander of the Indian Central Flying School at Sitapur) had been despatched from England with two officers, a party of men and three Maurice Farman aeroplanes, while two further Maurice Farmans, described as 'old but in flying condition', were acquired second hand from Italy.[181] Arriving at Alexandria on 17 November, disembarkation began the next day, and the force arrived at Camp Moascar, Ismailia, two days later. An airfield was established here, close to HQ Canal Defence Force and supported by good infrastructure, and the first flight took off on 27 November.[182] However, although from Ismailia, at a height of 4,000ft, the whole length of the Canal could be viewed, to conduct a proper reconnaissance the portions of the Sinai opposite Port Said and Suez would need to be visited. From Ismailia, this meant a flight of some 50 miles, taking up more than half the flight time of the (even then) outdated and decrepit Maurice Farmans.[183] Therefore, a programme was started to establish advanced landing grounds, and by the time of the Ottoman attack the RFC were staging their patrols through fields at Kantara, Suez, Mabeiuk (15 miles east of Suez), Ras el Nagg (35 miles east of Suez), and Er Rigum. This greatly extended the ranges possible, although a practical range of 40 or 50 miles into the desert was still imposed.

In December, reinforcements arrived, in the form of two more Maurice Farmans and a Royal Aircraft Factory BE2 (all minus their engines) with mechanics from the Indian Central Flying School, and a party of pilots (with engines) from the UK.[184] Now, regular patrols could be staged out into the desert, particularly (as can be seen by the disposition of most of the advanced landing grounds) the southern half of the Sinai, where seaplanes could not reach. While the French seaplanes kept track of the build-up of Ottoman forces around Beersheba and El Auja, from mid-January the RFC began to report on (and occasionally bomb) troop movements in the desert.[185] Through their services, General Maxwell was kept fully informed of Djemal's progress.

For defensive purposes, the base line of the Suez Canal was used. Actually, the Suez Canal is technically two different structures. The Ship (or Marine) Canal is the broad waterway used by shipping, and is usually what is meant (including in this work) by the term Suez Canal. However, just to the west runs the smaller, narrower Sweet (or Fresh) Water Canal. This is unconnected to the salt-water Ship Canal, instead being fed by the Nile. It was, and remained throughout the war, an important source of drinking water to the forces along the Canal and in the Sinai Desert.

The length of the Canal, from Port Said to Suez, is approximately 100 miles, but for nearly thirty of these it runs through the substantial and broad bodies of water of Lake Timsah and the Great Bitter Lake.[186] Unless the Ottomans hauled some substantial boats across the desert, these sections were safe, and could be lightly guarded. In November 1914 an additional flooded section was made by opening a cutting in the Canal near Port Said, inundating a further 20 miles of the Canal's frontage, down almost as far at Kantara. It had begun to seep away by January, but a second cutting at Kantara was made to reinforce this area.[187] Thus, only half the actual length of the Canal needed defending.

This was still a considerable stretch, given the troops available to General Maxwell. He was loath to commit the still partially trained British and ANZAC troops. Instead, Major General Alex Wilson, commander of the 10th Indian Division, was appointed General Officer Commanding, Canal Defences, and given command of the Indian infantry and cavalry in the country.[188] The Indians were short on supporting troops, so these were supplied by the British and, to a lesser extent, Egyptian armies, particularly artillery and engineers. Generally, Egyptian troops were not trusted, as it was thought they would be unwilling to fight fellow Muslims, and it speaks volumes about the seriousness of the shortages that Egyptian artillery, engineers and machine-gunners were deployed. In simple numbers, Wilson had 30,000 men at his disposal, and he split them between three defensive zones along the still approachable lengths of the Canal (*see* Appendix C). Behind him, he had a further 40,000 ANZAC and British troops to draw on if need be.[189]

Wilson's force worked hard to fortify the Canal, while also leaving it open for shipping. Trenches were dug along the western bank of the Ship Canal to provide a solid line of firing points to counter any attempts to cross it. On the eastern bank, strong points were constructed to cover the existing ferries and other infrastructure, and then to cover a series of new crossing points. Landing stages were built for ferries and the multitude of small boats that patrolled the Canal, many on loan from the Suez Canal Company. Several pontoon bridges were built, the central sections of which were removable to allow ships past. Gradually further trenches were added on the eastern bank, to cover the flanks of the new strong points, although most of these were only manned, and then sparsely, during daylight.[190] Beyond them, mounted patrols explored the desert. Behind the defences, the existing network of roads, railways and telegraphs was expanded to allow fast communications and movement. The whole defensive project was carried out by an overworked mixture of British, Indian, Australian and Egyptian engineers, aided by the troops available in each area.[191]

As early as 11 January 1915 the British began to prepare the ground for the public reaction to an attack on the Canal, and an announcement was made in the Egyptian press that one was expected.[192] Long-range reconnaissance began to show that Ottoman forces were gathering and from 18 January aerial reconnaissance began to plot large bodies of troops across the Sinai. On that day French seaplanes reported troops at Bir-es-Saba;[193] as they moved closer to the Canal aeroplanes of the Royal Flying Corps from Ismailia also picked them up. Even if aerial observation had not given warning, the advance elements of the Ottoman columns began to make probing attacks to test the British defences. Patrols clashed east of Kantara on the afternoon of 26 January and probes were made against outposts at the southern end of the line around El Kubri, just north of Suez, in the early hours of 27 January and also against the Kantara bridgehead the next day.[194] On 1 February, troop movements were seen in the desert opposite Ismailia and the following day patrols clashed in the area.[195]

As a response to these skirmishes and movements, the defences on the eastern bank of the Canal were manned (although many of the trenches continued only to be manned in daylight), and the strong points reinforced. British and New Zealand units were brought up and held in close reserve. Perhaps most importantly, the British and French navies were also called in. Apart from six RN torpedo boats that had been posted from Malta to patrol the Canal, and a flotilla of Suez Canal Company tugs and launches that had received a selection of heavy guns and machine guns and RN crews, now the big ships were called up.[196] Warships that had been held at Port Said and Suez entered the Canal on 27 January, and took up positions along its length:[197] the British battleships HMS *Swiftsure* and HMS *Ocean*, cruiser HMS *Minerva*, sloop HMS *Clio*, and armed merchant cruiser HMS *Himalaya*; the Royal Indian Marine armed troopship *Hardinge*; and the French cruiser *D'Entrecasteaux* and coastal defence ship *Requin*. Their guns would be used to make up for the army's shortages of heavy artillery, with HMS *Swiftsure* being first to open fire, supporting the 14th Sikhs during the attack on the Kantara bridgehead on 28 January,[198] and HMS *Clio* firing on an Ottoman troop concentration east of El Ferdan on 1 February.[199]

Now, all was ready on both sides. The Ottoman forces were fully gathered, and by probing the defences along a 75-mile stretch (from Ismailia down to El Kubri) had not only gained a clearer idea of British defences, but also muddied the waters as to where their main strike would fall. Those defences were now on full alert and, indeed, greatly strengthened.

Djemal began his attack after dark on 2 February, moving his men forward with the hope of launching them across the Canal before first light next morning. Confusion and delays followed, partly due to an unexpected sandstorm and partly due to a lack of training in handling the pontoons.[200] The ones used for the crossing were galvanised steel, 24ft long and 5ft wide, capable of carrying twenty to thirty men each, while rather less stable ones of kerosene tins and wooden planks were held back to be used to build a bridge once a crossing was made.[201] At around 3.25 a.m., sentries of the 92nd Punjabis at Tussum, at the southern end of Lake Timsah, heard movements and voices to the south of their position, later explained as Arab troops engaging, against orders, in their traditional chanting before battle. Major T.R. Maclachlan led a machine-gun team and half a platoon of his sepoys south, around 2,000yd (1,800m), where they opened fire at the vaguely seen figures. Fire was returned but the fighting soon petered out.[202]

Around 4 a.m. the sand storm thinned and the moon began to illuminate the desert. At 4.20 a.m., No. 5 Battery, Egyptian Artillery, which was placed on a high point on the western bank nearby, began to make out movement on the far bank, and also opened fire. As their shells tore into the main Ottoman force, most were seen to panic and scatter, leaving their pontoons on the sand. This was only the southern edge of the attack, and shortly after more boat parties were seen to advance on the Canal across a 1½-mile front to the north of them. The strong points on the eastern bank and the trenches on the western opened a devastating fire, again scattering most of the troops before they could reach the Canal, and sinking most of the pontoons that were launched. Only three boats made it across unscathed. The first landed at Mile Post 48.3, nearly on top of the heavily defended Post No. 6. Major O. St J. Skeen immediately led some of his 62nd Punjabis forward to meet the Ottomans head-on as they struggled up the bank, killing or wounding the whole crew. The other two boat loads landed further along by Mile Point 47.6, near Post No. 5. Here, Major M.H.L. Morgan and Lieutenant R.A. Fitzgibbon led men from the 62nd Punjabis and 128th Pioneers respectively in a counter-attack. Both of these officers were wounded, Fitzgibbon later dying of his wounds after running a considerable distance to take a message to No. 5 Battery. Four of the Ottomans were killed and six wounded and captured. It was not until after dawn broke fully that another twenty Ottomans were found sheltering under the banks and captured by the 2nd Rajputs. All three officers, as well as *Subedar* Kula Khan and *Jemadar* Sher Zaman Khan of Skeen's company, were Mentioned in Despatches for their courage in repulsing these attacks. *Bimbashi* I. D'E. Roberts of the Royal Artillery, attached Egyptian Artillery, and *Mulazim Awal* Effendi Helmi of No. 5 Battery were also Mentioned, the latter for standing by his post despite coming under close-range and heavy fire, until he was killed.[203]

Dawn found the first Ottoman attempt to cross the Canal thoroughly thwarted. The forces that had been sent forward with the pontoons, from the 73rd and 75th Regiments of the 25th (OT) Division, had been scattered, although some had taken shelter in the British trenches that had been left empty overnight. A large body of men in the trenches 200yd (180m) south of the Tussum post were cleared out by enfilading machine-gun fire, although another body of 350 Ottomans in trenches to the east of the post proved out of any line of direct fire. Two counter-attacks by the 92nd Punjabis were needed to clear this section of the defences, at 7 a.m. from the south led by Captain H.M. Rigg, and from the north at 11 a.m. led by Lieutenant J.W. Thomson-Glover. The fighting continued until 3.30 p.m., when the line was finally cleared, and seven Ottoman officers and 280 men led to the rear as prisoners.[204]

Meanwhile, a few miles south of Tussum, around Serepeum, a larger British counter-attack was staged across the Canal. At 6.30 a.m., two companies of the 2/10th Gurkha Rifles and two platoons of the 2nd Rajputs crossed the Canal and, after joining two companies of the 92nd Punjabis, began to sweep north along the east bank two hours later. They quickly ran into a large body of *Mehmetçik*, and possibly as much as two whole brigades of Ottoman troops were seen to move up to join the battle. The two platoons of 2nd Rajputs pushed forward a short distance, but stalled after their commander, Captain Reinfred Arundell, was killed. The rest of the force went to ground, and, after receiving further reinforcements from the 2/10th Gurkhas under Lieutenant Colonel F.G.H. Sutton, held off the Ottomans into the early afternoon. As the infantry battle raged, an artillery duel developed between the Ottoman batteries and the gunners of *Requin* and *D'Entrecasteaux*, the latter definitely getting the upper hand. As the big guns crashed overhead, Torpedo Boat 043, under Lieutenant Commander George Palmes RN, swept up and down the Canal strafing the abandoned pontoons, and any visible Ottomans, with artillery and machine-gun fire, and landing small parties to check trenches and make sure of their damage. Caught between the crossfire of the infantry and the warships, and harassed by Palmes, the main Ottoman force broke off the engagement at around 2 p.m. and withdrew, although *D'Entrecasteaux*'s long-range guns kept up a harassing fire for some time.[205]

Elsewhere, largely ineffectual decoy attacks were made far to the north and the south, to draw off British reinforcements. Down at El Kubri, some unenthusiastic infantry attacks made a fairly feeble demonstration but some more effective attacks were made in the northern areas. At Ismailia, at the northern end of Lake Timsah, the Ottomans did not advance until after first light, and were easily held off at around 800yd (730m) from the Canal by small arms and artillery fire. From 7 a.m., RIMS *Hardinge* engaged in a long-range artillery duel with some of the heaviest Ottoman artillery. This gradually grew more accurate until, shortly after 8 a.m., the ship suffered a series of hits. The first took away its wireless aerial and then two shells hit a funnel each. A fourth shell exploded over the foredeck, knocking out one of RIMS *Hardinge*'s guns and causing much damage. At 8.45 a.m., with eleven of the crew wounded (one of whom would later die), *Hardinge* was moved back out of range and the Ottomans would later claim to have sunk it.[206] *Requin* moved up slightly to fill the gap. After receiving several near misses, the Frenchmen managed to plot the position of the Ottoman 15cm howitzer battery at around 9 a.m. and knock it out at a range of nearly 6 miles. Soon after, HMS *Swiftsure* arrived to take *Hardinge*'s place, and *Requin* moved back south to support *D'Entrecasteaux*.[207]

Slightly further north, near El Ferdan, an artillery duel between HMS *Clio* and some Ottoman artillery saw the former suffer two hits before silencing the enemy, but although infantry were visible at a distance they did not press the attack. Further north still, at Kantara, infantry assaulted the defences between 5–6 a.m., but were fought off. At daylight, twenty dead *Mehmetçik* were found in front of the positions, and thirty-six unwounded prisoners were rounded up. A small attack was mounted in the afternoon, but was easily held off at nearly a mile from the defences.[208]

By mid-afternoon, Djemal Pasha was facing up to the fact that his attacks had failed. Surprise, such as it was, had been lost, and the British defences had proven to be much too strong for the resources he had at hand. Although many of his forces were still in good order and the 10th (OT) Division had not yet been committed, almost all of the pontoons had been destroyed. There was nothing more that could be achieved, and he ordered a general retreat.[209] Through the night of 3–4 February, a few light skirmishes took place, and the following morning strong patrols and detachments of Indians were sent out to thoroughly clear the eastern bank of the Canal. Over the next few days large parties of infantry and cavalry pushed out into the desert, watching the Ottoman retreat and fighting small actions with the Ottoman rearguard. A few score more *Mehmetçik* were killed, and several hundred captured in these actions. However, no general pursuit was ordered. This would later cause some controversy, and various excuses were given, all valid to some extent. For one thing, there was no convenient and fully prepared body of men ready to make such a move; the Indian troops were already fully committed to defensive positions and the British and ANZACs were not up to the task as yet. Equally, no training or preparations had been made to operate, support and supply a large body of British troops in the desert.[210] At a higher level, a certain defensive mentality was in force among commanders, particularly as the available intelligence had it that the Ottomans had had 100,000–250,000 troops in southern Palestine, and that anything from 40,000–100,000 had taken part in the offensive across the Sinai. This would mean that any pursuing force would be heavily outnumbered, and any move could leave the depleted defences of the Canal dangerously vulnerable to a renewed attack.[211]

The offensive failed to cut the Canal for any length of time or to spark an Egyptian uprising. Although the Canal was closed for a few hours on the morning of 3 February, no other disruption had occurred.[212] Indeed, on 31 January, even while the defences were being placed on full alert, the second of the great convoys carrying the Australian and New Zealand volunteers passed through the Canal. Strategically, the attack did have the effect of convincing the British authorities that the Canal was still vulnerable, and thus of the need to keep large bodies of troops in the country. But given that the vast majority of the troops in Egypt were only partly trained, and would not have been sent to France even if they could be spared, this was a limited achievement.

On a human level the defenders suffered twenty-five Indians, four British and three Egyptians killed, and 110 Indians, eighteen British and two Egyptians wounded. Ottoman casualties are less clear: both Djemal Pasha and Kress von Kressenstein would claim in their memoirs to have lost 192 men killed, 371 wounded and 727 missing.[213] British sources would record 238 Ottoman dead gathered for burial, not including those lost in the Canal, and over 700 captured.[214]

The weary Ottoman columns marched back into Beersheba on 15 February 1915. Djemal would write in glowing tones of how his force marched home in good order with heads held high, having suffered no privations during their desert march.[215] Aaronsohn, who saw the troops return, recalled that they were in a shambolic order, with morale low and rumours rife of the murder of German officers and harsh discipline being used to prevent mutiny.[216] Both, doubtless, exaggerated for their own reasons, and the truth was somewhere in between. In Egypt, the attack seems to have passed without too much notice, although the anti-British factions vocally exaggerated British casualties and, according to British civil servant Ronald Storrs, when Ottoman prisoners were marched through Cairo, they started a rumour that the 'prisoners' were actually Indian troops who had had their boots removed (an interesting suggestion of Ottoman supply problems, even at that early stage in the war) and uniforms roughed up.[217] The February assault would be described in the multi-volume British history, *Official History of the Great War: Seaborne Trade*, as:

> An event of first-class importance in the history of the war, since it averted once and for all the danger of a permanent interruption of the sea-trade to the East.[218]

In truth, this is a slight exaggeration, but it was the last serious attempt at cutting the Suez Canal for eighteen months, as both Entente and Ottoman attention would soon be directed elsewhere. However, smaller actions did continue. Bedouin were employed to smuggle mines into the Canal, using the same routes that had previously been used to smuggle hashish into Egypt. Only one of these attempts was successful, when the British steamer *Teiresias* hit a mine at the southern end of the Little Bitter

Lake on 30 June 1915. Although severely damaged, it was successfully towed up the Canal and across to Alexandria, but the Canal was closed for fourteen hours as a search was made for other devices.[219] Further into the desert, skirmishes with Arabs and a small Ottoman force, left under the command of Kress von Kressenstein for that purpose, continued, but were small enough and far enough away to pose no serious threat to the Canal. Safe from attack, Egypt would now turn to a new task, as base of operations for Britain's other Mediterranean adventures.

5

EGYPT BASE, 1915

The first few months of the war had found Egypt the scene of intense commotion. Between troop movements, and the associated building and expansion of camps, facilities and defences, and the fighting on the Suez Canal, the country had been a hive of activity. The rest of 1915 was to prove just as hectic, even chaotic, for the country.

Although the principal threat to the Canal had been thwarted for the time being, Egypt continued to be assailed by threats from almost all sides. In the east, Kress von Kressenstein's force in the Sinai would continue to probe the defences and skirmish with British, Indian and ANZAC patrols. On the western frontier, fighting would break out against the Senussi, who had the potential to not only seize the Western Desert, but also encroach into the Nile Valley and raise religious rebellion across much of the country. In the south, unrest would touch the borders of the Sudan. All of these threats will be examined in later chapters.

It was on a strategic level that the country was most important for the rest of the year and into 1916. The British forces in Egypt now found themselves as the central hub of a series of campaigns across the region. The most important were undoubtedly to the north, across the Mediterranean at Gallipoli and in Greece. Of lesser importance, at least in terms of the commitment of resources and troops from Egypt, were the campaigns to the south in Aden and Mesopotamia.

The Gallipoli campaign was (apart from some small raids elsewhere) conducted on the peninsula that ran up the northern side of the Dardanelles Straits, from the Aegean up past Constantinople and into the Black Sea. These had long been seen as a fast-track to the Ottoman capital, allowing an attack that could knock the Ottoman Empire out of a war with a single blow. The Royal Navy had run this gauntlet before, in 1807, without success, and during the 1906 Taba Crisis had been prepared to do so again. In the last weeks of 1914 and the early days of 1915, it again seemed a tempting option. With stalemate on the Western Front and the Russians in disarray on the Eastern Front, sending an Anglo-French fleet through the Dardanelles seemed like the solution to many problems. It could reopen lines of communication and supply with Russia, while at the same time easing the pressure on her hard-pressed armies by making the Ottomans divert troops from their campaign in the Caucasus. Better yet, with their capital standing defenceless under British and French guns, the Ottomans could even be forced out of the war altogether.

But if the Entente knew the importance of the Dardanelles, so did the Ottomans. Massive works had been undertaken to improve and expand the fortifications during the Balkans Wars, making them the most heavily defended point in the entire Empire.[220] The Straits were less than a mile wide at their narrowest point and heavy artillery batteries covered the whole area. Although much of the heaviest artillery was becoming outdated and ammunition was in short supply, reinforcements poured into the area in the autumn of 1914. When the Royal Navy sailed in to bombard the forts at the mouth of the Straits on 3 November, there was a garrison of some 40,000 men, most of them veterans of the Balkans Wars, and 103 artillery pieces in addition to those in fixed fortifications.[221] After this display of naval interest in the Straits, the garrison was increased, reaching close to 50,000 men and over 300 artillery pieces by February 1915.[222] Fresh positions were dug for the artillery, including for newly arrived German-made howitzers that could fire in high arcs from behind hills and ridges, safe from counter-battery fire from ships, whose guns had significantly flatter trajectories. The infantry dug trenches and built roads. Moving rapidly around the peninsula to repel landings was repeatedly practised.[223] Meanwhile, mine fields were laid across the Dardanelles.

In January 1915 proposals for a heavy naval demonstration against the Straits were laid before the British War Committee.* After much discussion in the higher circles of government, a full-blown attempt to force the Straits and sail on Constantinople was approved on 28 January. The fleet in the Aegean was now under the command of Vice Admiral Sackville Carden RN, who was ordered to attack with his force of mostly aged, pre-dreadnought warships (the more modern ships being kept in the North Sea for home defence), supplemented by trawlers sent out from the UK to act as mine-sweepers. On 19 February the first attack was launched but made little headway. The following day, Kitchener cabled General Maxwell in Egypt to inform him that a force was being put together to land and occupy the forts on the Gallipoli Peninsula, to support the RN's efforts. The Royal Naval Division** (RND) was being sent from the UK directly to the island of Lemnos, just off the mouth of the Straits, and Maxwell was ordered to prepare a force of 30,000 ANZACs, what would become the 1st ANZAC Division, under Major General William Birdwood to join them.[224]

Over the following month repeated naval attacks failed, although Royal Marine landing parties knocked out the aged forts at Kum Kale on the southern shore and Sedd el Bahr on the northern shore. After yet another failed attempt on the night of 13–14 March, Carden stepped down, suffering badly from the strain of command, and Rear Admiral John de Robeck RN took over control of the Anglo-French fleet. He made a concerted attack on 18 March, but a combination of minefields and the plunging fire of hidden howitzers wreaked havoc among his elderly warships. The French battleship *Bouvet* and the British battleships HMS *Irresistible* and HMS *Ocean*

---

*   The War Committee was the senior political body running the war effort. In December 1916 it
     was replaced by the smaller War Cabinet.

**   Made up from sailors and Royal Marines for whom no ships could be found. Instead, these
     unemployed seamen were equipped and retrained as infantrymen.

were sunk, while the French battleships *Gaulois* and *Suffren* and the battlecruiser HMS *Inflexible* were all badly damaged. It was a heavy defeat and proof that the Straits could not be forced by naval power alone.

In fact, plans were already well in hand to make a serious military commitment to the campaign. The 29th Division had already been despatched from the UK to reinforce the RND, and French troops were being gathered. Command of this newly forming Mediterranean Expeditionary Force (MEF) was given to the experienced General Sir Ian Hamilton. Mudros (Moudros), a harbour on the island of Lemnos some 50 miles (80km) west of the Dardanelles, was chosen as the base of operations, although at a meeting of senior staff on the island on 17 March it was decided that the facilities were too basic for the first task which would need to be undertaken: preparing the MEF for the actual landing. Maxwell offered Egypt as an alternative, and immediately began to evacuate his own garrisons from Alexandria and Port Said to make room for the new arrivals.[225]

The various convoys began to arrive on 27 March. First, the 8,000-strong Royal Naval Division arrived at Port Said. Next came the French division, formed from a mixture of Senegalese, Zouave and French troops, into Alexandria, followed on 29 March by the British 29th Division. This was formed of eleven regular battalions, brought home individually from India, and a single Scottish Territorial battalion.[226] Each convoy consisted of troopships and separate cargo vessels, but once in Egypt all of these ships were unpacked and reorganised. In order to be effective immediately on landing, the various supplies had to be divided between the troopships, so that each unit had with them exactly what they needed to support them for at least the initial phases of the operation. For a few days Port Said and Alexandria were a hive of activity, until, from 4 April, the embarkation of the invasion force began.[227]

The combined landings on 25 April 1915 on the Gallipoli Peninsula marked the start of a famously disastrous campaign. Poor planning at all levels has often been blamed for the confusion and mistakes that permeated the initial landings and subsequent attacks, although simple inexperience was also a significant factor. None of the units to arrive on the first day – French, British or ANZAC – had operated together before as single divisions, let alone as an army, and co-ordination and communications were poor. Meanwhile, the scale of the landings was unprecedented in living memory, and the art had been lost. Too many factors had been overlooked or ignored, and, faced by experienced and well-prepared Ottoman defenders, the landings stood little chance of success from the start. Even so, the campaign would drag on, with increasing numbers of divisions being committed, and steady reinforcement of the ANZAC contingents made.

Although extensive facilities would be established on Lemnos, the main base for the Mediterranean Expeditionary Force would be in Alexandria, under the command of Brigadier General C.R. McGregor.[228] While located within Maxwell's command, the base of the MEF was fully independent. Indeed, technically Hamilton had the power to requisition troops from within Maxwell's forces, which consisted of the Force in Egypt maintaining the garrison and the Canal Defence Force protecting the Suez Canal, or from the ANZAC Depot, another independent organisation under the direct control of General Birdwood. To say the least, lines of command and responsibility were blurred and confusion rife.

Maxwell managed to be surprisingly accommodating to Hamilton's demands for ever more men. Just two days after the initial landings, the 29th Indian Brigade was detached from the Canal defences and despatched to Gallipoli.[229] The next day, Hamilton followed up with a request for the urgent despatch of the entire 42nd Division, plus reinforcements for the ANZACs. On 29 April the 2nd (Yeomanry) Mounted Division began to arrive from the UK to join the Egyptian garrison, and its ships were immediately resupplied to carry the 42nd Division north, without even having time to reconfigure those that had been used to carry horses into a more suitable environment for men, nor indeed to thoroughly clean them. On 1 May, the Territorials and 3,000 Australians and New Zealanders sailed.[230]

Over the coming months, troops continued to pour into Gallipoli. Division after division sailed out from the UK, some directly to the Dardanelles while some of them put into Alexandria to rest or reorganise first. The units of Australian Light Horse and New Zealand Mounted Rifles still in Egypt were sent too (becoming the New Zealand and Australian Division), leaving their horses and a contingent of men to care for them behind. Meanwhile, more half-trained ANZAC units arrived over the spring to complete their training at the Depot near Cairo, eventually totalling enough men to form the 2nd ANZAC Division.[231]

Despite the continual hunger for fresh troops, the decision to send the 29th Indian Brigade was questioned in mid-May by Hamilton. Two of the brigade's battalions – the 69th and 89th Punjabis – were Muslim, and both Hamilton and Maxwell were worried about sending them to fight so close to Constantinople. However, to withdraw them from the fighting could be seen by not only the troops themselves, but also all of the Muslims in the Indian forces, as a criticism of their fighting abilities, further aggravating what the British high commanders (erroneously) saw as a fervent undercurrent of dissatisfaction at having to fight their co-religionists in Turkey. In the end, two understrength and battle-weary battalions of Indian troops were withdrawn from France and sent to Egypt,[232] from where the 1/5th and 2/10th Gurkha Rifles were sent to the 29th Indian Brigade. The two Muslim units were then withdrawn and sent to France, which no one could take as an affront to their pride.[233]

The movements of troops put a severe strain on the Force in Egypt and the Canal Defence Force. Although it was rightly considered that the campaign in Gallipoli would draw off Ottoman troops from Palestine and Syria, making another large-scale attempt on the Canal unlikely, the eastern defences were being stretched dangerously thin. In March 1915 the 30th Indian Brigade had been despatched to Mesopotamia, and in July the 28th Indian Brigade was temporarily sent to protect Aden.[234] A survey on 9 July showed that there were some 70,000 men, 36,000 horses and 17,000 mules available in Egypt. This number was deceptive: of these men, just 16,000 (including the soon-to-depart 28th Indian Brigade) were available for guarding the Suez Canal. A further 9,000 men from the 2nd Mounted Division and an independent Yeomanry brigade were deployed partly on the Canal and partly across the rest of the country on garrison and policing duties, while around 15,000 ANZACs at various stages of training were also available. Of the rest, 2,000 belonged to various supply columns or depots, while 28,000 were employed at the base of the MEF and not accessible for duties in Egypt. On top of these numbers, 11,000 men were in various hospitals, most of them casualties from Gallipoli.[235]

In real terms, the Force in Egypt was now much weaker than it had been during the February attacks on the Canal. At the end of July matters became worse still as Hamilton called for the Yeomanry units in Egypt to be dismounted and sent to him. Maxwell, under protest, began to make the arrangements, but Lord Kitchener stepped in to block the move. However, even this was only a temporary respite, and on 16 August over 5,000 Yeomen set sail.[236] At the same time, the ANZAC 2nd Division also began transferring to the Dardanelles.[237] Ronald Storrs would recall seeing these troops depart through Alexandria harbour, which was:

> Fuller than I ever remember to have seen it; but of Transports and Hospital ships. Muslims four years old stand upon heaps of coal and vociferate Tipperary* with perfect accuracy of time and accent, for half piastres flung them by departing warriors.[238]

Egypt's support for the Gallipoli campaign did not end at merely sending troops. From the first hours of the landings in April, a steady stream of casualties flowed back off from the beaches. As new ships arrived to land troops, they would be met with all manner of small craft packed with wounded, waiting to be evacuated. The MEF had, based on projected casualty rates, arranged for two hospital ships to accompany the invasion fleet, with a combined capacity of around 700 wounded.[239] However, the first seventy-two hours of fighting generated some 6,000 wounded personnel (as well as 2,500 men killed), and all manner of ships began to take casualties on board.[240] By the end of June, over 40,000 men had been killed or wounded in the Dardanelles, and an extraordinary expansion of the casualty clearing system took place. Additional hospital ships were acquired and fitted out. Some of the smaller vessels were to remain permanently offshore, acting as Casualty Clearing Stations offering basic treatment until evacuation could be arranged. Other ships would then collect the wounded for transporting to Mudros, and then on either to Malta or, more likely, Alexandria. It was a demanding and distressing job for the medical staff on board, who would be hugely outnumbered by their patients. Sister E. Campbell on board HMT *Caledonia* recorded in her diary in early August 1915:

> Worked to get ready for wounded which arrived in pm. 1380 of them mostly stretcher cases and very bad. Some brought on dead. Had 20 deaths during voyage … We spent all afternoon and night dressing wounds. We left at 8pm. Men in every corner of ship. Ward frightfully hot … MOs operated nearly all night.[241]

The rule of thumb was that if a wounded man was likely to take less than four weeks to recover, he would be held at Mudros. Otherwise, he was sent to the base hospitals two or three day's travel south.[242]

---

*   'It's a Long Way to Tipperary', a popular First World War music hall and marching song.

By July, demands were being made for over forty new hospital ships to be posted to the eastern Mediterranean, with some of them simply being temporarily converted merchantmen. The sudden need was due to the planned additional landings at Suvla Bay in mid-August, which it was expected would generate around 20,000 casualties from an attacking force of 80,000 men.[243] Shortages of medical staff and supplies and of shipping, and concerns about congestion in ports, meant that this number of ships was never reached.

In Egypt, an impressive expansion of the medical services took place, prompting one resident officer to remark that 'Egypt now became one vast hospital'.[244] Already the six Ophthalmic Travelling Hospitals and five Ankylostomiasis (tapeworm) Travelling Hospitals in the country had been diverted to military use, their mobile nature making them very useful during the attacks on the Canal in February.[245] Hospitals were established across the country, and schools, colleges and hotels (even the Heliopolis Palace Hotel in Cairo, then brand new and one of the largest hotels in the world) were converted, and space was given over in existing Egyptian civilian hospitals.* The Public Health Department provided vital aid in the early months, when equipment and staff were in very short supply. By the end of 1915, there would be some 35,000 hospital beds (including 17,000 in convalescent homes) in Egypt, as well as 18,000 beds on Malta.[246]

Another eager supply of help for the medical services were the large number of otherwise unemployed British women, mostly the wives of officers and officials. A Red Cross organisation sprang up across Egypt on the outbreak of war (followed in early 1915 by a Red Crescent Society, established by Maxwell with Prince Ahmed Faud (later King of Egypt) at its head, to provide for Ottoman prisoners of war[247]), but now a new enthusiasm swept the country. The sight of the wounded pouring in from the Dardanelles prompted many new members to flock to join, or to set up their own organisations or institutions to provide succour to the wounded, although this sadly led, apparently, to much bickering and politicking between different groups.[248] These civilians added immeasurably to the comfort of the wounded, and provided a level of aid that the military establishment was simply unable to supply themselves. One witness recalled:

> Casualties absolutely poured in. They unloaded them on to the quays where vans and lorries picked them up. In the meantime some had an hour or several hours lying unattended with the blazing sun tearing their nerves. So many wounds had developed gangrene on the voyage over, with a shortage of nurses and frequently no one at all to change the dressings. Here Mary's[249] mother-in-law Lady Carnarvon worked. She collected other women and sunshades and organised cups of hot tea to cool and refresh these unhappy men. She was tiny, and white-haired with a quiet manner: the heart of a lion and indomitable determination and very persevering.[250]

---

*   This sudden and, at times, uncoordinated requisitioning of buildings led to some very high rates of rent being paid by the army, and the establishment of the Board of Arbitration in the summer of 1915 to oversee and set the prices for all buildings and material requisitioned by the military in the future. See: TNA T1/11809.

Some ladies set up their own hospitals or convalescent homes, fighting initial military opposition to these ad hoc and unofficial establishments. Lady Margherita Howard de Walden, the wife of an officer in the Westminster Dragoons, set up a hospital in Maison Karam, outside Alexandria, in late July 1916, for example. She imported stores and staff from England, despite having been personally and directly forbidden to do so by the Director General of Army Medical Services at the War Office.[251] Her establishment was later incorporated into the system as No. 6 Convalescent Hospital.

The hospitals were a strange world to men who had spent months in the cramped and basic conditions of the small beachheads on the Gallipoli Peninsula; even the novelty of spending their nights in a proper bed, and between clean sheets, would be something of a culture shock. While no sinecure, army hospitals were still relatively comfortable places. Private William Lindsay of the Royal Scots recorded the daily routine in a letter home in August 1915:

> The hospital is in three blocks and is situated in large grounds. It was up till recently a private school and when I say grounds I mean playgrounds. We are not allowed to go outside and all we see of Eastern life is viewed from the top of a wall where we sit in the cool of the evening. Two pyramids can be seen from the ward in which I'm in [sic]
>
> 6 a.m. Reveille. Get up, wash and make bed.
> 7.30 Breakfast. Those on full diet go to dining hall, remainder dine in ward.
> Till 9.30 Help sisters and orderlies in tidying ward.
> 9.30–11 Doctor's rounds
> 12.30 Dinner
> 4.30 p.m. Tea
> 9 p.m. Bed
>
> I'm dressed in a shirt, pyjamas, socks and slippers and find it quite warm enough. We lie on our beds most of the day. Reading is our one and only way of passing the time. The Cairo newspapers are absolutely worthless and contain no news of Britain but we get some English papers a fortnight old ... I'm making fine friends here and though life is sometimes monotonous we are having a quiet and happy time. Last Sunday evening I went to church service. It was a Church of England minister and the service was very enjoyable.[252]

The monotony would become a problem for many of the convalescent homes, who would have to spend considerable time and effort trying to stop their charges entering Cairo or Alexandria to let off steam. As it was, the numbers who did manage to go out on a spree were enough to create an echo of discipline problems of the previous winter and spring. For the most part, better policing and legal reforms kept the trouble to the minimum.

Maxwell's campaign against disorder opened in March 1915 with a series of changes that drastically changed the nature of the law in British Egypt. Under the

Capitulations, the rules left over from the time of the Ottomans whereby most Europeans were effectively immune from Egyptian law, Egyptian police had been unable to enter, let alone interfere with, bars and businesses run by foreigners. Much of the strong, poorly brewed and often counterfeit alcohol that was having such a deleterious effect on discipline came from such establishments. On 18 March 1915, though, General Maxwell declared the Capitulations to be suspended in this area at least, and at the same time increased the maximum punishments for any wrong doing from fines of £1 and a week in prison, to £100 and six months imprisonment.[253] Just over a week later, the powerful spirit absinthe was banned completely.[254] Suddenly, quality control could be enforced on all alcoholic drinks, backed by the threat of substantial punishments, by the local civil authorities.

At the same time, there was a rapid expansion in the numbers of service police available, even if many of these were only temporarily assigned soldiers, with little training. By the time the MEF returned to Egypt in early 1916, Cairo and its environs was policed by British Military Police operating from Kasr el Nil Barracks (known as 'Castle Nit'), by patrols of between five and fifty men from the Australian Provosts, a Cairo Town Piquet of over 800 ANZACs, regular patrols along the surrounding roads and railways in and out of the city by the Australian Light Horse, and numerous regimental piquets and patrols to police individual camps.[255] As can be seen from the national make up of these forces, it was a recurrence of the wild behaviour of the ANZACs in particular that was feared. In this they were only partially successful. Birdwood would himself excuse the behaviour of his men, explaining that 'it was only natural that there should be a certain amount of breaking out when we got back to the "fleshpots of Egypt"'[256] from the rigours of Gallipoli. Others went even further in excusing them; one British Army officer, from the Grenadier Guards, on a tour of Egypt admired their spirit and actions greatly:

> They are fine keen men, those 'ANZACS' but a wild undisciplined crowd!! … They've painted Cairo pretty red, but I fancy they are better than they were! But their keenness to get to France, & the Bosche is quite marvellous; poor chaps, if only they knew!! But I have an immense admiration for them, as they have not made these huge sacrifices for themselves but for the Empire. It is a marvellous imperial spirit which has called on them to fight & nothing else.[257]

This particular officer, HRH the Prince of Wales, later King Edward VIII, had something of a 'wild' reputation himself, and his opinion was not entirely representative of the rest of the British Army. General Sir Archibald Murray, who commanded the MEF from January 1916, was certainly less tolerant, and complained to Birdwood on several occasions about the lack of military courtesies and basic discipline shown by the Australians.[258] While the widespread trouble and rioting of 1915 was not repeated, indiscipline was still a problem. The Military Prison at The Citadel in Cairo was soon at capacity, and an Australian institution had to be established at Ismailia to take the overflow.[259]

The conduct of his troops remained a major concern for Maxwell, particularly from the point of view of his role in liaising with the civil government of Egypt.

Throughout 1915 the country had remained remarkably calm on the whole, although with a couple of notable exceptions. There was some unrest and radicalisation among the student population,[260] and there had been two assassination attempts made, on 9 April and 9 July, against Sultan Hussein Kamel, and an attempt on Hussein Rushdi Pasha, the Prime Minister, on 10 August.

On a smaller, or more local scale, occasional hostility was encountered. Trooper C.H. Rastall of the QOWH, attached to the Military Police in Cairo, encountered the odd demonstration from the locals, which the MPs matched with demonstrations of their own:

> I had a narrow escape a few nights ago, two of us were riding through a native village when they started & stoned us from behind. One stone hit me on the side of the eye. My eye is black and blue now but you can guess we had our revenge. We both turned round & charged them. They went down like nine pins. My horse went into a stall & smashed it all down lamps & all the rest of it went to the sports.[261]

It is unclear whether incidents like these were evidence of systematic unrest or rather the acts of a few disgruntled individuals or the types of youths who can be counted on to throw stones at the police the world over. A clearer sign of genuine grievances was encountered by Lieutenant Algar Howard of the Royal Gloucestershire Hussars in May 1915. His unit, about 150 strong, was called out at 4 a.m. one morning in Alexandria:

> To quell a riot of Egyptian Labour Corps, who had refused to board ship [to Mudros] and escaped … They were armed with iron crow bars but were quickly disarmed and marched back to their boat. As they were still rebellious, a guard of 1 officer and 21 men were put over them.[262]

This episode was far from unique. Private Loudon of the Royal Scots:

> On 1st February [1916] 400 men of the 4th and 7th R.S. were marched with fixed bayonets to the barracks square of Egyptian reservists who had been called up, and were protesting at the duties to be performed, such as tending camels, and at the pay proposed. We had to order them to go inside the barracks, when guards were set on the doors to prevent anyone leaving. The guards' duties were taken over by Australians at 8 am next day.[263]

This was perhaps a foretaste of the increasing unrest of 1917 onwards, although there were equally examples of the Egyptian people welcoming British garrisons. At Beni Suef, on the Nile south of Cairo, the British established a garrison, a regional headquarters, and a hospital. The locals responded by raising money to buy fruit, cigarettes and other comforts for patients in the hospital, to buy and present a plot of land for use as a military cemetery (for which large numbers would turn out to pay their respects at funerals), and even to pay for a shelter to be raised at Mazura for the horses of the Yeomanry stationed there.[264]

Other parts of the country benefited from the war. Martial law was imposed by Maxwell with a light hand, even in clearly military areas. For example, there were few restrictions on travel within the defences of the Canal Zone, and only in September 1915 was access to Port Said and Suez restricted.[265] The restrictions on agriculture were also lifted, allowing greater proportions of cotton, which was much in demand and could secure a far higher price than foodstuffs, to be grown. Both food and cotton, and many other goods, could be sold to the army for a respectable profit, a market which was welcomed in many areas.[266] The relative decrease in food production and availability to the general public would become a problem further down the line, but in the short term farmers enjoyed a burst of prosperity. Meanwhile, the needs of the army for labourers and herdsmen, on short, three-month contracts, proved a welcome source of employment in the Canal Zone. Facing only short periods away from home and for decent wages, thousands of Egyptians welcomed a development that would, again, cause problems further down the line.

Back in the big cities, one of the problems was that many, indeed the majority, of the patients were recovering from illness rather than wounds, giving them a greater freedom of movements. Just over 25 per cent of the hospital cases from Gallipoli (and nearly 7 per cent of the deaths) were caused by dysentery alone,[267] while three times more soldiers were classed as casualties due to disease and illness than due to wounds.[268]

Efforts to alleviate some of the insanitary conditions in Gallipoli were made from Egypt. Apart from the constant flow of fresh and frozen food for the troops, the perhaps unlikely Egyptian export of fresh and clean water was also shipped across by the thousands of tons. As early as June 1915 a system had been established whereby the SS *Sunik* transported 6,900 tons of water at a time from Alexandria to Mudros, where it was cross-shipped to the SS *San Patricio*. From here, two smaller tankers transported the water to Gallipoli, and kept a third small tanker that was moored permanently off ANZAC Cove topped up. However, it was estimated that the army's needs, currently around 650 tons a day, would soon go up, and with it the amount of shipping needed. While new tankers were procured, all transports and merchant ships sailing to Mudros out of Alexandria were ordered to scrub out their ballast tanks and refill them with fresh water.[269]

The strain on the military institutions of Egypt would soon become even greater. In September 1915 events in the Balkans sparked a chain of events that would make conditions in Egypt more difficult. Bulgaria formally joined the Central Powers in early September (although the Bulgarians did not officially declare their entry into the war until October), thus opening a direct line of communications and supply between Germany and the Ottomans.[270] To counter this new threat, and to bolster the now dangerously exposed Serbians, the Entente powers began to lobby Greece to enter the war. The Greek government was torn between their pro-German King Constantine (Kaiser Wilhelm II's brother-in-law) and a pro-Entente prime minister, but on 5 October the Entente intervened directly. Troops of the French 156th Division and the 10th (Irish) Division, withdrawn for the purpose from Gallipoli, began landing at the port of Salonika (Thessalonika), and were soon joined by a Composite Yeomanry Regiment, made up of men from the detachments left in

Egypt by the 2nd Mounted Division. Eventually, six divisions of British troops would be part of the multi-national force stretching across southern Greece and southern Albania (although the Greeks themselves would not enter the war, on the side of the Entente, until 1917). Although the area occupied included the port itself, towns and large areas of countryside, it was decided that this campaign too would have its base area in Egypt.[271]

In Alexandria in particular, this put further pressure on the already overcrowded harbour and port facilities, and on the logistical organisation being built up there. At least it led to a simplification of some of the military structure. In October, the Levant Base was organised, under direct War Office control to co-ordinate and satisfy the logistical needs of the forces in Egypt, Gallipoli and Salonika.[272] The only exception to this was the sourcing of local produce from within Egypt, which remained with the Force in Egypt, whose supply officers at least knew the local markets and could provide a more efficient service.[273] But while logistics were simplified the rest of the command structure remained complicated, and caused confusion at every turn. At times, some subordinate commanders could be unclear as to which headquarters they actually belonged.[274] At Port Said, for example, command passed from the Canal Defence Force to the Force in Egypt to the Levant Base and finally to the Egyptian Expeditionary Force all within the space of one month in early 1916.[275]

By November 1915 it was clear that the Dardanelles campaign was a failure. In October, Hamilton had been replaced by General Sir Charles Munro, in an attempt to breathe fresh ideas into the campaign; instead, Munro agreed with Hamilton that the only sensible course was to withdraw. After much debate at higher levels, the decision was made to prepare to pull all remaining troops out of the Dardanelles to Egypt to rest, be re-equipped and retrained. In the two most successful operations of the entire campaign, Suvla Bay and ANZAC Cove were evacuated in late December and Cape Helles in early January 1916.

While the focus of the army, and the public, remained on Gallipoli, those men left in the 'fleshpots' of Egypt were hardly on a sinecure. Defences had to be maintained (and expanded), and the daily routine of training and care of equipment continue. This could be particularly arduous at the depots of the mounted units who had been sent to Gallipoli, leaving a small detachment to care for all of the horses. F.S. Hook was a driver with the 2nd South Western Mounted Brigade Field Ambulance. Although he took part in the usual rifle drill, inspections and parades, the bulk of his time (even into the heat of the day when most infantrymen would be doing as little as possible in the shade) was taken up with his wagons and particularly his mules:

Getting monotonous, so must describe routine & surroundings & let it stand until it gets more interesting. Reveille 4.30 a.m. Roll Call 4.45. Exercising Mules & sometimes Wagon drill until 6 when breakfast. 6.45 Stables. Water & Feed & attempt at grooming until 8. 8–9 Harness cleaning. 9. Finish & go down camp & undress – to lie down until 11.30 when tea arrives. 12 Stables. Water & Feed. 12.15 Finish & lie down until 5 p.m. when Dinner arrives 5.30 to 6.30. Stables. Water Feed & Grooming. Lights out at 9.30.[276]

If the chores and routine were repetitive, the food was not much better. Although the army went to lengths to obtain fresh food whenever possible direct from Egyptian farmers it still lacked variety. Lance Corporal R. Loudon of the 4th Royal Scots recorded his daily rations while at a training camp near Cairo, which, though wholesome, were deeply repetitive:

> Our rations in camp were tea, bread, bacon (or two eggs), cheese and jam for breakfast; tea, bread, cheese and jam for lunch (at 1 p.m.), and stew, or beef cooked in soup, and potatoes for dinner (at 5 pm). There was a YMCA hut in camp where we could purchase a cup of tea, and various titbits, very cheaply.[277]

Further out on the frontiers and front lines, the diet could be drearier still. In the Western Desert, for example, there were no local sources of food beyond what could be traded with desert tribes (many of whom had been driven away by the fighting with the Senussi – *see* Chapters 8 and 9), and supplies had to be brought out from Alexandria by boat or rail. Private W.R. Bowden of the Royal East Kent Mounted Rifles was in the garrison at Sollum, after the fighting with the Senussi had moved on to other areas. Here, the poor diet combined with the monotony could have a deleterious effect on morale, and state of mind. In November 1916 he wrote home how:

> Things are awfully slow here, same old life day after day. It would be alright here if only there was more shipping, our boats never bring enough grub we are always running short of potatoes & onions. Fancy onions being scarce in Egypt. It's a good thing we are able to get things from the canteen. Our grub hasn't been fit for a dog this week.[278]

Under such circumstances, tempers could fray and spirits sag. Even the smallest change, or most basic entertainments, was a much needed tonic to the boredom. The following month, Bowden recorded:

> It's damn rotten slow here … We are having two sports days [and] I hope to win a quid or two. I am jolly glad they are doing something to make us forget Christmas time. Besides, the sports will arouse the Chaps … they are getting irritable & always arguing & falling out. We are all glad when bed time comes, shut eye is the best pastime in Sollum … The fleas & lice are a pest. I caught 8 in my shirt just now (lice I mean) and I guess there will be reinforcements there by the morning. My gawd what a life. It makes me laugh to think of home & being clean again. Still, we keep smiling and grumbling.[279]

Indeed, things could have been worse. Sollum was, at that time, at least safe. In plenty of other places around the edges of Egypt during 1915 and 1916, things were far from as settled.

6

SIDESHOWS

While the Sinai Desert offered the most direct route between the two main bellig-erents, and the Western Desert offered the Ottomans an opening into the very heart of Egypt (*see* Chapters 8 and 9), these were not the only areas to see campaigning. Fighting also occurred further south, in the Sinai Peninsula. This area, being moun-tainous and well south of the main routes between Egypt and Palestine, was largely overlooked during the war, although the number of monasteries and other religious sites and routes for traders and visitors meant that it was far from empty. From 1916 the Imperial Camel Corps (later Imperial Camel Corps Brigade) would send regular patrols – known as 'Pilgrim Patrols' – through the area to keep an eye on, and occa-sionally skirmish with, the local tribes.[280] The small clusters of European or Russian monks and nuns, and the traffic between them, proved very useful to the British as the basis of an intelligence network.

On the outbreak of war, a military intelligence section had been established with the HQ of the British forces in Egypt, co-located with them in the Savoy Hotel, Cairo. The Director of Military Intelligence was Colonel Gilbert 'Bertie' Clayton, while Philippides Bey, the Chief of Police, operated his own internal network.[281] Clayton reported to both General Maxwell and to General Sir Reginald Wingate, the Governor of the Sudan. Under him he initially had Colonel Alfred Chevalier 'Wallier' Parker, former Director of the Police School in Cairo, and by the end of 1914 reinforcements had arrived from the UK. Lieutenant Colonel Stewart Newcombe, Royal Engineers, a man whose life reads like a *Boy's Own* adventure, led the party and became joint-deputy to Clayton. With Newcombe came two men who had explored the Sinai and southern Palestine with him shortly before the war, ostensibly examining archaeological sites while Newcombe collected intelligence. These were Lieutenants Leonard Woolley and Thomas Lawrence.[282]

Through the early months of the war, Parker, who knew the area well, developed an intelligence network that was based through St Catherine's Monastery and Convent, on Mount Sinai. This network had existed even before the war, being used to keep tabs on tribal news, feuds and rivalries, and also any Ottoman or German interfer-ence in the region.[283] Information came out from the monastery down to the fishing village of Tor, which lay on the Gulf of Suez and acted as a landing point, and quarantine site, for pilgrims visiting Mount Sinai. From here, information was collected by passing British patrol ships. However, Tor came under threat in early 1915; almost the entire Egyptian police garrison had deserted from the village in December 1914, and were only replaced with some difficulty by Egyptian troops, there being no British or Indian units to spare.[284]

In February a force of some 150–200 Arabs with a small number of Ottoman troops arrived at Jebel Hamman, where they could threaten not only Tor, but also the Russian Convent at the Mount of Mosses. For political reasons, the Russian nuns had to be protected, but perhaps more importantly control of Tor could not be lost. Not only would it severe communications with the monks-turned-agents at Mount Sinai, but also provide an ideal spot to launch mines into the Gulf of Suez.[285]

On 10 February 1915 half a battalion of the 7th (Duke of Edinburgh's Own) Gurkha Rifles under Lieutenant Colonel C.L. Haldane was pulled out of the line on the Suez Canal, and embarked on HMS *Minerva*. The plan was to land them north of Tor, to swing around the Arab force and attack it from the rear. In the event, the weather was too bad and the sea too rough to land them at the intended site, at the base of some cliffs, and instead at 1 a.m. on 13 February the force was put ashore by boat in the harbour at Tor. Once ashore, 'without mishap though a few men were extremely seasick', the force was joined by a company of the 2nd Egyptian Regiment and a detachment from 136 Battery Royal Field Artillery.[286] Guided by Parker, a night march of 9 miles was completed to bring the force to the original intended position, inland of and behind the camp, which lay in a horseshoe-shaped gully at Jebel Hamman.

At 6 a.m. the attack began with the Gurkhas on the right and in the centre and the Egyptians on the left of the line. They advanced virtually in silence as the Gurkhas moved into the camp, using their kukri knives rather than their rifles to kill or subdue any Arabs they found.[287] Once through the camp, firing broke out from the surrounding hillsides. With the centre of the line still engaged in the camp and the right encountering stiff resistance, it was left to the Egyptian troops to swing around the Arab flank and force them from their positions among the rocks. Once in the open, a general pursuit was made, and by noon the enemy troops were completely overwhelmed or scattered.[288] Estimates vary but over 100 Arabs were captured (including an Ottoman major) and between sixty and ninety killed.[289] A considerable amount of stores were captured or destroyed, for the loss of one Gurkha, Rifleman Aganraj Rai, killed and one wounded. By 5.30 p.m. the expeditionary force was back on board HMS *Minerva*.[290]

Further south and east, the southern tip of the Arabian Peninsula also saw fighting. For over a hundred years the barren rocks of Aden were a byword in the British Army as a harsh posting. First acquired in 1839, Aden (at this time simply the town and harbour, on the end of an isthmus standing out from the coast but with a somewhat ill-defined landward border) was a coaling station on the route to India, and occupied a strategic position at the base of the Red Sea. In November 1914 Ottoman forces in the Yemen under Ali Said Pasha began to threaten the British-held island of Perim, about 100 miles west of Aden. The 29th Indian Brigade was diverted from a passing troop convoy to land and deal with the threat, chasing the gathering Ottomans inland before returning to the ships and continuing to Egypt.

In June 1915 the threat re-emerged with Ottoman probes against Perim Island, and indications that a force was moving against the town of Lahaj, about 20 miles north of Aden, and whose Sultan was friendly to Britain. While an appeal was made to the government of India (which was responsible for the administration of Aden, but which passed the request on to Maxwell in Egypt), the Aden Moveable Column was put together from the garrison. The Aden Troop, a cavalry force of around seventy men, was immediately despatched north, followed by the main column on 3 July.[291] This consisted of around 1,000 men, under the direct command of Lieutenant Colonel Pearson, including a mixture of Welsh and Indian infantry,[*] supported by machine guns, six field guns and four mountain guns.[292]

While the Aden Troop rode on Lahaj, the Moveable Column marched to the village of Sheikh Othman, about 6 miles from Aden and the head of the colony's water supply system. Even this short march was a trial, conducted during the hottest part of the year in the late afternoon when, while the sun was starting to cool, the sand which had been absorbing the heat all day now radiated it back. At Sheikh Othman they received news that the Sultan of Lahaj's own forces had engaged Ottoman troops to the north of the town, and so the machine guns with the column were despatched by motor car to support the Aden Troop, although some of the cars became bogged down in the sand along the way.[293] After a short rest, at 3.30 a.m. the column started to move again, reaching Bir Dir Amir during the cool of the morning. It was over the next leg, the final 6 miles to Lahaj, that the poor preparations of the column became evident. Too little carrying capacity for water had been arranged and too little rest had been given, and the heat began to take a terrible toll. The official historian of the 23rd Sikh Pioneers recalled that 'the going was terribly heavy, and men fell out rapidly while the sun grew fiercer and fiercer'.[294] The water supply was kept at the head of the column in an attempt to entice men to keep marching, but when, at around 11 a.m., they began to reach Lahaj, most were utterly worn out.

Around midday the first skirmishes were fought with the Ottoman advance guard but throughout the afternoon men from the column were still straggling into Lahaj. Indeed, by nightfall as many as half of the men, plus half of the artillery, had still not caught up. Those exhausted men that had arrived were placed in defensive positions on the northern edge of Lahaj. When the Ottoman force, consisting of around 1,000 regular troops with as many Arab irregulars and six artillery pieces, began to attack at around 5.30 p.m., the British force was slowly pushed back through the town and forced to abandon two of its remaining mountain guns.[295] Then the Arab cameliers, supervising the animals that carried most of the column's food, water and ammunition and who had been left without an escort, panicked at the first fall of Ottoman shells and fled with their charges.[296] Worse still, in the confused street fighting, the Sultan of Lahaj was shot and killed by one of his own men.

---

[*]   Parts of 1st Brecknockshire Battalion, South Wales Borderers, and parts of 109th Indian Infantry, 126th Baluchis, and 23rd Sikh Pioneers.

With his men on their last legs, with no food, water or ammunition, and with his ally dead, Pearson decided that his position was hopeless. Having marched and fought under the searing heat for two days, Pearson abandoned much of his remaining supplies and several machine guns, and fell back to Sheikh Othman on 5 July. By 7 July his force, now reinforced by part of the small remaining garrison of Aden, had fallen back further still, to Khor Makhsar, at the very top of the isthmus.[297]

The Ottoman forces were now in a position to cut off the main water supply into Aden, as well as the caravan routes on which the town relied for much of its food.[298] So on 13 July 1915 the 28th (Field Force) Indian Brigade[*] under General Sir George Younghusband was despatched from Egypt, along with the Berkshire Battery RHA from the 2nd Mounted Division. In the early hours of 21 July, Younghusband's force swept through the lines at Khor Makhsar and pushed the heavily outnumbered Ottoman forces out of Sheikh Othman with very little resistance. Once recaptured, the water supply was repaired, the caravan routes reopened, and proper defences prepared to counter any future attacks.[299] This was deemed to be enough for the time being, and, there being no great tactical advantage to be gained by it, no attempt was made to recapture Lahaj.[300]

With the borders of Aden secure, Younghusband and his brigade returned to Egypt, but two Ottoman divisions, the 39th and 40th consisting of around 5,000 men combined, remained active under Ali Said Pasha in the Yemen. Around 2,000 Ottoman troops supported by 500 Arab irregulars remained in positions around Aden, and in early 1916 further small scale skirmishing occurred north of Sheikh Othman as forces from Aden, including the locally recruited 1st Yemen Infantry, pushed the defensive perimeter a few miles further out.[301]

Ali Said Pasha now became increasingly cut off from Constantinople and would be completely isolated from any other Ottoman forces by the end of 1916. In the spring of 1916 he attempted to forge better ties with the tribes of Yemen and the southern Arabian Peninsula, and a meeting for local tribal leaders was arranged at Lahaj to discuss relations. Unable to make any effective demonstration on land, the Aden garrison called in the Royal Navy to help disrupt the Ottoman proceedings, and in late March the seaplane carrier HMS *Raven II* arrived. From 1 April the Royal Naval Air Service spent several days dropping over ninety bombs on Ottoman positions at Subar, What and Figush, and dropping propaganda leaflets to the Arab population. Having made their point, HMS *Raven II* returned to Port Said on 3 April.[302] Two months later, a second demonstration of British power was arranged, this time with the seaplane carrier HMS *Ben-My-Chree*. Six days of operations, dropping high explosive and petrol bombs on troop positions and increasingly valuable supply dumps, culminated on 13 June when a wireless-equipped aircraft acted as spotter for the *Ben-My-Chree's* guns to shell shore positions. This completed, the ship carried on to support the rebellion of the Sharif of Mecca.[303]

Aden was not the only area where air power would prove to be a cost-effective alternative to ground forces. The Sudan remained surprisingly quiet during the First

---

[*]   51st and 53rd Sikhs, 56th Punjabis and 1/5th Royal Gurkha Rifles.

World War, especially considering the lengthy wars fought in the late nineteenth century between Anglo-Egyptian forces and those of the Muhammad Ahmad bin Abd Allah ('the Mad Mahdi') and his successor, Abdallahi ibn Muhammad, who led Islamic uprisings against Egyptian rule. However, one of Abdallahi's followers, Ali Dinar, had fled south after their final defeat at Omdurman in 1898 and taken over the Sultanate of Darfur, whose borders began about 500 miles south of the Sudanese capital of Khartoum. Darfur was twice the size of the United Kingdom, had a population of less than one million, a slave army of around 10,000 men formed around a core of Dervishes, and was largely empty and waterless. The flat, dusty landscape was only broken by a mountain range (Jebel Marra) to the north and west of the capital, El Fasher, and with nothing of any value in the country, Britain and Egypt were both happy to leave Ali Dinar to it. According to the Foreign Office brief on the Anglo-Egyptian Sudan, Ali Dinar 'for the most part was left to go his own way', noting for anyone who was interested that 'his religious zeal was fervent; his harem large'.[304]

As a religious man with a proven anti-British track record, Sultan Ali Dinar was an obvious target for Ottoman pressure. As early as January 1915 the British Governor General of the Sudan, Wingate, was writing to the War Office voicing concerns over German attempts to stir Ali Dinar into rebellion, a concern which grew through the spring and summer.[305] In February 1915 Enver Pasha also opened a correspondence with the Sultan, and links began to be formed with the Senussi, who would later supply Ali Dinar with arms. In July, Wingate was complaining that Ali Dinar had 'written me a series of most insulting letters' in which he had 'entirely repudiated all allegiance to the Sudan'.[306] Within weeks, he would declare open hostility and a *jihad* against the British in the Sudan.[307]

There was little that Wingate could do for the moment, as his own resources were limited (at the same time as he reported Ali Dinar's insulting letters, he was also reporting ammunition stocks for the Egyptian and Sudanese forces under his command at just 200 rounds per man). However, through late 1915 Ali Dinar's continued defiance, and stated intent that he was going to invade the Sudan, created rising unrest in the western Sudan. In December, it became clear that an invasion attempt was indeed likely,[308] and Wingate began to reinforce the border.

From January 1916 a column of approximately 2,000 Egyptian and Sudanese troops began to be gathered under Lieutenant Colonel P.V. Kelly at Nahud, about 90 miles east of the frontier. In mid March, Kelly struck west with a small mounted column, and seized the wells at Jebel el Hilla, just over the border into Darfur. This secured a water source, although supplies of all kinds remained difficult. The rainy season would not start until June, and Kelly was faced with either advancing now and potentially facing severe shortages, or waiting until the summer deluges turned the ground to mud and washed out what few roads existed.[309] Movement was hard enough already. From Jebel el Hilla, the nearest railhead was nearly 300 miles behind them, and everything had to be moved the remaining distance over dirt tracks by camel or carefully driven light lorries.[310]

These factors made the addition to his force in May even more unlikely. On 11 May, two RFC BE2s arrived at a landing strip at Jebel el Hilla, while two further aircraft were held in reserve at Nahud. For them, this was the end of a journey that had been meticulously planned by Major P.R.C. Groves of HQ RFC Egypt, and commanded by Captain E.J. Bannatyne of 'C' Flight, No. 17 Squadron. Their deployment had involved a four-day, 800-mile journey by sea from Suez to Port Sudan, and a six-day, 900-mile transit by train to Rahad. There, the aircraft had been reassembled and flown the remaining 350 miles, with Sudanese troops acting as observers to show the pilots the way.[311] At least one of the pilots, Lieutenant John Slessor, had had serious doubts about this method:

> I was not sure that this was an awfully good idea. *Bashawish* Badda had never before seen anything more mechanised than a camel in his life. I need not have worried. The old boy wormed himself into the front seat between the centre-section struts without turning a hair and took me straight to Hilla, following the rather indistinct tracks through featureless bush country.[312]

Meanwhile, all of their supplies followed by those same tracks, including two hangars broken down and divided among fifty-six camels. All fuel, ammunition, bombs, tools and technical equipment, as well as food and water, eventually arrived by the same method, although at least some of the supplies suffered from the heat. Despite being wrapped in grass matting, the average can of petrol lost about 50 per cent of its contents to evaporation.[313]

From 12 May, daily reconnaissance flights were made over El Fasher, keeping track of Ali Dinar's movements and dropping propaganda leaflets to maximise the psychological effect of the aircraft.[314] On 15 May, Kelly began his advance, capturing the wells at Melit unopposed three days later. After a pause to rest his troops, the advance restarted on 22 May, coming into contact with the Darfuri main force later that day at Beringia.

Despite being in strong defensive positions and, at around 3,600 men, outnumbering Kelly, Ali Dinar's force attacked in true Dervish style. They threw themselves directly against the rifles, machine guns and artillery of the Sudanese force with fanatical bravery, in a fashion that made Slessor later sum up the average Darfuri as a 'very good fighter but a rotten soldier'.[315] After sustaining this attack for forty minutes, Kelly ordered his men to counter-attack, and the Darfuri force broke and fell back in disarray. It was estimated that the Darfuris had suffered around 1,000 casualties, while Kelly's force reported just twenty-six.[316]

The advance on El Fasher now continued, and the following morning Kelly was outside the capital. Ali Dinar was personally leading a force of 2,000–3,000 men acting as a rearguard at Baggara, but this force was spotted and attacked by an RFC patrol:

> I came upon this rather disorganised rabble and added to their confusion with my four little 20lb Hales bombs. I had bad luck with Ali Dinar himself. We had been specially briefed about him – his large banner and his splendid white Bishareen camel; and there sure enough he was in the midst of this milling crowd of demoralised Dervishes. Much more by good luck than good judgement I made a remarkably

good shot with my last bomb and blew his camel to pieces, but Ali Dinar miraculously got away with it.[317]

Kelly entered El Fasher without opposition. The pilot who had proven so decisive
had been wounded in the leg by ground fire, and was invalided back, eventually all
the way to the UK. He would later receive the Military Cross for his action, and in
the fullness of time would successfully lead RAF Coastal Command during the most
critical phase of the Battle of the Atlantic in 1943, become Chief of the Air Staff from
1950–52, and retire as Marshal of the Royal Air Force Sir John Slessor.

After Ali Dinar fled with his remaining followers into the desert, he opened negotiations with Kelly. Initially these went well, and in late June the RFC contingent
was withdrawn back to Egypt.[318] However, by August, it was clear that he was just
playing for time, and while his followers had been wracked with dissent and many
had deserted, he still had over 1,000 men with which he conducted raids. In October
a force was despatched under Major H.J. Huddleston to corner Ali Dinar, and a
series of skirmishes followed in which large amounts of Darfuri supplies were captured. It was clear that the Sultan was deeply unpopular with the local population,
who offered information and material aid to the Sudanese. Finally, on 6 November
1916 Huddleston caught up with the Sultan's main body at Jebel Juba. After a brief
exchange of fire, the Darfuris scattered, and on advancing into their camp Ali Dinar
was found dead.[319]

Apart from the use of air power, the campaign in the Darfur had been a classic
example of one of Britain's 'small wars', using superior organisation and firepower to
overpower a more numerous but less-well-armed and less-well-supplied local force.
Elsewhere, and also under the Sudan's sphere of operations, a totally different campaign had just begun; one which would see the position almost reversed. In Arabia,
Britain would side with, supply and offer guidance to, a disorganised collection of
Arab factions in opposition to the Western-style Ottoman Army.

With the failed campaign in Gallipoli, the Arab Revolt has come to dominate
(largely through the exploits of one man) the popular image of the First World War in
the Middle East. The origins of the revolt can be traced back decades, if not centuries,
in an area where a handful of large, and dozens of smaller, tribes and factions vied
constantly for power. The size, borders, and importance of each tribe varied greatly
over time, as did their higher allegiances. The Ottomans had nominally controlled the
Arabian Peninsula for some 400 years, but the control was generally tenuous and in
name only; the various tribes and chieftains were scattered, independently minded,
and relatively poor. They were hard to control and not worth the effort of building
the infrastructure that would be needed to impose such control. Over time, some
areas had even drifted away to other powers; Britain gained Aden in the 1830s, and by
the early twentieth century also had significant influence and power with many of
the states and tribes on the Persian Gulf coast.

The exceptions to this where the two Islamic Holy Cities, Mecca and Medina, on
both of which the Ottomans kept a solid grip. In 1908, a railway was built with aid

from Germany down through the Hedjaz* to Medina to strengthen Ottoman control over the area, although plans to extend it further south to Mecca were interrupted by political problems and a coup in Constantinople. The Ottomans had their own governor for the region, but the real local power in the Holy Cities was Sharif Husein ibn Ali, the Emir of Mecca. Appointed to power as Emir (Governor) of the areas around Mecca and Medina in 1908 by Sultan Abdülhamid, Husein was also the Sharif, a title given to members of one of the two traditional ruling families who claimed direct descent from the Prophet Muhammad. As both a Sharif and the Emir, he had considerable standing (although not always popularity) within the Muslim community, and arguably more religious power than the *Caliph* himself. After Abdülhamid was deposed in 1909 and his brother Mehmed V installed as Sultan and *Caliph*, Husein began to be viewed with increasing suspicion from Constantinople. This coincided with a rise in Arab nationalism across the whole of the Ottoman Empire, partly a reaction to the new pro-Turkish government and the development of several major grievances in the Hedjaz region in particular. The building of the railway not only infringed on the traditional political freedoms of the local tribes, it also affected them economically. The Bedouin had made their living for centuries by acting as guides and escorts to convoys of pilgrims or alternatively by ambushing and robbing them. The railway denied them of both incomes.[320]

By the spring of 1914 unrest and discontent had reached a point where Sharif Husein sent his son Abdullah ibn Husein to Cairo to sound the British out on supporting a revolt in Arabia. At that time, the two empires were at peace and no such help could be offered by the British authorities.[321] However, friendly relations were still maintained and a lengthy correspondence began after the outbreak of the war. Relations with Arabia were traditionally run by the Indian government but in March 1915 the responsibility for most of the peninsula was transferred to Egypt, where Sir Henry McMahon (aided by the Governor General of the Sudan, Sir Reginald Wingate) could open a more direct dialogue. The Emir wanted British money and weapons to support a rebellion against the Ottomans, and in the long term British support for an independent Arab homeland covering Arabia, Palestine, Jordan, Syria and Mesopotamia. He was reluctant to move without British support but the British were unsure of what they had to gain.

Militarily there was very little of any significance in Arabia. The Ottomans had laid mines in the Red Sea from the coast but the risk from these was minimal, while the garrison (including Ali Said Pasha's troops in the Yemen) amounted to only four weak divisions.** This was a small enough force that operations to tie them down could easily cost the British more then would be gained, while if the Ottomans did send large reinforcements and crushed the rebellion, the political and propaganda results could be a boost for Constantinople.[322] The principal benefit to be gained, apart from

---

*   'Hedjaz' literally translates as 'the barrier' and denotes the region (dominated by the Hedjaz or Sarawat Mountains) that runs down the eastern shore of the Red Sea into the Arabian Peninsula.

**   The 21st and 22nd (OT) Divisions in the Hedjaz, and the 39th and 40th (OT) Divisions in the Yemen.

nuisance value against the Ottomans, was the propaganda element. In 1914 the Emir had refused to endorse the Ottoman call for a *jihad*, undermining the appeal and incidentally further souring relations between himself and Constantinople. If the British could be seen to be helping to defend the freedom of Mecca and Medina, the political benefits would be significant among the Muslim populations of India, Africa and Asia. At the same time, having the Emir of Mecca in open rebellion against the *Caliph* would be a major embarrassment for the Ottomans.

In October 1915 an agreement was reached. In slightly hazy terms, the British promised to support the Arabs' claims to the stipulated areas in principle, with the caveat that they would not be able to condone any changes that would clash with the interests of their French allies. While not the ringing endorsement he had hoped for, the Emir was enough of a politician to realise that this was the best that could be expected. However, unknown to him, a separate, secret set of negotiations ran from November 1915 between Britain and France on the future control of the region, and which came to a significantly different arrangement. Finalised as the Sykes-Picot Agreement[***] in May 1916, it was endorsed by the Russians and envisaged carving the region up far more to the advantage of the Entente powers than of the Arabs. However, the ramifications of these two agreements, and the later Balfour Declaration of 1917,[****] and how to reconcile them, lay in the future. In 1916, it was enough that Britain had agreed to support the Emir, and by May 1916 was already providing him with gold and weapons.

The spark for the revolt came in the summer of 1916. The Emir's third son, Feisal, had visited Constantinople in the spring, among other things to justify why his father was continuing to resist Ottoman demands for political support and to send more men for the war effort. On his return through Syria, Feisal witnessed a series of harsh punitive actions ordered by Djemal Pasha against the Arab populations in that country, who were rumoured to be planning their own revolt. Further south he saw a force of some 3,500 Ottoman troops apparently being gathered for despatch to Arabia to reinforce the 13,000–15,000 troops already there. In fact, this force was intended for use in Yemen and to support an infiltration into East Africa[323] but the threat was enough. On 5 June 1916 the Emir's first and third sons, Ali and Feisal, raised the flag of rebellion near Medina, the northern of the two Holy Cities.

The Arab force initially numbered between 30,000–50,000 men – Bedu who largely came and went as they pleased and showed frustratingly little discipline or consistency. They were poorly equipped, with very few modern rifles and no artillery or machine guns. Although they outnumbered the Ottoman garrison in the Hedjaz, the lack of modern weapons was a severe handicap. On 9 June Arab forces attacked the Ottoman garrisons at Mecca and Medina, both reduced as the Ottoman governor and many of his troops had already withdrawn to their summer quarters at Taif, in the cooler mountains. At Mecca, it took three days' fighting before the Ottomans could be defeated and the town seized. At Medina, repeated attacks failed in the face of superior Ottoman firepower.

[***]   After the two primary negotiators, Sir Mark Sykes and M. Georges Picot.

[****]   This Declaration announced British support for 'a national home for the Jewish people' in Palestine.

A priority had to be opening a secure line of communications with the British in the Sudan, to allow material aid to flow in. On 9 June about 4,000 tribesmen of the Harb tribe attacked the port of Jeddah, west of Mecca. The Ottomans, well dug in, resisted fiercely, even after the arrival on 11 June of HMS *Fox* and RIMS *Hardinge*, which began to bombard the defences. On 15 June HMS *Ben-My-Chree* also arrived and seaplanes from the ship flew bombing operations.[324] The next day, from lack of water as much as the attacks, the garrison of some 1,400 men surrendered, and their rifles, artillery and machine guns passed into Arab hands. With a secure port, supplies and support began to flow in. Over the coming weeks, the ports of Rabegh (100 miles north of Jeddah) and Yanbu (a further 100 miles north) were also captured.

The ports allowed British aid to pour in (and the Arabs to relieve themselves of their Ottoman prisoners; those who did not volunteer to join the revolt, as many ethnic Arabs did, were shipped out to Sudan), and also allowed the arrival of several French military advisers. The Arabs were inundated with the supplies needed to keep the revolt active: rifles, machine guns, artillery and ammunition for them all; millions of pounds of rice and flour; grenades, explosives and detonators; wagons, boots, saddles, mess tins, buttons and waterbottles.[325] There was considerable concern about the deployment of British troops, due to the possible upset that could be caused by Christian troops fighting in Islam's most holy sites.[326] Instead, Muslim Egyptian troops were sent to operate the heavy weapons, and in time train the Arabs how to use them. The only white British personnel who were deployed in these early days were an adviser, Lieutenant Colonel Cyril Wilson, and an intelligence officer, Lieutenant Colonel Alfred Parker. Later, others would join them, and in November 1916 a detachment of six aircraft from No. 14 Squadron RFC would be despatched to operate from Rabegh, and later Yanbu.[327]

The opening of the ports also allowed a significant propaganda victory. In September 1916 over 1,000 Egyptian Muslims travelled on pilgrimage to Mecca, while over 2,000 travelled from India. More than 6,000 others came overland from outside Arabia. The success of the pilgrimage gave a significant boost to the status of the Emir and strengthened his claims to represent Islam better than the *Caliph*.[328]

However, militarily the campaign was not going very well. The garrison at Medina stubbornly held out against two forces totally around 12,000 Arabs, led by Abdullah and Ali, while even with Egyptian artillery bombarding them the Ottoman force at Taif, the governor's summer residence, held out under siege until late September. By October, morale was crumbling, as were the numbers of Arabs willing to continue the fight. Only Feisal, with 8,000 men at Yanbu, was enjoying any success, and a British delegation was sent to assess the situation more thoroughly. Ronald Storrs was sent as the political representative, and he took with him a young officer from the Arab Bureau, which had been set up in February 1916 to provide intelligence on and propaganda support for the Arabs. This officer was Captain Thomas Lawrence, who had learnt Arabic and a certain amount about the Arabs themselves during his travels as an archaeologist before the war.

Storrs and Lawrence met with all three of Sharif Husein's sons, who were now in positions at Jeddah (Ali), Rabegh (Abdullah) and at Yanbu (Feisal). Talks were held and options discussed, and at the end of the month both of the British representatives returned to Cairo. It was clear from their (and other) reports that the revolt was almost certainly doomed unless changes were made. The Arabs could not face and defeat the Ottoman forces in open battle, and Lawrence suggested that an alternative approach was taken. He advocated hit-and-run tactics, utilising the superior mobility of the Arabs to run rings around the Ottomans, and deny them the opportunity of bringing their heavier firepower to bear on the lightly armed tribesmen. The alternative would be to commit large numbers of British troops, which the political situation in the Hedjaz, and the military situation in Egypt, simply would not allow.[329]

In December Lawrence was sent back to Feisal to give this advice, which at first was ignored. Instead, after another defeat, Feisal fell back to Yanbu, where another British adviser, Bimbashi Herbert Garland, was busy organising a defence. Luckily for the Arabs, at about this time the Ottoman forces also began to lose their momentum, particularly due to drastic supply shortages. In the breathing space provided, a further appeal was made to Feisal, and a plan was conceived to make a 200-mile dash up the coast and capture the port of Wejh. On 4 January 1917 Feisal, with Lawrence, left Yanbu with 8,000–10,000 Arabs. His march north through areas still nominally controlled by the Ottomans was a public display of defiance that boosted the morale of the tribes. The journey took several weeks, during which time contact was maintained with a Royal Navy force offshore. Consisting of HMS *Fox*, HMS *Espiègle*, and RIMS *Hardinge*, this flotilla was to co-operate in the attack and took on 500 Arabs for a seaborne landing at Wejh. The date for the attack was set for 23 January, although in the event Feisal's force was a day late. Unable to feed the Arabs any longer, Admiral Wemyss decided to attack anyway. Under the cover of fire from the ships offshore, the Arabs and 200 armed sailors were landed under the command of Major Charles Vickery and Captain Norman Bray, and the town was stormed and captured. The following day, Feisal's force also arrived and took up positions in the town.[330]

Seizing Wejh had been a masterstroke and would prove to be a turning point in the Arab Revolt. From here, 100 miles north of Medina, a 200-mile long stretch of the Hedjaz railway was open before them. The Ottoman forces in Medina relied on this single track for all of their supplies and potential reinforcements. Lawrence returned to Cairo at the end of January 1917 but other British officers arrived in his place. Lieutenant Colonel Stewart Newcombe and Bimbashi Garland (who blew up the first train on the Hedjaz railway a few weeks later) trained and led the Arabs in the methods that would allow them to attack the railway with near impunity. The Ottomans now lost the initiative entirely and were forced to concentrate on defending their supply lines. Other offensive operations ceased and the Arabs were given the time and space they needed to raise and train a proper army (partly with the help of Ja'far al-Askari – *see* Chapters 8 and 9). This army would later, with the help of Lawrence, who would return again in a few months, push the Ottomans out of Arabia and, working closely with the British forces in Palestine, sweep up through Jordan and into Syria.

7

THE CANAL DEFENCE ZONE, 1916

While the fighting raged in Gallipoli, and on Egypt's western border, the troops in the Canal Zone were also kept busy. New railways and roads were laid and new defences constructed both on the western side and on the eastern, pushing out into the desert. Enemy action was fairly muted, although Kress von Kressenstein had maintained a small force in the Sinai after the repulse of the attack on the Canal in February 1915. Several encounters occurred between forces of Ottoman soldiers and Bedouin tribesmen on the one hand and (mostly) Indian troops on the other, while a number of attempts were made to mine the Canal. As the military forces in Egypt – including not only troops but the warships that had proved so effective in February – were stripped out and sent to the Dardanelles, these actions caused considerable worry, although in the event the Ottomans were also feeding their resources into the Gallipoli campaign and were in no position to exploit the situation.

Patrolling beyond the Canal was difficult, if only from a logistical point of view. To support a Yeomanry regiment for one week in the desert required a large body of camels to provide water and fodder. These camels in turn needed further camels to carry their own supplies, and so on, until a figure of some 900 animals was reached.[331] Patrols therefore tended to be small, falling back if they encountered serious opposition in order to return to the main defensive lines to call up reinforcements. On 22 March 1915 for example, *Havildar* Subar Singh and eight men of the 56th Punjabis encountered a force of 400–500 Ottoman and Arab troops east of El Kubri. The *Havildar* skilfully extracted his men, although not without some difficulty, and fell back to the Canal. It was known that a force of up to 4,000 Ottomans, with artillery, were based in the hills at Nekhl, 70–80 miles to the east, and it was feared that Singh had encountered the advance guard of this force, marching to make another attempt at cutting the Canal. A column* was assembled, and all of the available warships scraped together into defensive positions. The mobile column moved out to meet the Ottomans, and did so 9 miles east of the Canal, routing the enemy and

---

* Consisting of two squadrons Hyderabad Lancers, 1/5th (Lancashire) Battery, 51st and 53rd Sikhs, half of the 1/5th Gurkha Rifles, and a detachment Bikaner Camel Corps, all under Lieutenant Colonel G.H. Boisragon.

inflicting around fifty casualties for the loss of three Indian soldiers killed and sixteen wounded. The Ottomans left a large stock of ammunition behind, which was carried back to the Canal or buried.[332]

Similar encounters occurred east of Ismailia in late April, and at Bir El Mahadat, east of El Ferdan, in late November. Both times, Ottoman and Arab forces numbering 200–300 were encountered, and mobile columns despatched to successfully see them off.[333] Not all of the enemy forces encountered were so large, and indeed the smaller ones were often more cause for concern. On 9 March 1915 eight mines were found floating in the Red Sea, obviously set adrift with the hope of being hit by Entente shipping heading to or from the Canal.[334] This led to renewed fears that small groups could evade the defences and lay such devices into the much narrower Suez Canal, where they would be more likely to be struck, and indeed a foundering ship could potentially block the entire waterway. These fears were exacerbated when, just six days later, the torpedo boats used to patrol the Canal were withdrawn for use in the Dardanelles, although a scratch force of small boats was organised to take their place.[335] Meanwhile, the danger of snipers or ambush led to the requirement that all ships passing through the Canal should have their bridges and other vulnerable areas protected by sandbags.

In early April, fears of mines were first proven when a patrol found tracks leading to the bank of the Canal near Kantara, and, on following them some 15 miles out into the desert, a large packing crate was found. The Canal was immediately dredged and a mine recovered. Further attempts followed in late May and early June, and on 30 June the Ottoman's only success was scored, when the steamer *Teiresias* struck a mine in the Little Bitter Lake. However, the ship did not sink and the disruption caused was minimal.[336] In August, the game was changed slightly, when Arabs (presumed to be former hashish smugglers, using their old routes to avoid British patrols) swam across the Canal and placed dynamite charges on the railway north of Kantara. Although these exploded under a passing train, they were poorly laid and no damage was caused.[337]

While patrols skirmished on the western side of the Sinai, the Royal Flying Corps increasingly took the fight to the eastern side. Moving on from reconnaissance work, with the occasional dropping of bombs on targets of opportunity, by the spring of 1916 specifically targeted long-range raids on Ottoman camps and infrastructure were being staged. The aircraft detachment in Egypt had formally become No. 30 Squadron RFC in March 1915 but in October had been despatched to reinforce the Indian forces in Mesopotamia.[338] To take its place, a whole new organisation arrived from the UK from November. The newly created Fifth Wing, under Lieutenant Colonel Geoffrey Salmond, consisted of Nos. 14 and 17 Squadrons and 'X' Aircraft Park. Arriving by sea in the middle of the month, No. 14 Squadron and the Wing Headquarters established a new airfield at Heliopolis, outside Cairo. The Aircraft Depot, responsible for keeping the squadrons supplied and providing repairs for aircraft too badly damaged to be patched up by their units, took over an old iron foundry at Abbassia. In mid-December, No. 17 Squadron also arrived, and was sent to Heliopolis. By this time, No. 14 Squadron's aircraft had been unpacked, rigged and were operational, with one flight being posted out to Ismailia.[339]

In February 1916 HQ Fifth Wing moved to Ismailia as well, where it could liaise better with the army's headquarters, and in July the organisation was expanded to include the whole of the region. The new Middle East Brigade, under the newly promoted Brigadier General Salmond, now encompassed No. 30 Squadron and the Aircraft Depot in Mesopotamia, No. 26 (South African) Squadron in East Africa and No. 17 Squadron, which was being despatched to Salonika. In Egypt, it included the Fifth Wing and the Twentieth Reserve Wing. The Fifth Wing, now under Lieutenant Colonel Philip Joubert de la Ferté comprised of No. 14 Squadron, No. 1 Squadron Australian Flying Corps (which had just arrived to replace No. 17 Squadron[340]), 'X' Aircraft Park, and the newly formed 'X' Aircraft Depot, which was the central supply hub for the whole brigade. The Twentieth Reserve Wing included Nos. 21, 22 and 23 Reserve Squadrons. These training squadrons would form the basis of a flying training programme in Egypt.[341]

Regular flights by the RFC's (and later AFC's) BE2s now patrolled the Sinai, bombing and strafing Ottoman forces when they could be found, and also conducting a photographic survey of the desert on which to base the new maps that the army was preparing.[342] The two-seater BE2s were poor performers even by 1916 standards, although they would continue to form the backbone of the RFC in France and elsewhere into 1917, and the average patrol could only reach 100 miles out, as far as Hassana and Nekhl. To make it this far, the observer had to be left behind and an extra fuel tank installed in his place, with usually enough weight saved to add a small bomb load too. Bombing Ottoman camps did little material damage, although both sides would find that even the smallest bombs falling on their troops had a disproportionate impact on morale. Lieutenant Cedric Hill, an Australian serving with No. 14 Squadron, recorded the effect when he attacked a camp near El Arish in April 1916:

> It is lovely in the early morning flying over the desert and I had a pleasant hour and a half trouble-free flight before sighting the camp which I could see long before I reached it. I decided to give the Turks a surprise so I sneaked up on the camp by flying very low and as I passed over it with what I hoped would be an impressive roar I dropped a bomb in the middle of it.
>
> It was extraordinary what effect one bomb could produce. It was just like hitting a beehive with a brick. What had looked like a peaceful camp a few minutes ago was now alive with people rushing about in all directions. Judging by the various states of dress I think most of the people who popped out of the tents must have been in bed or just getting up when the bomb exploded.[343]

Very occasionally the material benefits were more substantial. In January and February 1916 the pilots of No. 14 Squadron had watched a new reservoir being built at Hassana, about 90 miles south-east of Kantara. Several attempts were made to destroy it with bombs, and eventually, after much practice near his own airfield, on 26 February Hill dropped a 20lb bomb into the centre of the structure. While a small charge by any standard, it was enough to blow a hole in one wall that allowed around half of the carefully hoarded water to run off into the desert.[344]

For over a year, the only active danger to these flights, apart from the weather or mechanical failure, was ground fire (Hill was shot down in this way in May, and captured). But in April 1916 air opposition began to arrive. Although the Ottomans had their own air service, this was fully committed on other fronts, and recourse had to be made to their German allies. In January, Flieger Abteilung (FA) 300 'Pasha' was formed in Germany from aircrew with combat experience, under the command of Hauptmann Hans-Eduard von Heemskerck.[345] It was equipped with six Rumpler C.1 two-seaters and two Pfalz E.II single-seat fighters, both of which types outclassed the RFC's BE2s. After a protracted journey south, the squadron arrived at Beersheba in early April, where an airfield had been constructed to house it.

Within weeks FA300 was active, flying reconnaissance operations for the Ottomans (their first patrol crossed the Suez Canal on 20 April), gathering intelligence that would prove critical to the attack on Katia and Oghratina later that month. As the Ottoman forces advanced, forward operating bases were established at El Arish, Bir el Abd, and just outside Katia. Bombing and strafing attacks against British ground forces, Egyptian ports, and Entente vessels offshore now became commonplace. In early May, two German raids were made on Port Said. In retaliation, on 18 May 1916 a mixed force of six of No. 14 Squadron's BE2s and one Short 184 and two Sopwith Schneider seaplanes from HMS *Ben-My-Chree* attacked the airfield and camps at El Arish. One of the seaplanes, carrying a wireless set, 'spotted' for the guns of the monitors M15 and M23 and HMS *Espiègle* offshore. Unfortunately, most of the German aircraft at El Arish had already been withdrawn to Beersheba, but bombs were dropped and shells directed on camps and columns of marching men.[346]

Further large-scale raids were carried out by both sides over the summer, with Port Said and El Arish receiving regular attention. Later in May a new airfield was established at Port Said, with a half-flight from No. 14 Squadron, to protect the port. Direct telephone lines were laid to the British advance positions in the Sinai to provide adequate warning for the British aircraft to climb high enough to intercept in-coming German aircraft. Later, the RFC would establish an early-warning system of wireless posts right along the length of the Canal.[347] However, apart from a few notable exceptions (such as on 1 June when eight members of the 1st Australian Light Horse Brigade were killed and twenty-two wounded, plus nearly forty horses, or the raid on El Arish on 18 June that cost the RFC three out of the eleven BE2s despatched[348]), casualties on both sides remained light. The principal contribution of the flying services was in reconnaissance, intelligence gathering, and nuisance value, as their very appearance tended to create disproportionate concern among those below.

While enemy action was a constant threat, on a daily basis the main danger to the troops defending the Canal was simply the desert itself. Those troops who had been in Egypt since 1914 or early 1915 had by now, to some extent, become acclimatised, but it was a very different experience to be positioned on the edge of the Sinai to being in the training camps of Cairo. Although, it is true that some elements remained the same, such as the ubiquitous, maddening flies. Out on the edge of the Sinai, 7–10 miles south-east of Suez at Ayun Musa, Gunner Anthony Bluett opined that

It is no light thing that sends a strong man into hysterics or drives one sobbing from his tent, to rush about the camp in a frenzy of wild rage. Yet the flies did this – and more.[349]

As those close to the Canal worked to improve the defences and infrastructure, others were posted further out and had to start from scratch. In this position, in a feature-less desert ('as flat and bare as a billiard-table'[350]), Bluett's unit of the Honourable Artillery Company, along with an Indian infantry battalion, had to construct their own encampment. Being in front of the line and relatively close to the Ottoman force at Nekhl (with whom they frequently skirmished, with little result, on patrol), the camp had to be fully defensible as well as capable of being lived in, and with an almost total absence of building materials in the area, this meant digging everything into the ground:

> There followed days of unremitting toil … With bowed backs and blistered hands [we] shovelled up half the desert and put it down somewhere else; the other half we put into sandbags and made gun pits of them. We dug places for the artificers, kitchens for the cooks, walled-in places for forage, and but for the timely arrival of a battalion of Indian infantry we should have dug the trenches round the camp; we were mercifully spared that, however. By way of change we dug holes: big holes, little holes, round holes, square holes, rectangular holes; holes for refuse, wide, deep holes for washing-pits; every kind of hole you can think of and many you can't. Day by day the sun waxed stronger until work became a torture unspeakable and hardly to be borne. With the slightest exertion the perspiration ran in rivulets from face and finger-tips; clothes became saturated and clung like a glove to our dripping bodies; and if a man stood for a time in one place the sand around was sodden with his sweat.[351]

Over these holes canvas tents were erected, which could prove heat-traps during the day. Although the sides could be rolled up to let a breeze through, and tricks were picked up such as hanging a porous stoneware jug of water just inside the door to cool the air, they were far from comfortable. Elsewhere, where more foliage was available, even if only from scrub bushes, shelters could be made that allowed the air to circulate more freely. George Wright, an officer in the QOWH, described such a bivouac in a letter home:

> Imagine a grove of palm trees and amongst them a hole dug in the ground roughly six foot square and two foot deep with a roof of branches cut from palm trees, the whole containing a bed, chair and table. It is cool in the day and quite warm at night.[352]

On the other hand, palm trees could be deceptive:

> Providence perpetrated a huge practical joke when it designed the palm to be the only tree which will grow in the desert. From a distance it looks well, but when the

weary traveller approaches and proposes to rest beneath its shade, he finds he has to choose between the thin shadow of the trunk, not wide enough to shelter him, and the little blob of shade given by the clump of leaves at the top; this latter, coming from a point high above ground, moves round with the sun so quickly that you are hardly settled in it before it has glided away, and you must chase it round in a great unrestful circle.[353]

Shortages of water were a fact of life, even if it still caused constant complaint throughout the army. The official ration was one gallon (4.5 litres/8 pints) per man per day, but it often came up short of this. Drinking was discouraged during daylight hours, and while marching or manoeuvring men often had to make do with just the water they carried. The historian of the 5th Highland Light Infantry recorded:

A single water-bottle, once filled, is but a poor supply for a long day under the Egyptian sun. Marching over heavy sand in the hot hours, even when the haversack has replaced the pack, soon produces an unparalleled drought. Sweat runs into a man's eyes and drips from his chin. It runs down his arms and trickles from his fingers. It drenches his shirt and leaves great white streaks on his equipment. And while so much is running out, the desire to put something in grows and grows. The temptation to take a mouthful becomes well nigh irresistible, and once the bottle of sun-heated chlorine-flavoured water is put to the lips, it is almost impossible to put it down before its precious contents are gone.[354]

All of the wells that the army would use in the Sinai were heavily chlorinated to kill off diseases but at the same time making the water from them almost undrinkable.

Water for hygiene reasons varied in quality and availability. In some areas, where water was totally absent, the average soldier simply had to do without. In large areas, however, water that was undrinkable could be found under the desert by digging down from a few feet to a few yards. Not being fit for human consumption, it could be used for hygiene purposes instead. As well as the obvious benefits on physical health, this water could also have an immense effect on mental health too:

Fortunately there was washing-water in abundance, as we quickly discovered in our digging operations. Two or three feet down the sand was quite moist, and if the hole was left for a time, brackish water percolated through in sufficient quantities for a bath. It was the daily custom, after evening-stables, to rush across to the washing-pits, peel off our saturated clothes and stand in pairs, back to back, while a comrade poured bucket after bucket of water over our perspiring bodies until we were cool enough to put on a change of clothes ... You, who dwell in temperate climes, with water – hot and cold – at a hand's turn, will perhaps accuse me of labouring the point. I cannot help it; no words of mine can express what it meant to have that clean feeling for just an hour or two. It was ineffable luxury; it helped us to endure.[355]

At the best of times, sand got everywhere and caked the soldiers and their clothes. Cloth would stiffen and become harsh on the skin, but at least uniforms could be cut down. Sleeves and trouser legs gradually got shorter in many units as soldiers sought to become more comfortable. Other kit was also shed as it became unnecessary or adapted to the desert. For example, buttons, buckles and other metalwork such as swords would be painted black or dark green, not only to prevent reflections that could give positions away to the enemy, but also to help deflect heat and stop the men from burning themselves on them. But if the heat could be deflected in some way, the sand could not. The worst experiences of many involved sandstorms:

> Sandstorms were just as uncomfortable and of those I had several experiences, we rode into the storm wearing goggles fitted with side pieces which were part of our equipment and afforded some protection to the eyes; ears, nose and mouth however were still exposed to the elements and the only way to get relief was to bend the head forward, the poor horses had no protection against the deluge of sand which travelled at a terrific pace. One storm which struck us in the night uprooted bivouacs, and left the place in a terrible mess, so much sand was on top of me that I had to be dragged out of the debris which had been my bivouac. A lot of hard work had to be put in after a sandstorm, however well protected our rifles were they always needed a thorough overhaul, and the horses also needed a spring clean.[356]

Perhaps worst of all was the *khamsin* (also commonly known in Egypt as the *khamaseen*), the hot wind from central Africa that blows up through Egypt between March and May. These typically lasted around three days and when the wind 'blew it was like a blast of heat from a ship's furnace'.[357] Men would be unable to move, with visibility at zero, and could only sit and wait out the phenomenon in their tents or whatever other cover they could find as the hot sand whipped around them:

> Our tempers became very ragged, and though we had hutted together for some weeks, this afternoon we could have murdered each other. Things got worse and worse, until it was difficult to keep one's sanity.[358]

When the elements were not trying to cook, blast or generally drive men mad, the local wildlife would try to do them harm. Blankets, boots and any other equipment left on the ground would have to be carefully checked for scorpions and large, poisonous spiders.

On the other hand, though, the animals and insects of the desert could also provide some entertainment and relief, although attempts to use them to vary and supplement diets were not always very successful. Oskar Teichman, Medical Officer of the QOWH, discovered that the flamingos that inhabited the Canal were 'of no use as food'.[359] In fact, according to Trooper Hatton, flamingo meat would turn green on being cooked and 'was as tough as old boots, and of a similar flavour'.[360]

Some animals had practical uses – chameleons proved useful in keeping flies at bay. If one was suitably harnessed and placed on a branch tied to a tent pole, it would deal with any insects that flew into the tent. But mostly, the local fauna was good for diverting tired, bored and uncomfortable troops. Fights between various combinations of scorpions, tarantula spiders, and chameleons (which turned aggressive during the mating season) were common, and could see some heavy betting. For the more patient (and army life, particularly in a desert, did encourage patience), tortoise racing was popular:

> Tortoise racing was a slow business, but eminently sporting, because the tortoise is so splendidly unreliable. On one occasion one of the competitors in a big sweep-stake was discovered to consist of a shell only – the tortoise who had once dwelt therein having died and turned to dust. In consideration of this it was given a start of six inches, but long odds were offered against it. However, at the end of the time limit – eight minutes – no competitor had moved at all, so that the tortoiseless one was adjudged the winner amid great applause.[361]

For some of the mounted units, the adrenaline rush of tortoise racing simply was not enough. In March 1916 the slightly pre-emptively named 'First Grand Palestine Race Meeting' was held. This included the Sinai Grand National, won by Captain Gooch of the Warwickshire Yeomanry on Clautoi. Polo was also popular, as was hunting. The Royal Gloucestershire Hussars (RGH) had managed to bring two hounds – Tripe and Onions – with them, and these were used by the officers of the RGH and other units of the 5th Mounted Brigade to hunt pi-dogs and jackals. For the more pedestrian units, football, rugby and cricket were all popular pastimes, heat and dust permitting.

The routine of military life also remained the same, and for those close to the Canal defences, this included the inevitable fatigues and working parties, loading, unloading and moving military stores. The process continued day and night:

> The scene was the goods yard of the railway where trucks had to be loaded with great bales of forage, sacks of grain, or cases of bully and biscuit for the personnel at railhead. Snatched from the tender care of their officers, the men were delivered over to NCOs of an unknown breed ... with a highly technical jargon picked up in happier days in the goods yards of English railways. Great naphtha flares cast a blinding light, dispelling the friendly gloom on which every right-minded private relies, if unlucky enough to have to work at night. The still air is solid with dust, increased every moment as GS wagons, each drawn by a team of maddened mules, entered the yard at a hand gallop, scattering all in their path. The atmosphere is one of strenuous profanity, most uncongenial to the unhappy infantry.[362]

Through the winter of 1915–16, the troops on duty with the Canal Defence Force experienced a complete change of pace. As an evacuation from Gallipoli began to look more likely, and the possibility of having to fight another campaign in the Sinai grew, a programme was started to greatly expand and improve the Canal's defences. In pure tactical terms, this meant pushing the line of first defence out to 11,000yd (10km) from the Canal into the desert. This would prevent a repetition of February's events when Ottoman artillery was able to get into range of the Canal. A second, supporting line would be established about 4,500yd (4km) out from the Canal, and then the existing line on the eastern bank of the Canal itself would become the last line of defence. In logistical terms, this required a massive effort. Works were put in hand not only to support the troops on the eastern side of the Canal, but also to expand the entire infrastructure of the Canal Zone.

To staff and maintain the growing network of railways and other technical systems that kept the defences on both sides of the Canal supplied, a search was made of the entire Egyptian garrison. Men with suitable experience and skills in not only engineering and railway work, but also bakers, miners, electricians, draughtsmen and others were pulled back from their units and reassigned, in a move that struck many as being unusually organised and logical for the army to make. Indeed, the move seemed to fly in the face of the traditional 'predilection of the army for putting square pegs into round holes'.[363]

The backbone of this network was an upgrading of the road and railway network, with the full support of the Egyptian Works Department and the State Railway. New railways were built to connect the garrisons and supply dumps in the Western Desert and down the Nile Valley, although the principal effort was made on the western side of the Suez Canal. The main Cairo–Ismailia railway was only single-track along its last 50 miles, from Zagazig to Ismailia. In just thirty-six days, between December 1915 and January 1916, some 15,000 men worked to dig out 12m cubic feet (340,000 cubic metres) of earth and move 150,000 tons of material to double this track. That completed, the branch line from Zagazig to As Salhia was extended all the way to the immense supply depot being assembled at Kantara, and much of the connecting railway along the western bank of the Canal was also improved. In all, 250 miles of new track was laid, while 100 miles of roads were improved, metalled or constructed.[364]

To move supplies across the Canal, the wharves and landings on the banks were improved, and the bridges strengthened. In all, eight pontoon bridges would be built across the Canal, in additional to numerous passenger and freight ferries and one rail-ferry. Three of the bridges were capable of carrying heavy artillery, and the other five of taking troops and vehicles. All were built to be detached at one end and swing aside to let past the organised convoys of shipping that ran through the Canal to a regular schedule.[365] On the eastern bank new depots were constructed at regular intervals, allowing local supplies to be built up. From each of these, 2ft 6in-gauge railways were built stretching out to the second and first lines of defence, transporting rations, ammunition, construction materials and water to the forward positions.[366] From February 1916 a new line, of the heavier 4ft 8½in gauge, was started at Kantara, running out into the desert towards Katia. This line would eventually run all the way into Palestine, and would form one of the two lifelines of the army once the coming desert campaign began.

The second lifeline was a water pipe than would run beside the railway. So far, drinking water for the army, and its livestock, to the east of the Ship Canal had been collected from the Sweet Water Canal on the western side, and then shipped across in boats. For the relatively small numbers of troops operating in the desert in

1915, this was a workable system, but it was unsuitable for any serious operations. From November 1915 a much more substantial water supply system was assembled. Pumping stations were constructed along the Sweet Water Canal that fed water through extensive filtration systems to remove debris, wildlife and parasites, and to treat it with chlorine.[367] From there, it was pumped through pipes that lay across the bed of the Ship Canal and into massive, 50,000 gallon (225,000 litre) capacity reservoirs on the eastern bank. It was then piped out to the forward areas.[368] Just linking these together needed over 150 miles of piping.[369]

The main pipeline that would eventually stretch across the desert was slower starting than the railway. Whereas the army could draw upon the Egyptian State Railways and local industry for the rail network, only a limited supply of the 12in-diameter pipes that were needed could be obtained quickly, with 130 miles of piping arriving from India.[370] Further progress had to wait until 20 September 1916, when the first consignment of 5,000 tons of pipes from America were offloaded at Kantara. To some extent the pipeline also had to follow after the railway, due to the method of laying it. The pipes, each one weighing half a ton, were loaded onto rail trucks, and the trains steamed slowly into the desert. Egyptian labourers rolled the pipes off the truck and onto the sand at the correct intervals, while further gangs connected them together. The speed of this process meant that it took less than a month to lay the first 25 miles, to Romani where advanced reservoirs had been dug in preparation. A series of pumping stations and reservoirs, each with a capacity of over 440,000 gallons (2 million litres), would eventually punctuate the length of the pipeline and railway as it crossed the 100 miles of desert all the way to Palestine.[371]

8

THE SENUSSI WAR

While Britain was concentrating on defending the Suez Canal, and then on forcing the Dardanelles, the western side of Egypt lay wide open. Officially this should not have been a problem. Libya belonged to Italy and the Italians were neutral for the first months of the war and then joined the Entente (although their May 1915 declaration only actually committed them to a war with Austro-Hungary; they would not declare war on the Ottoman Empire until August). However, Italy's grasp on the country was far from firm and the Ottoman influence had the potential to be strong. The real power in this question lay with the Senussi.

The Senussi were a religious group, an orthodox branch of the Islamic Sunni.[372] They were established in the early 1800s by Sayyid Muhammed bin Ali al-Senussi, and named after him.* Starting in Algeria, they spread along the caravan and trade routes of North Africa through the nineteenth century, setting up hostels and religious schools for the itinerant Bedouin tribesmen of the region. Their influence spread far, including deep into Egypt, and in the early twentieth century turned military. The Grand Senussi had turned a deaf ear to appeals for help from the Islamic uprisings in the Sudan in the 1880s and 1890s (whose teachings were broadly heretical to orthodox Muslims), but when the French invaded Zawiya in 1901 the Senussi took up arms. In 1911 the Italians invaded Libya and the Senussi turned their guns on this new invader. After the withdrawal of the Ottomans and their signing of a separate peace in 1912, the Senussi provided steady leadership for the continuing resistance, holding out in the desert regions while the Italians held most of the towns and coast, each unable to dislodge the other.

When Sayyid Muhammed al-Mahdi died, his son, Sayyid Muhammed Idris, was only 11 years old. By common consent, the leadership therefore passed to al-Mahdi's nephew, Sayyid Ahmed al-Sharif. The agreement was that Sayyid Muhammed Idris would be al-Sharif's successor, although as Idris came of age, many Senussi began to believe that he should take over immediately. This division, and the level of support for the pro-British Idris, would be an important factor later on. Having said that,

---

* The term Senussi can be interchangeably used for both the sect and the leader; for clarity the leader will be referred to as the Grand Senussi.

the Grand Senussi and the majority of his followers harboured no ill-feeling against the British and were reluctant to cause trouble. However, in 1914, they were seen as being a perfect candidate for the *jihad* planned by Berlin and Constantinople. Even before the war, Ottoman and German envoys were sent to speak with the Grand Senussi, including the orientalist and eccentric Baron Max von Oppenheim. After the outbreak of the war in Europe further envoys were sent, including the no less colourful Baron Otto von Gumpenberg and Otto Mannesmann. On the Ottoman side, in January 1915, staff officer Ja'far al-Askari was sent to Libya with Nuri Bey, the younger brother of Enver Pasha. Nuri had served with the Senussi beside Enver during the war of 1912, and had remained after Enver had returned to Constantinople. With all of these envoys came further Ottoman officers, specialist soldiers (such as machine gunners or artillerymen), weapons, ammunition and gold. However, efforts to persuade the Senussi to join the *jihad* against Britain failed.

For their part, the British knew what was going on. In late 1914, the Grand Senussi had established his camp at Amsa'id, just across the border from the Egyptian Coastguard post at Sollum, and the commander of that station, Lieutenant Colonel Cecil Longueville Snow, kept a close eye on proceedings. The British remained largely unconcerned. For all that Prime Minister Herbert Asquith considered an attack on Egypt from the Western Desert to be 'a species of nightmare', he also considered that 'any force that had been held up by the Italians could not be of very much value'.[373] It was also considered that the terrain in the Western Desert was unsuitable for campaigning, overlooking the fact that the Bedouin were born and bred to such conditions.

The terrain in western Egypt was particularly difficult for military operations. Along the coast was a thin strip of land with water sources that could be exploited. Just inland was a long range of bare, craggy limestone hills, ranging from 50 to 150 miles deep. This coastal strip could be traversed by the grandly named Khedival Road, running from Alexandria 280 miles west to Sollum, and then on across the Libyan border. One driver recalled that this was 'not a metalled highway. It had been made by throwing aside the stones on the desert, or dumping them on the patches of soft sand.'[374] It was easy for vehicles to become bogged down or puncture tyres on the smaller rocks, but it was better than nothing. A narrow-gauge track, the Khedival Railway, ran parallel with the road for the first 100 miles or so, while telegraph lines ran along the coast to the border. For moving troops or equipment out to Sollum, or to the post at Mersa Matruh about 160 miles west of Alexandria, by far the quickest route was by sea.

South of the hills was the desert. Unlike the Sinai Desert, the Western Desert is hard-surfaced and rock-strewn. Several large oases – some of them covering dozens of square miles – were spread across western Egypt, and much of the central region was dominated by the Qattara Depression. A few tracks crossed these empty expanses and the population consisted of nomadic tribesmen. It would be a very difficult place to campaign in.

Over the summer of 1915, the Grand Senussi came under increasing pressure. On at least one occasion the Germans tried to force the Grand Senussi's hand: on 16 August 1915 two British submarines, the *B-6* and the *B-11*, were close to the Libyan shore between Sollum and Tobruk, having been forced to take shelter by bad weather.

While on the surface, the crews spotted figures, including at least one white man, waving flags and gesticulating onshore. The commander of *B-11*, Lieutenant Norman Holbrook RN VC, took a boat in to investigate, but became suspicious and returned to his submarine. As they reboarded *B-11*, a hidden machine gun opened fire, killing one British sailor and wounding two more. The white man had almost certainly been Otto Mannesmann.[375] This incident had led to a flurry of diplomatic activity between Britain and the Senussi, causing Maxwell great concern, but eventually it blew over.

Slowly, the Grand Senussi began to lean towards the Ottomans and Germans. Several factors were at play here. Britain was now allied to their old enemy, Italy, and at the same time looking increasingly weak. The campaign in the Dardanelles was clearly failing, while between that, the new campaign in Salonika and the growing offensive in Mesopotamia, Britain's resources in the region were stretched dangerously thin. The Senussi, on the other hand, were growing in strength. On 10 October the Senussi defeated a large Italian force near Tripoli, boosting their confidence, and by early November Lieutenant Colonel Snow was estimating that some 2,500–3,500 Senussi fighters were now gathered at Sollum, including 1,500 *muhafizia* (formally trained and uniformed regular troops) with another 600 under training. Each man had a modern rifle, courtesy of the Ottomans, the Germans or defeated Italian troops.[376] What Snow did not know, was that just up the coast a further camp held some 700 Ottoman troops, with six field guns and two machine guns (and it would become clear after the fighting began that numerous other machine guns were held elsewhere).[377]

In the end, the war was sparked by the actions of a German submarine, *U-35*, under *Kapitänleutnant* Waldemar Kophamel. His assignment had been to carry supplies and Ottoman personnel to the Senussi, while escorting several sailing vessels carrying similar cargos. He delivered his own cargo into Bardia, just west of Sollum, although the vessels he was escorting went astray. His job done, Kophamel left Bardia on the morning of 5 November 1915 to seek targets along the coast. Shortly after 10 a.m., he torpedoed the British armed boarding steamer HMS *Tara*, commanded by Captain Rupert Gwatkin-Williams. A converted passenger steamer, as SS *Hibernia* she had been operated before the war by the London and North Western Railway, sailing between Holyhead and Dublin. Most of her crew where Welshmen who had served on her pre-war, and for the past year had been operating her on anti-submarine patrols in the Irish Sea. HMS *Tara* had only arrived in Egypt a fortnight before, to take over the Alexandria–Sollum patrol route.

Of the 104 men on board, 92 managed to abandon ship, although not without some injuries. Most made it into lifeboats, and when Kophamel surfaced he allowed those men who could not find a place in one aboard his own ship. Taking the lifeboats under tow, he set course back to Bardia, where the survivors were handed over to the Senussi. These men would be led into the desert, eventually being held captive at a barely habitable spot called Bir Hakim. Over the coming months they would be held on increasingly short rations (although their captors faired little better) and in poor conditions. Several would die of injuries or illness in captivity.[378]

Although the fate of survivors of HMS *Tara* (and several survivors from the horse-carrier SS *Moorina* sunk by *U-35* a few days after, who later joined the *Tara* men) would become an issue towards the end of the campaign, it was Kophamel's next action that would cause the British the most immediate anxiety. Leaving Bardia, he steamed into Sollum harbour shortly after 5 p.m., and having established that there were no shore defences, began a forty-five minute bombardment with his 7.5cm deck gun. Two Egyptian Coastguard motor cruisers were moored up, and one, the *Abbas*, was sunk and the other, the *Nour al-Bahr*, severely damaged. The coastguard station, on the cliffs overlooking the natural harbour, was shelled, as were the tents of the garrison. Miraculously, no one was killed but considerable material damage and confusion was caused.[379]

The news took a day to reach Alexandria, due to damage to the telegraph wires, but when it did arrive caused a considerable stir, as it did in London. Coincidentally, the War Committee meeting in which the Prime Minister gave the opinions quoted above had also been held on 5 November, and he had been typical in denigrating the possibility of open war with the Senussi. Only at the insistence of the Chief of the Imperial General Staff, Sir Archibald Murray, who had been briefed by Lord Kitchener (absent in the Dardanelles at the time) had the matter been taken seriously.[380] It was now clear that military action was needed, but transferring troops from France was out of the question, while the British forces in the eastern Mediterranean and Persian Gulf were already overstretched. It was proving difficult to adequately garrison the Suez Canal, and now suddenly the backdoor to Egypt was wide open.

The first force to be despatched was the Emergency Squadron of the Royal Naval Armoured Car Division (RNACD). This consisted of six Rolls-Royce Armoured Cars, built on the chassis of Silver Ghosts and equipped with a Maxim machine gun, and around twenty supporting trucks, including an ambulance and two wireless vehicles. These travelled by rail to the end of the Khedival Railway – the coastguard station at al-Dab'a – and then by the rough Khedival Road. The road proved too poor for the armoured cars, which only made it as far as Sidi Barani, about 60 miles east of Sollum, and only a half a dozen supporting vehicles made it into Sollum itself on 11 November.[381] Two days later the Coastguard cruiser *Rasheed* arrived, bearing two Krupps field guns and around twenty Egyptian soldiers. The garrison now stood at around 100 Egyptian Coastguard or Army personnel and a score of British personnel from the RNACD with their lorries, supported by two field guns and two Maxims.

Over the next two weeks, the situation continued to be confused. The telegraphs lines along the coast were cut numerous times, sentries at Sollum and friendly Bedouin camped at Sidi Barani were assaulted, and many of the coastguard stations came under sporadic rifle fire. At the same time, Snow met with Ja'far and other Senussi officials, and received a letter of apology from the Grand Senussi himself. However, it was increasingly clear that, in the circumstances, the far western coastguard stations were dangerously exposed. The road could easily be cut, while it had been proven that German submarines could equally cut the sea routes. On 22 November the garrison of Sidi Barani was pulled out by road, and along the way fourteen officers and 120 rank and file from the Egyptian Coastguard deserted to the Senussi, taking 176 camels and all of their arms and equipment with them.[382] On the same day the Coastguard station at Baqbaq, about half way between Sollum and Sidi Barani, was also evacuated, and the garrison commander also deserted to the enemy.[383] On 23 November, the garrison at Sollum, minus the two Krupps guns (and fourteen Egyptian soldiers who were forgotten about and later arrived, very annoyed, at Mersa Matruh[384]) embarked on the *Rasheed*. As they pulled out of the harbour, jubilant Senussi poured in.

The British presence in the Western Desert was now concentrated at Mersa Matruh, where supplies and forces could be more easily consolidated. On 20 November Major General Alexander Wallace was told to form the Western Frontier Force (WFF) from the scraps of the units left in Egypt. A Composite Yeomanry Brigade was formed, consisting of three Yeomanry regiments and one Australian Light Horse (ALH) regiment, drawn together from the rear depots of twenty or more cavalry units, plus the Notts Battery of the Royal Horse Artillery (RHA), and placed under Brigadier General Julian Tyndale-Biscoe. The infantry (15th Ludhiana Sikhs, 6th Royal Scots, 2/7th and 2/8th Middlesex Regiment) were formed into a brigade under Brigadier General George Charles, the 5th Earl of Lucan, with support troops drawn from the Australian forces and the Egyptian Army. A further force of the 2nd Battalion, New Zealand Rifle Brigade (NZRB), a company of the 15th Sikhs, detachments of the Bikaner Camel Corps and an Egyptian artillery-manned armoured train was put together to guard the lines of communications.[385]

Apart from the 15th Sikhs, an experienced regular battalion that had already seen action in France, and the Bikaner Camel Corps, the rest of the Force had little active experience. Some units had a few men who had been evacuated from Gallipoli as sick or wounded and had recovered, but the 2nd Battalion NZRB had only been in Egypt for a matter of days. The three commanding generals all had experience from fighting on the North West Frontier of India, which would prove useful. In early December the WFF was despatched to Mersa Matruh, along with two BE2cs from No. 14 Squadron RFC. By the middle of the month, they had been reinforced by A Battery, Honourable Artillery Company (HAC) and two 4in guns from the Royal Marine Artillery, while the 161st Brigade (four battalions of the Essex Regiment) which had recently returned from Gallipoli had been added to the force defending the road and railway back to Alexandria, based (with two more aeroplanes from No. 17 Squadron) at Hammam.[386]

In order to restore British prestige in the region, it was decided to make an early demonstration, no matter how small, in the area. The RFC reported a camp of around 400 *muhafizia* about 25 miles west of Mersa Matruh. A force was put together under the command of Lieutenant Colonel John Gordon of the 15th Sikhs. It was planned that he would march along the line of the telegraph wires with two companies of his own regiment, while a force of the 2nd Composite Yeomanry Regiment, a detachment of the RNACD and the Notts Battery RHA moved along the Khedival Road, a few miles inland. They would meet and spend the night at Umm al-Rakhm, 12 miles west of Mersa Matruh, before carrying on to investigate the Senussi camp.

The force left Mersa Matruh at 7 a.m. on 11 December 1915, and marched west. Unfortunately, the reported camp of 400 Senussi was only a small part of a much larger force; approximately 1,000 *muhafizia*, 900 tribesmen, a cavalry company, two mountain guns and four machine guns were in fact operating in the area,[387] and their scouts soon spotted the column, under Major J. Wigan of the Berkshire Yeomanry, on the Khedival Road. This force was moving at speed, and their own scouting was suffering as a consequence. The RNACD detachment had moved up to 2 miles ahead of the main body, and when a large detachment of the Senussi launched an ambush near Wadi Senab the force was spread out and Wigan was unable to organise a coherent response. The severely broken ground beside the road left the RNACD unable to manoeuvre at all, while it was only after several hours that the Yeomanry managed to push the Senussi back enough for the artillery to deploy. Even when the guns were in action, progress was slow as the Senussi withdrew into the gullies and caves of the broken ground.

Lieutenant Colonel Gordon and the 15th Sikhs were 6 miles away and unable to intervene, proceeding instead to Umm al-Rakhm. Back at Mersa Matruh, around 9 miles east, Wallace could hear the firing and despatched the RFC to investigate; on hearing their report a squadron of the ALH was sent to reinforce them. Arriving around 3 p.m., they found the Senussi still slowly retreating and turned their flank. The Senussi now melted away, leaving the British force too exhausted to pursue. Marching on, the cavalry and artillery reach Umm al-Rakhm after dark.[388] It is perhaps surprising that such experienced officers as Wallace and Gordon had allowed their already small force to become so spread out and disjointed across broken country. The cost was heavy – sixteen killed and seventeen wounded, the dead including the irreplaceable Lieutenant Colonel Snow, former commander at Sollum whose local knowledge and contacts would be sorely missed. The British would estimate that the Senussi had lost eighty men killed, as well as seven taken prisoner, but this is likely to be an exaggeration.

The next day was spent resting in camp, scouting the local area, and awaiting a supply convoy escorted by three companies of the 6th Royal Scots. On 13 December the force took to the field again, albeit leaving one company of the Sikhs at Umm al-Rakhm to guard the baggage (a questionable idea given that these were the more experienced soldiers available to Gordon) as well as the Royal Scots' machine-gun section. At 9 a.m. the column marched west again, with a broad cavalry screen ahead and an advance guard of the remaining company of Sikhs. To the south of the road was a narrow plain with a line of hills and ridges beyond, and a piquet of two platoons of the Royal Scots guarded this flank.

At 9.15 a.m., scarcely 2 miles had been covered when a Senussi force of between 1,000–1,500 men, with artillery and machine guns, under the command of Ja'far open fired from a line of ridges just south of the road near Wadi Hasheifiat. Advancing in good order, the Senussi pushed in the Royal Scots' flank guard, which fell back in disarray. No. 2 Company of the 15th Sikhs swung south immediately, and seized a series of knolls that dominated the area between the road and the ridge line. From here they could enfilade any Senussi attack across the small plain, firing into their exposed flanks. However, they could also be enfiladed from the Senussi-held hills themselves. Gordon ordered the Royal Scots to advance in support, but they could make no headway against the Senussi machine-gun fire. At 10.15 a.m. Gordon ordered the Sikhs, under Captain Hughes, to withdraw. Hughes answered that to do that would mean abandoning his wounded, and declined to do so.

By now Gordon was sending urgent messages back to his camp at Umm al-Rakhm for every spare man to be sent, and about 180, including seventy-five members of the Australian Service Corps and the machine-gun section of the Royal Scots, were despatched. However, they too became pinned down by well-sited Senussi machine guns. For four hours the deadlock lasted until, eventually, the RHA managed to deploy their guns under cover and, supported by the guns of the newly arrived HMS *Clematis* offshore, began to lay an accurate fire against the Senussi positions. Ja'far now began an orderly retreat, holding up the half-hearted attempts to pursue.

The British losses were surprisingly light, considering the circumstances. Nine men had been killed, and fifty-six wounded. These were loaded onto HMS *Clematis*, and, after spending the night on the battlefield under sporadic artillery fire, Gordon withdrew his column back to Mersa Matruh. Senussi casualties were estimated at 250 killed, although Ja'far would later claim figures for killed and wounded at less than fifty.[389] As a demonstration to reassert British prestige, the expedition had been a failure. If anything, the Senussi were now in higher spirits than after the evacuation of Sollum; they had twice met the British in the field and had the best of the encounters.[390]

For the next ten days the British licked their wounds, while the weather turned cold and wet. At Mersa Matruh reinforcements arrived in the form of the 1st Battalion NZRB, while sniping was common at night and cavalry patrols fought occasional skirmishes during the day. Ja'far had established his main force – probably 3,000–4,000 strong – at Jebel Medwa, a height that stretched across the Khedival Road some 6 miles south-west of Mersa Matruh. Wallace determined to assault this position on 25 December, and again split his forces to do so. The right-hand column,[*] under Lieutenant Colonel Gordon, would advance straight down the Road and attack the positions on Jebel Medwa head-on. Meanwhile, the left-hand column,[**] under Brigadier General Tyndale-Biscoe, would swing deep into the desert and come up from the south, behind the Senussi position. From offshore, and at a range of 10,000yd (9,000m), HMS *Clematis* would provide fire support.

The troops were roused at the unpopular hour of 3 a.m. on Christmas morning and the march was soon underway. The flanking column ran into problems very quickly, being delayed by difficulties in getting their guns and wagons through the Wadi Toweiwia. The squadron of the Herts Yeomanry fell so far behind during this operation that in the end they joined Gordon's column. This force had made good progress, despite some light skirmishing between the advance guard and Senussi piquets in the predawn. At 7.30 a.m. the assault on Jebel Medwa began, with the Sikhs, supported by the New Zealanders, advancing up the road, with the Royal Bucks Hussars and the 2/8th Middlesex attacking on the left flank. The RHA battery and the Royal Navy gave supporting fire, while the Senussi artillery replied in kind. After a disjointed

---

[*]   Royal Bucks Hussars (Yeomanry), 1 Section Notts Bty RHA, 15th Sikhs, 1st Bn NZRB, 2/8th
        Middlesex Regt, Notts & Derby Field Ambulance, Water Section Australian Train.

[**]   Bde Staff and Signal Troop Composite Yeomanry Bde, 2 Trps Duke of Lancaster's Own
        Yeomanry, 1 Trp Derbyshire Yeomanry, 2 Trps City of London Yeomanry, 1 Sqn Herts
        Yeomanry, Composite Regt ALH, Notts Bty RHA (less one Section), Yeomanry Machine Gun
        Section, Yeomanry Field Ambulance.

and prolonged attack, the Senussi began to fall back and shortly after 10 a.m. Jebel Medwa was in Sikh hands. From there, the Senussi could be seen escaping down the Wadi Majid, which ran north from behind the ridgeline. Of Tyndale-Biscoe's flanking column there was no sign, and so Gordon ordered his own forces to pursue. In the bed of the Wadi they found the Senussi camp, which they burned.

The flanking column had been delayed by the terrain, and then by stiff resistance from a force of Senussi cavalry soon after dawn. Contact was finally established shortly before 1 p.m., but the two forces did not link up until 3 p.m. By then, it was too late, and the remaining Senussi force had escaped north along the coast, where the pursuit was broken off at around 5 p.m. As with previous encounters, exhaustion and lack of water prevented the British from continuing and destroying the enemy. Still, some 300–400 Senussi had been killed, and around eighty taken prisoner. British casualties had been thirteen killed and fifty-one wounded. It was, at last, a clear British victory, and Ja'far recorded that after this action (known after the Wadi Majid rather than Jebel Medwa) the Bedouin began to drift away in increasing numbers.[391]

After the victory at Wadi Majid, the British forces returned to Mersa Matruh. The weather continued to be cold and wet, turning the desert to mud. One gunner recalled how 'it rained all day and almost every day; tents were waterlogged and one moved about in a slough of sticky mud. We ate mud, we drank it in our tea, we slept in it.'[392] The mud limited mobility, as did the continuing lack of pack animals. Although small patrols continued to operate in the local area, the British remained restricted to an area two to three day's march from Mersa Matruh, due to the impossibility of carrying enough food and, particularly, water to go any further. On the positive side, reinforcements began to slowly arrive from the troops evacuated from Gallipoli. This meant, especially for the infantry, a greater proportion of experienced troops, and for the cavalry in particular a much higher level of unit cohesion could be obtained.

On 19 January 1916 the RFC found Ja'far's new camp, some 22 miles south-west of Mersa Matruh, near Halazin. This spot had been chosen for its defensible nature; surrounded by high ground that shielded the camp, while closer in were numerous lower-lying areas that were now flooded and all but impassable. Nevertheless, Wallace determined to attack as soon as possible, and at 4 p.m. on 22 January led his Force out. Again, the British were split into several columns, with Lieutenant Colonel Gordon commanding the right-hand column[***] and Brigadier General Tyndale-Biscoe on the left.[****] Wallace remained a few miles behind with a Reserve force[*****] and an escort for the baggage.[******] After spending the night about halfway to their objective, the Force started out again at 6 a.m. on 23 January. The road was poor and the going rough, so much so that the detachment from the RNACD was forced to turn back.

[***] 1 Sqn Duke of Lancaster's Own Yeomanry, Notts Bty RHA, 15th Sikhs, 2nd Bn SA Infantry, 1st Bn NZRB.

[****] Bucks Hussars, 1 Sqn Herts Yeomanry, 1 Sqn Dorset Yeomanry, 1 Sqn ALH, 2 Trps Surrey Yeomanry, machine gun section, A Battery HAC (less 1 Section).

[*****] 2 Trps Herts Yeomanry, 6th Royal Scots (less 2 companies).

[******] 2/8th Middlesex Regt (less 2 companies).

Mud slowed progress and at Halazin Ja'far received plenty of warning of the approach. He deployed his 3,000 men along a crescent of hills one and half miles long, about 3 miles south of his camp, with the flanks arching out on either side towards the enemy. His field artillery and machine guns were placed at the centre of the line, where they could rake the ground ahead of them, which was 'absolutely flat, covered with small stones and small scraggy bushes about one foot high; and it was totally devoid of any cover'.[393]

When the British approached, at 10 a.m., Tyndale-Biscoe (to whom Wallace had delegated battlefield command) ordered a direct assault by the infantry in the centre, while the cavalry were positioned on the left flank. The 15th Sikhs were again placed in the forefront, with New Zealand and South African troops in support. There must have been a sense of déjà vu as they advanced across the flat plain against well-positioned Senussi troops on the high ground, although a new twist was a constant mirage that made the enemy positions hard to spot by either the infantry or the British artillery.

To begin with the battle went well for the Senussi. By noon the British had made very little progress and Ja'far decided that now was the time to add to the pressure. While Nuri Bey took two of their five machine guns out to the right flank, Ja'far took infantry and cavalry out to the left, and they began to turn the British flanks. Tyndale-Biscoe extended his own flanks to counter them, and a series of leapfrogs led to each flank becoming increasingly extended, until the British left flank found itself in serious trouble. On this flank, the cavalry were driven back until they were at a right-angle to the front line, and the guns of the HAC had to be turned ('and extremely difficult it was to move in the mud') and found themselves 'firing over open sights – and as any artilleryman knows, when that happens the enemy is quite near enough'.[394]

The success of the flanking moves proved in the end to be turning point for the Senussi. As each flank became more extended the centre of the line grew weaker. Nuri's removal of two of the machine guns greatly decreased the weight of fire being thrown against the Sikhs, New Zealanders and South Africans, and slowly progress was again made. The Senussi centre was pushed further back until, shortly before 3 p.m., it had fallen back into the main camp. However, they maintained their discipline, Maxwell later reporting to London that their retreat 'was conducted with great skill, denying our efforts to come to close quarters'.[395] From the camp, the Senussi melted away into the desert and eventually reformed about 20 miles away. Once again, the British were too exhausted to follow up their success, and, ironically given the mud that impeded every move, had too little water for an extended operation in the desert. After spending the night at the Senussi camp, they returned to Mersa Matruh the following day.[396]

British casualties had been heavy at Halazin, with thirty-one killed and nearly 300 wounded, but Senussi prisoners estimated their own losses at 200 killed and 500 wounded. Whatever the actual figures, a turning point had now been reached.

9

RETAKING THE WESTERN DESERT

After the action at Halazin, the Western Frontier Force (WFF) was finally in a position to begin to retake lost ground. It was a clear British victory, and back at Mersa Matruh the essential elements for an advance back to Sollum were now being gathered. Not least, some 2,000 animals arrived from the Camel Transport Corps, giving the British the capacity to operate for more than a few days away from their base at a time. Further reinforcements arrived, including the Cavalry Corps Motor Machine-gun Battery, whose armoured cars had had some of their metal plating removed to make them lighter than those of the RNACD, which they now replaced. Two more battalions of the South African Brigade – the 1st and 3rd Battalions – joined the 2nd Battalion already present, although at the same time the 15th Sikhs, who had undoubtedly borne the brunt of the fighting so far, were withdrawn. Another change came when Wallace, in his late fifties and feeling both the strain of campaigning and the effects of an old wound, ask to be relieved. On 10 February 1916 Major General William Peyton arrived to replace him.[397] An experienced officer who had spent time campaigning in India, Egypt and the Sudan, he had just returned from commanding the 2nd Mounted Division in Gallipoli. All was set now for the army to retake Sollum.

After Halazin, Ja'far and Nuri Bey had withdrawn their forces to near Sidi Barani, about 90 miles west of Mersa Matruh, while a smaller Senussi force was known to be at Sollum, a further 60 miles west. Maxwell and Peyton faced the options of either driving the WFF directly west along the coast to Sidi Barani, or conducting a joint operation, with the Royal Navy (RN) simultaneously landing troops at Sollum. There were concerns still about German submarines operating off the coast, and about the mouth of Sollum harbour being mined, so in the end the former option was adopted, and the RN confined to cautiously ferrying men and material between Alexandria and Mersa Matruh.[398]

Starting on 13 February 1916, a series of camel convoys began to build-up a forward base at Unjeila, about half way between Mersa Matruh and Sidi Barani. On 22 February, Brigadier General Henry Lukin, commander of the South African Brigade, arrived. Although he lost his 2nd Battalion on the same day, to escort an empty convoy heading back to Mersa Matruh, he took command of all of the troops present,[*] and prepared for the next move. The RFC had discovered Ja'far's camp at Agagiya (al-Aqaqir), 15 miles south-east of Sidi Barani and just south of the Khedival Road. Leaving the New Zealanders and the Royal Scots to guard the camp, he marched with the rest of his force along the coast in two stages, before setting up camp about 8 miles north of Agagiya, at the mouth of the Wadi Mehtila, on the afternoon of 24 February. His plan was to rest his forces during the next day until after dark, and then conduct a night march and attack the Senussi camp at dawn.

At Agagiya, Ja'far and Nuri Bey now had just 1,600 men, including only 400 *muhafizia*, one mountain gun and three machine guns. Supplies were also getting short. At the two previous engagements the Senussi camps had been overrun, losing large quantities of ammunition, as well as tents, food and other equipment. Now, the supplies coming from Libya were getting increasingly sporadic and morale and discipline was suffering. However, on receiving word from Bedouin scouts on 25 February that Lukin's force was advancing along the shore, Ja'far gathered his heavy weapons and marched out to meet him. They came across the camp on the Wadi Mehtila late on 25 February, too close to dark to make an attack, and had to satisfy himself with shelling the camp for several hours. The British, unable to locate the mountain gun in the increasing darkness, had to endure the bombardment, although due to an error by the gunners most of the shells landed beyond the camp and only one man was killed.[399]

With the element of surprise lost, Lukin abandoned his plan to make a night march, and did not start his force moving until 5 a.m. on 26 February. At that time, cavalry scouts were sent south to locate the enemy camp, followed a few hours later by the infantry. On the way, they joined up with a detachment of armoured cars and motor ambulances that had journeyed along the Khedival Road. At this point, Lukin's force was about 4 miles north-east of the Senussi camp, and half way between the two Ja'far had established his main force, entrenched and behind barbed wire, on a cluster of sand dunes. As usual, the ground in front of these was wide open and without any cover. Regardless, Lukin deployed his infantry for a frontal assault, with the 3rd Battalion South African Infantry taking the lead supported by the 1st Battalion and several armoured cars. On his left flank he deployed his single squadron of the Royal Bucks Yeomanry with two armoured cars, and on his right three squadrons of the Queen's Own Dorset Yeomanry with two more cars.[400]

The attack opened at shortly after 11 a.m., with the infantry advancing in the centre. On the right the Dorset Yeomanry and armoured cars swung around into the sand hills on the Senussi left flank, where the Yeomanry dismounted and took up positions to pin down that side of the enemy line. Ja'far reacted by launching a flanking attack on the other side, momentarily pushing the weaker cavalry and armoured car force opposite them back until South African infantry came up to bolster the line. Ja'far's attack was pushed back, and as it did so the centre also began to melt away. Although the retreat by no means became a rout, the heart had clearly gone from the Senussi, and by just after 3 p.m. the South Africans had taken the sand dunes, and

---

[*]   1st and 3rd South African Bns, 6th Royal Scots, 1st Bn NZRB, Dorset Yeomanry, 1 Sqn Bucks Yeomanry, Notts Bty RHA (less 1 Section).

advanced to the far side overlooking the Senussi camp. To the south, they could see the Senussi baggage train and remaining forces streaming off into the desert.[401]

For the first time, though, a British force was in a position to mount a proper pursuit. The Dorset Yeomanry, under Lieutenant Colonel Hugh Souter, were under orders to intercept any retreat, and had moved slowly around until they were south of the Senussi camp. Souter advanced cautiously, keeping his horses as rested as possible, observing the ground, and waiting for the Senussi rearguard to get well clear of any trenches, barbed wire or other obstacles. Finally, shortly after 3 p.m., he saw his chance. From a range of about 1,000yd (900m), over flat, open ground that sloped up slightly away from him, Souter could see the rearguard, commanded by Ja'far himself and consisting of 150–200 men (some British accounts say 500) with three Maxim machine guns. Souter ordered his men to mount, and began his advance. One of his officers, 2nd Lieutenant J.H. Blaksley, recalled:

> We were spread out in two ranks, eight yards roughly between each man of the front rank and four yards in the second. This was how we galloped for well over half a mile straight into their fire … At first they fired very fast and you saw the bullets knocking up the sand in front of you … But as we kept getting nearer, they began to lose their nerve and (I expect) forgot to lower their sights. Anyhow the bullets began going over us and we saw them firing wildly and beginning to run; but some of them – I expect the Turkish officers – kept the machine guns playing on us.[402]

Souter himself later reported:

> The attack was made in two lines, the horses galloping steadily and well in hand. Three maxims were brought into action against us, but the men were splendidly led by their squadron and troop leaders, and their behaviour was admirable. About 50 yards from the position I gave the order to charge, and with one yell the Dorsets hurled themselves upon the enemy, who immediately broke.[403]

As the Senussi line dissolved, the ranks of the charging cavalry broke with them. Most of the officers had been killed, wounded or had fallen behind during the charge (Blaksley had two horses shot from under him) and too few remained to keep control of their men. Instead of reforming, the troopers followed their own targets, separating and becoming easy targets for any of the Senussi who kept their heads. Thankfully, the psychological as well as the physical impact of the charge, of a solid body of mounted men smashing into their position at speed, had shaken most of them too badly. Blaksley:

> The Senussi were running in all directions, shrieking and yelling and throwing away their arms and belongings; the Yeomen after them, sticking them through the backs and slashing right and left with their swords … Some stood their ground, and by dodging the swords and shooting at two or three yards' range first our horses then our men, accounted for most of our casualties.[404]

Casualties were heavy, although perhaps lighter than would be expected when charging horses against machine guns. The speed of the charge certainly helped, and perhaps the Senussi did not have a chance to adjust their sights properly as Blaksley suggests, as would also happen at Beersheba the following year. The wide spacing of the troopers also almost certainly helped, negating some of the advantages of the machine gun's rate of fire by being unable to cover more than one or two horsemen with a single burst. Fifty eight of the 184 Yeomen who had taken part in the charge were killed or wounded but the Senussi rearguard was broken. Not only that, but their leader was lost. As Souter charged into 'the middle of the enemy's lines my horse was killed under me, and, by a curious chance, his dying strides brought me to the ground within a few yards of the Senussi General, Gaafar [*sic*] Pasha'.[405]

Ja'far, already wounded, surrendered easily, along with several of his officers. In all, thirty-nine prisoners were taken and it was estimated that some 500 other Senussi had been killed or wounded. Apart from the thirty-two killed and twenty-six wounded of the Dorset Yeomanry, fifteen British (mostly South African) troops had been killed, and 111 wounded. Although Nuri Bey escaped (despite rumours of his death), the Senussi forces along the northern coast had been broken. The road to Sidi Barani was now open, and British forces retook it on 28 February 1916. Ja'far entered captivity in Egypt, which he later left to join the Arab Revolt as a senior officer.

After a few problems establishing reliable supply lines, Peyton concentrated his forces at Sidi Barani on 7 March. Further changes had occurred, with the 1st Battalion NZRB being replaced by the 4th South African Infantry, and the arrival of the Hong Kong and Singapore Mountain Battery (known as the 'Bing Boys' due to the noise their small mountain guns made), the Australian Camel Corps, and the 2nd Mounted Brigade. All was now set for the final advance on Sollum, although care would be needed with the terrain and water supplies. The line of hills, now almost a continuous cliff, that ran along the coast moved closer to the sea as it neared Sollum, leading to fears that the Senussi would once again seize the high ground for any coming fight. Therefore, a plan was drawn up for the WFF to climb up onto the plateau that ran along the tops of the hills, and advance on Sollum that way. There were some doubts as to the water supplies available on the plateau, but officers who knew the area assured Peyton that there would be enough. Even so, the WFF was split into two columns, marching a day apart, so as not to over-tax the water supply. In front would be Lukin with the infantry and slower moving units (except some armoured cars for scouting), while Major General Lord Hampden would follow behind with the cavalry and light artillery.[406]

Almost immediately the plan had to be changed. On reaching the crest of the plateau, Lukin discovered that the water supply was seriously inadequate to support even his own force, let alone Lord Hampden's. On 12 March he sent half of his infantry back down onto the coastal plain, where it now formed a third column under Peyton's own control, while the cavalry column also returned to this route. Continuing with just the 1st and 4th Battalions South African Infantry, the Hong Kong and Singapore Mountain Battery, and a Field Ambulance, Lukin found it a struggle to find even enough water for this depleted force, and when they linked up with the other two columns on 14 March at the Halfaiya Pass, about 3 miles southeast of Sollum, his force was suffering badly. Armoured car Driver Sam Rolls recalled:

> As soon as we halted the men of the South African battalions stumbled towards us hurriedly and unsteadily, gasping out, 'Water! Water! For the love of God, water!' Their tongues hung out of their gaping mouths … Flesh and blood could not stand this sight … Others, and still others, came straining over the edge of the cruel precipice and stumbling towards us, crying like babies and gesticulating like madmen … until they could drag their tortured bodies to where we had halted.[407]

Orders had been given to conserve the water carried by the armoured cars but in the face of such suffering waterbottles and even the radiators of the engines and the coolant systems of the machine guns were emptied.

The Senussi had not made any attempt to stop any of the columns and that afternoon Sollum was reoccupied. Two miles further west, at Bir Wair, Nuri Bey's camp was found to be deserted, with fresh tracks leading off towards Libya. A captured Bedu confirmed that Nuri and his followers had retreated that way the previous day.[408]

Peyton turned to his armoured car unit. This was under the command of Major the Duke of Westminster, who, like some of his crews, had transferred into the army from the RNACD. Peyton ordered him to take his vehicles, nine armoured cars and one Model T Ford with a machine gun mounted on the back, to pursue Nuri with a wonderfully vague 'reasonable boldness'. The armoured cars had been of mixed use so far in the campaign; their high speed was often negated by the rock-strewn or boggy terrain, and only really at Agagiya had they played a significant role in any action. Now, though, with the end of the Khedival Road merging into the Enveria Road at the Libyan border and proving to be a rough but useable track, the cars could come into their own. Pressing ahead at speeds ranging from 20–40 miles an hour, Westminster's convoy passed large numbers of Bedouin drifting in the same direction, presumably fugitives from Nuri's army. These were ignored and 25 miles west of Sollum, at Bir 'Aziz, the Senussi camp was found.

The armoured cars tore straight into the Senussi camp. Caught entirely by surprise, many Senussi fled, although the Ottoman crews of the remaining field guns and machine guns rushed to their weapons, and for the most part stood by them until killed. The armoured cars charged through the camp in line abreast, and Sam Rolls leaves a vivid description of being inside them:

> The reek of burnt cordite, blending with the stench of our hot, sweating bodies, made us gasp for fresh air, but with the armour lid closed down there was little chance of getting any. The heat, a combination of that given out by the racing engine and that of the sun on the steel cylinder, added to the din of the stuttering gun and the clatter of the ammunition belts, made the conditions nerve-shattering. Hot, empty cartridge cases frequently fell on my bare neck, and into my shirt, stinging my flesh; and the general sensation inside our war chariot was infernal.[409]

Nuri's force was estimated at 150–200 *muhafizia* plus Ottoman specialists. As the cars swept all before them and then continued to harry the survivors for another 10 miles or so into the desert, around fifty were killed and another forty captured. All of their remaining heavy weapons – three field guns and nine machine guns – were captured, along with precious stores and ammunition. Although Nuri Bey escaped, the power of the Senussi along the Egyptian coast had been broken.[410]

Several matters remained unsettled. The first was the safety of the crew of HMS *Tara*. Documents were discovered at Sollum that allowed the position of their camp at Bir Hakim to be estimated, and two Arab guides found who were reasonably confident that they knew the way. Again, this job called for the speed and range of the Duke of Westminster's armoured cars. Supplemented by ambulances and trucks, plus the Duke's own Rolls-Royce Touring Car, to make a column of forty-three vehicles, the rescue party left Sollum in the early hours of 17 March 1916. They drove while the moon shone, and arrived at Bir Aziz, where the Berkshire Yeomanry and the Australian Camel Corps had established a forward base, just as it set. The convoy stopped and breakfasted, waiting until there was again enough light to navigate by, as strict orders had been given not to use headlights in case they were spotted by the enemy.

The convoy sped across the featureless and barren desert for the rest of the morning and half the afternoon, relying on the somewhat shaky memories of the two Arabs who had claimed to have visited Bir Hakim many years before. Although the convoy had three days of water, only enough petrol for 300 miles could be carried, and while the prisoners were estimated to be only 75 miles south-west of Sollum, the nature of the ground led to frequent detours. It was a vast relief when, at 3 p.m. and with 120 miles covered on the ground, the tiny collection of buildings at Bir Hakim was spotted.

If it was a relief for the rescue party, it can be imagined how the prisoners felt. For nineteen weeks they had been held in the middle of nowhere, on starvation rations of a little rice and occasional meat, bolstered by whatever wildlife (generally snails) they could catch. It was little consolation that their captors had been left in the same plight, and having shared all that they could with their prisoners were equally half-starved and ragged. However, it had been hoped for weeks that fresh supplies would be sent in from the coast. When the first, and even the second and third, cars appeared on the horizon, hope soared that this was the long-promised convoy of food and medical supplies. But instead, recalled Captain Gwatkin-Williams:

When we saw first ten, then twenty, then thirty, forty and finally forty-three cars come rushing up, we began to get a glimmering of the truth, a half-fearful hope that the impossible *had* happened. It was then that out little world turned itself inside out, that we saw the heavens opening, and gazed terrified lest they should close again. We had to ask our saviours 'Are we free?' and when we were told 'Yes,' we did not believe them!

I cannot remember even the cars coming up to us. I have a vague recollection of the whirr of motor engines, of the presence of a crowd of vehicles, and suddenly they are there! Near by was a Red Cross ambulance to which the men pushed, and presently some came away from it, and it dawned on me that they had open tins of food in their hands. Forgetting my dignity, I also rushed to the car and snatched what I could get, and then came running back to the officers' tent, a tin of chicken in one hand, a tin of condensed milk in the other; these two I ladled indiscriminately with a piece of stick on to a hunch of bread and gorged![411]

The euphoria was tempered only by the rash actions of the armoured cars. Tragic first impressions led to a perhaps understandable, of not condonable, misunderstanding. Rolls recalled:

We charged right up to the well mounds, and before we had halted we were surrounded on all sides by a throng of living skeletons. They were clad in old burnouses, rice sacks and the tattered remains of blue uniforms ... Then there was no room left in us for compassion. We fended them off with firm and hasty hands; the engines roared, and we shot away after the creatures who had had it in their power to turn our fellow-countrymen into whimpering scarecrows ... The guards were running with their women and children, running for their lives. We did not look to see who or what they were – this was no politicians' game; at last we had something really worth fighting for. Men, women and even children were mown down ruthlessly by our guns, in that mad hustle for revenge ...

Of course, it was all a mistake, as such things usually are. The Senussi had not ill-treated their prisoners as they understood treatment. These desert people starve every day of their lives, according to our notion of feeding. They had given their prisoners what they had themselves, and treated them decently, according to their own notions. It was beyond their power to do more. But it was a long time before I understood this.[412]

With food and clothing distributed, and the worst medical cases taken into the ambulances, Westminster was keen to get moving again. 'So we packed up our little belongings, and still stuffing down food, and in many instances smoking two cigarettes at once, we stowed ourselves away in the various vehicles of the convoy.'[413] Within half an hour, the column was fully loaded and back on what passed for the road. They arrived at Bir Aziz in the early hours of 18 March, rested for a few hours, and then entered Sollum later that morning to a rapturous reception.[414]

This meant an end to major operations on the coast, and most of the troops returned to Alexandria. However, a garrison was installed in Sollum, from where they continued to carry out patrols and raids across the area. Several raids were made into Libya to intercept Senussi supply convoys or depots that were supporting Nuri Bey's continuing fight with Italy. From July 1916, these operations began to be made in conjunction with the Italians, with whom Britain now signed an agreement (later joined by the French) not to make a separate peace with the Senussi.[415]

If the coast was peaceful, there was still the issue of the oases of the Western Desert, which the Grand Senussi had begun to occupy in February. A small British force, consisting of the 1/1st North Midland Mounted Brigade[*] and the 159th Infantry Brigade,[**] had already been deployed down the Nile Valley to protect against any attack from this direction, but to begin with there was little offensive action that could be taken. Half a dozen or so large oases dominate the Western Desert, and between them water and shelter was extremely scarce. While the desert-bred Senussi could navigate and traverse this area with relative ease, the British troops were neither trained nor equipped to operate in such extreme conditions. In March, the Southern Force was organised to co-ordinate operations in this area, under Major General John Adye, although, with the end of major operations on the coast, this command was merged into the Western Frontier Force (still under Peyton) at the end of the month. Troops were now transferred from the coastal region, and on 15 April 1916 the southern oasis at Kharga, from which the Senussi had withdrawn, was reoccupied by the British using an existing light railway from the Nile to the oasis. Another light railway was now begun from the Nile at Beni Mazar towards the oasis at Bahariya, while a line of blockhouses was constructed in a parallel line to the south, running west from Samalut. From these, patrols monitored the areas between them, sweeping out each morning and following any tracks that were discovered.

In early May, Peyton was transferred and, after several others held the command in quick succession, command of the WFF fell to the Canadian Major General Sir Charles Dobell. Now reinforced with camel troops and armoured cars, Dobell began to push patrols further out into the areas between the oases, using the range of these troops to begin to dominate the region, cutting Senussi communications and intercepting supply convoys. It was dangerous work, not because of the Senussi, but the very desolation of the desert itself. One of the cameliers recalled how 'there was no water, no growth and no sign of life, nothing but sand, gravel, rock and during the day-time a burning shimmering heat which distorted everything into fantastic shapes and images'.[416]

By the time that Dobell passed command of the WFF on to Major General William Watson on 4 October, several thousand Senussi were still active across the Western Desert, but they were facing a severe shortage of stores, and sickness was rife.[417] Between 8 and 10 October 1916, the Grand Senussi and his commanding general in the area, Muhammed Saleh Harb, drew their forces back to Siwa. Ten days later, Camel Corps and armoured car patrols retook Bahariya and Dakhla, and a month later Farafra. Small numbers of Senussi were captured, but the important thing was that the civil authorities were restored, and the Senussi pushed back away from the Nile Valley. The following February, a raid (again of camel troops and armoured cars) would strike at Siwa, routing the final Senussi troops out of Egypt and back across the Libyan border.

In May 1916 the Grand Senussi's cousin, and to many the rightful Grand Senussi, Sayyid Muhammed Idris, had approached the British authorities in Egypt with peace overtures. Throughout, he had been vocal in his opposition to the war with the British, and as the summer wore on more and more Senussi turned from their defeated leader

---

[*]   Lincolnshire, Staffordshire and East Riding Yeomanrys.

[**]   1/4th and 1/7th Cheshire Regiment, 1/4th and 1/5th Welsh Regiment.

and joined Idris' ranks. Talks, which included the Italians, dragged on through the rest of 1916 and into 1917, with most of the sticking points concerning the Italian side of the negotiations. Finally, in April 1917, peace was signed.[418] Sayyid Ahmed al-Sharif, still calling himself the Grand Senussi, withdrew into the desert, where he maintained a futile resistance until escaping, by submarine, to Constantinople in August 1918.

The later stages of the Senussi campaign had been dominated by a strange combination of brand-new war machines – the armoured cars – and one of the oldest tools of war – the camel. It is probably fair to say that the latter were the more versatile, for while armoured cars were suitable only on certain types of terrain, the camel, as the ship of the desert, was made for these conditions. Indeed, their very form was shaped to the needs of desert life alone, and certainly had no consideration to aesthetics:

> The Arabs say that at the Creation, when the beasts of the earth were formed, there were left over a lot of remnants out of which was made a camel, and the parts are not hard to find. The head of a sheep was placed on the neck of a giraffe, which was attached to the body of a cow, and the neck bent itself in shame at being put to such a use. The tail of an ass was appended, and the whole was set on the legs of a horse, which ended in the pads of a dog, on each of which was stuck the claw of an ostrich, and the monstrosity, evidently being considered a failure, was banished to live in the desert where no other quadruped could exist, and where its solitary existence gave it 'the hump'.[419]

Small numbers of camels had been used by the army in Egypt since the start of the war, particularly by the Bikaner Camel Corps, and by the Egyptian armed forces and Coastguard. Perhaps surprisingly (and Maxwell would be criticised for this), the mass purchase of camels for military use was not started until November 1915 when an order was placed for 20,000 camels to carry supplies.[420] Even in Egypt the procurement of camels was not that easy. Egypt's main supply of animals came from Arabia, and the war had cut off this route. Instead, camels had to be purchased and transported from the Sudan, Somaliland, and even India to reach the amount needed. In fact, a total of 150,000 were gathered in December 1915 and January 1916, of which a mere 13,000 were considered as fit for active duty. Mange was a particular problem, with some 60–70 per cent of Egyptian camels suffering to some degree. In the end, many of the less severe cases had to be purchased anyway simply to make up numbers, and in the first three months of 1916 alone 16,067 were treated in the army's three Camel Veterinary Hospitals.[421]

Those that were purchased were mainly put to use in carrying supplies, under the auspices of the Camel Transport Corps, a part of the Egyptian Labour Corps. By the end of 1916, around 30,000 camels were in use, with around 20,000 Egyptian drivers to manage them. Initially, Egyptians were hired on a three-month contract, but as the war spread across the Sinai and into Palestine in 1917, this was increased to six months. Pay was good but conditions fairly poor, and much depended on the officers and NCOs, all Europeans, in whichever of the (eventually) seventeen companies a driver was attached to. The standard of European staff varied drastically, as did their knowledge of Arabic and the Egyptians, although often just as bad were the Egyptian overseers recruited from the ranks, especially as the Corps continued to expand. Discipline could be harsh, with beatings by overseers as a standard tool of encouragement, and floggings for more serious offences.[422] From a military point of view, these units added immensely to the mobility and reach of the British forces in Egypt, and in both the Senussi and Sinai campaigns their ability to move supplies (particularly water) would often prove a crucial factor in operations.

Other camels were siphoned off to be used by the various camel companies that were created in the summer of 1916. The brainchild of Lieutenant Colonel Clement Leslie Smith VC MC, they were initially largely recruited from the Australian cavalry units. Only individual companies were formed at first, for use in the Western Desert, but these were brought together into a Composite Camel Battalion during the advance into the Sinai. Thereafter various temporary camel battalions saw service until, in January 1917, the Imperial Camel Corps Brigade was formed. Again the troopers, or 'cameliers', were drawn mostly from Australian units. Of the four battalions, two and a half (ten companies) were Australian, one half (two companies) consisted of New Zealanders, and the final battalion (larger than the others at six companies) was drawn from British units. During the Sinai campaign, an Imperial Camel Corps Brigade was formed, made up from three battalions on rotation, while the fourth operated elsewhere.

To begin with, most of the new cameliers, although volunteers, found their new duties hard to warm to. Camels were certainly not as likable as their horses had been, although Australian Oliver Hogue found that the initial revulsion did slowly wear off:

> We hated the thought of 'em. We hated the sight of 'em. We hated the smell of 'em. We hated the shape of 'em. The very idea of association with such brutes was hateful to us – at first.
>
> But the time was not far distant when we were to forget all our initial antipathies. Familiarity bred content. The law of compensation was in operation. A beast with so many obvious vices as a camel must have some compensating virtues. But it *did* take time to unearth them.[423]

The swaying motion of the camels also took a lot of getting used to, as did the dangerous and unpredictable natures of male camels in particular. On the other hand, there were obvious and undeniable benefits. The cameliers could carry on their mounts food and water to stay out for five days as well as 250 rounds of ammunition, far more in both cases than cavalry could. Their durability and stamina, and firepower if need be, made them perfectly suited for the long-range operations that characterised the campaign to push the Senussi from the oases of the Western Desert, and would later prove equally useful in patrolling and monitoring the Sinai Peninsula. Because, while a final end was being put to the Senussi threat in the west, the war had also been developing rapidly in the east.

10

THE WAR AT SEA

With the Suez Canal cleared of enemy-owned shipping, and the battlecruiser SMS *Goeben* and light cruiser SMS *Breslau* cleared from the central shipping lanes, the attention of the Entente powers turned in early 1915 to the peripheries of the Mediterranean. For the British this remained a secondary theatre with the most modern ships and the bulk of the fleet remaining in the North Sea ready to counter the formidable German fleet, should it ever venture out to sea. The sea war in the Mediterranean was instead, nominally at least, under French control, based out of the British island base of Malta.[424] In practice, differing British and French interests and concerns increasingly led to this single command turning into a loosely co-ordinated set of sub-units largely following their own national interests.

The major concern in the early months for the Entente powers was the threat posed by Italy and Austro-Hungary, who were ideally placed to dominate the whole area. Italy had been bound to Germany and Austro-Hungary, under the Triple Alliance, since the 1880s, although technically this was a defensive agreement. On the outbreak of war Italy prevaricated, based partly on its long standing rivalry with Austro-Hungary, and using the excuse that the other two powers had declared war first, on Serbia. In the end Italy would enter the war on the Entente side in May 1915. While the large Austro-Hungarian fleet was still dangerous, the threat was at least now bottled up in the Adriatic, with only a narrow entrance to be patrolled rather than the whole Italian shoreline. This entrance would see an increasingly heavy Entente presence in what would become known as the Otranto Barrage: a densely patrolled zone just off the heel of Italy.

Britain's concern with the Mediterranean was two-fold. Firstly, there was the through-trade with the eastern Empire. Before the war, between one-fifth and one-sixth of Britain's wheat came from India via the Suez Canal (and, after the American wheat crop failed in 1916, substantial amounts had to come from Australia, too[425]). Huge amounts of raw materials had also came up through the Canal; from the Malay Peninsula alone came some 86 per cent of Britain's block tin and (with what is now Sri Lanka) half of all rubber imports.[426] The war also required the speedy movement of tens of thousands troops from India, Australia and New Zealand, as well as horses for military use. And, of course, that other vital ingredient for victory, tea, also flowed through the same channels. These materials would now be desperately needed for Britain's rapidly expanding military and war economy, and taking the shortest and quickest route to their destination was paramount. If nothing else, the sooner ships could arrive in Britain, the quicker they could be despatched on another voyage. Shipping levels would be an ongoing concern for the British Government through-out the war. While numbers of available merchant ships spiked in 1914 and early 1915, as captured enemy vessels were pressed into service, for the rest of the war the increasingly effective German submarine campaigns would see a steady decrease in the tonnage available, straining the economy considerably. By the end of 1916, ships were being lost at three times the rate at which they could be replaced.[427]

The second, albeit closely linked, concern was the support of the British expedi-tionary forces in the Mediterranean: in Egypt, in the Dardanelles, and in Salonika, and through the Red Sea to Mesopotamia. The two northern campaigns relied heav-ily on the Egypt Base for their supplies of food, water and munitions, as well as an evacuation route for their sick and wounded. Keeping the sea lanes open and material flowing north from Egypt across the sea was important, but so too was moving the supplies to Egypt in the first place. Needless to say, most of the army's materiel was imported to Egypt from elsewhere, at increasingly considerable trouble and expense. For example, to ship a single horse from Argentina (which, with Australia, was the main source of supply) the cost rose from £5 in 1914, to £15 in January 1916.[428] Part of the cost increase was forced on shipping companies by the rise in insurance pre-miums which were an inevitable by-product of the submarine campaign, but simple profiteering was also a major factor, and affected shipping of all sorts.

Another major import from South America was meat for the army; about 35,400 tons of the 82,000 tons consumed by the forces in the Mediterranean in 1916.[429] In June 1916 the forces in or controlled by Egypt (including the Salonika garrison and the Royal Navy, but not other Entente forces) had a reserve of just twenty-four days' rations available in stores onshore, or on ships about to unload in the harbour. If the full supply of stores was diverted to the Egyptian Expeditionary Force, it could be stretched for over two months, but as the Salonika force was down to fifteen days' reserves, this could not happen.[430] For any army to plan protracted offensive action, particularly over such barren areas as the Sinai Desert where no other sources of food may be found, with such limited reserves of foodstuffs for their troops would be a risky business. It would not take too many resupply ships being sunk in the Mediterranean (particularly as ships capable of keeping stores frozen were at an absolute premium) for the army to find itself unable to feed its troops at even a basic level. The alterna-tive, which the Admiralty were in favour of, was to send the meat ships from South America to Egypt via South Africa, but this would take much longer and would also have the effect of leaving the army perilously low on rations in the short term.[431]

The submarine campaign was not the only cause of shortages, although it was certainly the most dramatic. The ever-hungry Entente war machine demanded increasing amounts of food and raw materials as the war progressed, and the com-paratively small size of the French and Italian merchant fleets led to British ships being diverted to carry Entente cargoes. For example, of the 82,000 tons of meat in 1916, 27,700 tons went to French forces, and 700 tons to the Italians.[432] Another was the limited portion of even British shipping that the government could afford to hold at any one time. By the end of 1916, 31 per cent of the British merchant fleet had been requisitioned for military use by the British or Allied governments. Another 27 per cent were directly under government control for specific purposes, chartered for certain cargoes or routes. The other 42 per cent was released to free trade, usually to and from Britain, but about 10 per cent were engaged purely between foreign ports.[433] Chartering or requisitioning a greater proportion of shipping would cost too much directly, especially as shipping companies raised their rates to meet demand. It would also cost too much indirectly; British wealth was based on trade, and already too many markets were being lost, and with them the revenue that was vital to pay for the war effort.

If physically moving the supplies to Egypt was an ordeal, getting them ashore could be equally traumatic. Alexandria acted as the main depot port for not only Egypt, but also Salonika (where the comparatively shallow harbours caused their own problems) and Gallipoli, with Port Said as an important secondary port. In 1915, when the two above operations began, the Royal Navy was so overwhelmed, globally, that the organisation of the harbours in Egypt was left to the army. Both ports quickly became seriously congested through sheer weight of traffic, leading to delays in loading and unloading that did not help the general shipping shortage.[434] As the flow of stores increased, greater numbers of Egyptians were hired to act as labourers to load and unload ships, move stores around the harbour, and to load the trains and vehicles that connected the depots with the troops in the field. The piecemeal nature of this expansion led to numerous teams working on the same jobs for different pay and conditions, and reporting to a variety of army organisations.

In January 1916 the end of the Gallipoli campaign allowed many of the RN staff from Mudros to be sent to Egypt. Here, Rear Admiral Reginald Allenby[435] arrived to command the RN depot at Port Said and act as Principal Naval Transport Officer for the whole country. This was no easy task. In Egypt he found near chaos, with a lack of co-ordination between the different army departments causing space to be wasted on ships, trains and in storage warehouses, leading to delays and wastage. His attempt to impose a single, unified system very quickly ran into problems as each existing department fought to defend their own empire, especially against naval interlopers. Indeed, the army complained to the War Committee that the navy was itself causing chaos by trying to overturn existing arrangements that had stood for two years. Further concerns were raised about the financial responsibility of the navy trying to handle army stores, and who should pay for breakages or losses. In the end, a dual system was established where the RN had responsibility for unloading ships, and moving materials onto the quay. From there, the army had responsibility for moving the stores onwards to their final destinations. This political wrangling stretched on well into the summer, with resulting delays and frustrations.[436]

For the Germans and the Austro-Hungarians, these supply lines, and the concentrations of ships off the Dardanelles, were increasingly tempting targets. There was considerable scope to disrupt not only local campaigns, but the wider Entente war effort. Raiding with surface vessels was not an option; they would be too difficult to slip past the Entente patrols at the mouth of the Adriatic, and too easy to hunt down once in the Mediterranean. Submarines, however, were a different matter.

The submarine fleet of the Austro-Hungarian Empire was small and out of date, even by 1914 standards. Poor designs and temperamental equipment meant that they were as much a danger to their crews as the enemy, with engine fumes building up inside the hull when submerged. Still, in December 1914 the *U-15* managed to torpedo and damage the French dreadnought *Jean Bart*, although the first real success did not come until April 1915. On the night of 26/27 April, the submarine *U-5*, under the command of *Korvettenkapitän* Georg Ritter von Trapp, sank the French armoured cruiser (and flagship of their 2nd Cruiser Squadron) *Léon Gambetta*, killing Rear Admiral Victor Baptism Sènés and 684 of his 711-man crew. This was Austro-Hungary's first naval success of the war, and the first of many for von Trapp, who, as well as becoming a noted singer, became the Empire's leading U-Boat ace with 44,595 merchant tons sunk to his credit by the end of the war.[437]

Austro-Hungarian efforts were soon swamped by those of their German allies. Already in March 1915 the Germans were transporting submarines in pieces by train to the naval base at Pola in the Adriatic. Three boats of the UB1 type were to arrive this way, although a fourth, the *U-21* under *Kapitänleutnant* Otto Hersing, sailed directly from Germany. Leaving Ems on 25 April, it sailed around Scotland and down to the Mediterranean, arriving at the Adriatic base of Cattaro on 13 May. Refuelled and resupplied, it almost immediately put to sea and sailed for the Dardanelles, where it scored a double success by sinking the British battleships HMS *Triumph* on 25 May and HMS *Majestic* on 27 May. Although a notable victory, these actions also had the effect of making the Royal Navy in the Aegean utterly paranoid about submarines getting in amongst the supply and support ships off the Dardanelles. Small craft were rushed to the area in large numbers, mounting patrols of such intensity that it proved impossible for submarines to operate in the area after that.[438]

There were still rich pickings elsewhere. The constant streams of merchant ships were all fair game under the prevailing interpretations of international law on the matter. Actually, the internationally recognised rules of naval warfare were in themselves rather vague, and more like generally accepted guidelines than actual laws. Under what were known as Blockade or Cruiser Rules, merchant ships were supposed to be stopped and their cargoes and papers examined to determine their destination and the status of their load. If they were clearly neutral or the cargoes for non-military uses they were to be set free to go on their way. If the ship was bound for a hostile nation bearing war materials, they were to be taken under the command of a prize crew to sail to the nearest friendly harbour. There were various rules on what cargoes could be seized as war materials and which should be let through. These were frequently contradictory; after all, food could be used for either military or civilian purposes, for example. A further problem was that submarines carried very small crews already, so they could not spare any to form prize crews. It was accepted that submarines would have to sink any confirmed enemy ships, but it was expected that they should warn the target vessel and allow the crews to abandon ship before opening fire.[439]

These rules would cause constant problems for Germany through the war. As the Entente powers began to arm merchant ships, or even dress heavily armed ships up like merchantmen to create traps – the so-called Q-Ships – it became increasingly dangerous for submarines to surface and close with their targets. Far safer was it either to fire torpedoes when submerged, or to surface and use their deck guns from a distance. Torpedoes were big and costly, and submarines could only carry a very small supply, but the deck guns did not have the same limitations. Either way, it meant opening fire without first ascertaining the destination or cargo of the vessel. In the Atlantic, the sinking by submarines of ships either under US colours or carrying US citizens, most notoriously the *Lusitania* in May 1915, led to frequent complaints from the Americans, causing the Germans to fluctuate between observing Cruiser Rules or conducting unrestricted submarine warfare. In the Mediterranean, there were very few US or other neutral ships (although the sinking of the New York-bound *Arcona* in November 1915 was a notable exception), and the German Navy gave greater freedom to its captains to conduct operations in their own preferred manner.

By October 1915 the Germans were operating a fleet of five standard and two mine-laying submarines from the Adriatic, of whom around half were at sea at any one time.[440] A year later, this had grown to sixteen standard submarines, most of a much larger and more modern type, and ten minelayers.[441] The more modern submarines were of the 'Thirties Class', armed with four torpedo tubes (two in the bow, two in the stern) and a 105mm deck gun. Although only six torpedoes could be carried at a time, a considerable amount of shells could be, and with a top speed of 16½ knots on the surface or 9½ knots submerged, and a range of nearly 4,500 miles, they were a formidable threat.[442] Between October and December 1915 alone, eighty ships were sunk by German submarines or submarine laid mines in the Mediterranean, totalling 293,423 tons. This constituted 82 per cent of British shipping losses world-wide in that period.[443]

Different captains developed their own preferred methods. The greatest submarine captain of his, and indeed all, time, was *Kapitänleutnant* Lothar von Arnauld de la Perière, who commanded *U-35*. He set repeated records through his career in the Mediterranean, sinking mostly merchantmen as well as a few warships. His most successful cruise was between 26 July and 20 August 1916 when he accounted for fifty-four ships (both steamers and sailing ships), totalling over 90,000 tons. His technique during this and his other voyages was to surface and stop ships, regardless of the risks to his own vessel.[444] He would later recall quite matter-of-factly of his record-breaking cruise:

> My cruise was quite tame and humdrum ... We stopped ships. The crews took to the boats. We examined the ships' papers, gave sailing instructions to the nearest land, and then sank the captured prizes.[445]

By the end of the war, de la Perière had wracked up a score of 194 ships sunk, over 450,000 tons.

Others were less humane in their methods. Several submarine captains made it onto the British list of war criminals, including *Korvettenkapitän* Max Valentiner, who had been responsible for sinking the *Arcona*. As the third most successful commander of the war (136 ships, 293,000 tons), Valentiner preferred to sink his prey without warning, and without allowing an evacuation first. In particular, the British wanted to hold him to account for the sinking of the P&O liner *Persia* on 30 December 1915. The ship was sunk without warning between Port Said and Crete, leading to the deaths of 334 of the just over 500 people on board.[446]

A few days after the sinking of the *Persia*, the tramp steamer *Coquet*, bound from Spain to Rangoon with over 6,000 tons of salt, was intercepted 200 miles east of Malta by the *U-34*, under *Kapitänleutnant* Claus Rücker. The British Captain, Arnold Groom, obeyed instructions from the surfaced *U-34* to heave-to and abandon ship. Two boats were lowered into the rough sea, and the thirty-one crew members disembarked. Rücker now ordered the boats to pull alongside his submarine, which they did with great difficulty as the sea ran high. While Rücker interviewed Groom, the two boats were sent, with German sailors onboard, back to the *Coquet*, where the crew were allowed to salvage personal items, and the ship was searched and looted by the submariners, who also laid scuttling charges. On returning to the submarine from the now-sinking *Coquet*, the boats and crew were searched and all charts or equipment that could be used to aid navigation (apart from one rather unreliable compass) was confiscated. Both boats were now leaking after banging repeatedly against the submarine's hull, while the weather was worsening considerably. Despite this, Rücker cast the boats loose and sailed off to find fresh targets.

Groom was now left with few options. His two boats had sails, and with a strong wind blowing from the north-west, the only viable one was to set sail for the North African coast. They had been cast loose on the late afternoon of 4 January 1916 and shortly before nightfall a ship was seen. Attempts to signal to it failed, and night, and temperatures, soon fell. The boats were leaking badly and despite having men constantly on bailing duty, the icy water was soon rising up the crew's legs. Cold seeped through every man and conditions were terrible. The two boats became separated, although they briefly rejoined each other on the morning of 6 January. The Captain and Chief Officer Griffiths, commander of the second boat, agreed to separate again, in order to maximise their chances of meeting another ship. Griffith's boat faded over the horizon, and neither he nor any of the other thirteen men on board were ever seen again. For the men in Groom's boat, the ordeal continued:

> Everybody chilled to the bone with that northerly wind blowing right through our saturated clothes; we all used to look forward to the daylight coming, in the hopes of seeing a little sun; but it was nearly always covered with clouds. Several of us had excruciating pains in the ankles, knees and wrists; the poor little Italian boy was crying all one night with them in his sleep, and, of course, I could do absolutely nothing for him.[447]

Provisions were strictly rationed to two and a half biscuits and a half-pint of water per day, although the water ration had to be increased later.

Finally, on the morning of 10 January land was sighted, and after hours of heaving the boat through the breakers and rocks of the shoreline, they landed at dusk. The next morning Groom made contact with an Arab and discovered that they had landed in the Gulf of Sirte in Libya. The Arab agreed to guide two of Groom's Greek crewmen to the nearest Italian garrison, while the other fifteen survivors waited on the shore. For most of these men, the worst was still to come.

On the next morning a large group of Arabs appeared on the skyline and opened fire at the merchant crew's camp. Groom was wounded and fell unconscious, and on waking much later he discovered two of his crew dead and two more badly wounded. Of the other ten men there was no sign. An Italian ship arrived that afternoon to rescue the survivors, although one of the wounded men died as he was being lifted aboard. It was ascertained that the other ten survivors had been carried off into the desert by the Arabs. These men faced a three-week trek across the desert before finally arriving at Jedabiah, about 120 miles from Benghazi. Here they were held in squalid conditions with a number of Italian prisoners by the Senussi. Kept on starvation rations, they were set to work rebuilding an old Italian fort, and anyone who attempted to escape was brutally flogged. One sailor died from an infected injury. Conditions improved slightly in April 1916, with the arrival of Nuri Bey (fresh from his defeat at Bir Aziz) and some German officers. Apparently under Nuri Bey's influence, arrangements were eventually made for the release of the merchantmen, and in late July 1916 they were handed over to Italian troops.[448]

The submarines would have the upper hand throughout 1915 and 1916, and only slowly in 1917 would the tables turn. Despite the Entente powers having near complete surface control of the Mediterranean, the weapons at their disposal to tackle submarines were limited. While it is true that submarines could only stay submerged for a limited amount of time, and had to surface regularly to freshen their air and charge their batteries, their very low profile made them hard to spot at a distance. On the other hand, the billows of smoke emitted by steam-driven ships made them very easy to spot from far over the horizon, allowing the submarines not only to home in easily on new targets, but also submerge in plenty of time to hide from potential attackers.

Once submerged there were very few ways to detect submarines although visual spotting was often possible. Although the range of view was limited from the deck of a ship, aeroplanes (land-based, flying boats and seaplanes were all used) and airships could cover much larger distances. Once a submerged target was spotted, bombs and depth charges (neither of which, in the sizes that could be carried by aircraft, were particularly effective) could be dropped, and wireless sets could be used to call in warships. The feathering wake left by periscopes cutting through the water could also be a giveaway.

While the 'Mk. 1 Eyeball' was the most common tool used, technology could also be employed. Slowly, the Otranto Barrage was built up across the mouth of the Adriatic, although this would not get into full swing until 1917.[449] Nets and minefields were laid, while patrols of trawlers dragging nets, which sometimes had explosive charges

attached, swept along, hoping to catch a submarine. Perhaps the most advanced tool in the Entente arsenal was the hydrophone. These underwater microphones could detect the noise of submarine engines and provide a basic bearing to the target, although they also picked up the noises of other ships, sea life, and the movement of the water. For most of the war they could only be used in fixed points off coastlines, although eventually models were developed that could be used by slow-moving ships.

Efforts were made to improve the co-ordination and distribution of patrols in the Mediterranean, as a deterrent to submarine raiding. In December 1915 the Sea was divided into eighteen zones split between the British, French and Italians.[450] Within these areas, each nation patrolled the shipping lanes and issued warnings to divert merchantmen away from areas where submarines had recently been active. The results were negligible. The technology did not exist to hunt submarines effectively, and there were simply not enough warships available to provide a thick enough blanket of patrols to deter attacks. On top of this, the designation of fairly set shipping lanes simply made the submariner's job of finding targets that much easier.

In March 1916 this system was refined at the Malta Conference. The number of zones was reduced to eleven but the problems of having fixed shipping lanes and patrol routes remained, and the level to which it allowed any co-ordination between the Allies is debatable.[451] What is interesting is the division of areas of responsibility. In the eastern Mediterranean, the French had responsibility for the area east of a line running from El Arish up to Cyprus, and then on to Rhodes. This left the entire Syrian, Palestine and southern Turkish coast in their control, in line with ancient claims held by the French to have special interests in Syria in particular. The French also had control of the waters around Greece and Albania, and off southern Italy. Italy had the Libyan coastline and the Adriatic. Britain had the central regions of the Sea, the coast off Egypt, and the Aegean, including the western coast of Turkey, known as the Smyrna coast.

The French had been active in the waters off Syria since the start of the war, with a squadron under Vice Admiral D'Artige du Fournet operating out of Port Said by the end of 1914. In September 1915 it was ships from this squadron that were contacted by survivors from the area of Musa Dagh, south of Alexandretta, where Ottoman troops had attacked the Armenian population. With British help, the French managed to evacuate 4,000–5,000 Armenian men, women and children from the enclave, which had been holding out for some forty days. The survivors were taken to Egypt, where the British authorities took them in and provided a camp at Port Said. Over the coming months various attempts were made to recruit the men for use in Salonika or the Sinai campaigns but without any success. Indeed, the British authorities found the attitude of the Armenians, who seemed to show almost no interest in any form of work, deeply frustrating. The French would meet with more success by using a somewhat subtler approach. In late 1916 and early 1917 many from the camp joined *La Légion d'Orient*, later renamed *La Légion Arménienne*, fighting with distinction in Palestine and Syria.[452]

The French also provided escorts for the small British force that still operated off Palestine and Syria once the Dardanelles campaign had begun. These were the seaplane carriers used to monitor Ottoman troop movements and coastal defences.

Initially the *Aenne Rickmers* (later HMS *Anne*) and the *Rabenfels* (later HMS *Raven II*) operated with largely Greek Cypriot crews under a few RN officers, and under the control of the army intelligence organisations and, ultimately, General Maxwell. In January 1916 HMS *Ben-My-Chree* arrived from the Aegean, and soon after HMS *Empress* was sent out from the UK. One of HMS *Ben-My-Chree's* officers, the novelist Erskine Childers, assessed the work of HMS *Anne* and HMS *Raven II*; he discovered that although over 270 flights had been made from the two ships, the reports and documentation produced was haphazard and no photographs had been taken. On application to the army and naval authorities, it was decided to group the (soon-to-be) four carriers together into the East Indies and Egypt Seaplane Squadron. Under the command of (Acting) Commander Cecil John L'Strange Malone, they would now come under direct RN control.[453]

The seaplane carriers now operated in a more organised fashion, ranging from the Sinai coast up to Smyrna, and occasionally being despatched to the Red Sea. Their home base was in Port Said harbour, although advanced bases were also established on Castellorizo, an island off the south coast of Anatolia, and on Ruad, a tiny island city 2 miles off the Syrian shore, about 75 miles north of Beirut. Seized by the French in September 1915, this island was used as a base for French naval and intelligence operations for the rest of the war.[454] Escorts were usually provided by French destroyers, although RN sloops were also used, and occasionally other British ships were attached for specific tasks, such as the attack on El Arish in May 1916. For the crews, life was cramped and uncomfortable and the flying dangerous. The aircraft used were often old and decrepit, and operating them far from easy. Aircraft were winched overboard and took off and landed from the sea. In rough weather this could be a fraught business. Even more dangerous was the possibility of coming down over the desert, deep behind enemy lines and far from help. Contingency plans were in place but it would be a desperate venture. Flight Lieutenant G.B. Dacre recalled:

> This desert flying is no joke as one depends entirely on one's engine. There is just a chance that a seaplane of our type can be landed without doing in pilot and passenger, so precautions have been taken. We take wireless, so that we can send back our position when a breakdown occurs ... Also, we are armed and take a water bottle and food and a pocket compass. It might be possible to walk back to the coast, but walking in the wilderness where no life is to be seen is very heavy. The ship will remain off the coast for 3 days and nights, at night with a searchlight and we have Very Light [flare] pistols. It might be possible to walk to some of the camel tracks and hold up a party, pinch their camels, food and trek back to the coast.[455]

While seaplane crews probably had the worst of it, sailors in line ships, be they the big line-of-battle ships, the smaller destroyers or the tiny trawlers and sloops, were also fairly uncomfortable. In the modern age of gun turrets and thick metal hulls, life below decks could be stifling. Whereas in the old days gun ports along the sides of the ships could be opened to allow a breeze to come through, now the lower decks were sealed off. This was where sailors slept (still in hammocks) and ate, and the atmosphere, even without the stifling Mediterranean heat, could be thick and unpalatable. In many ships sailors were allowed to sleep on deck instead, as long as they kept out of the way. On a day-to-day basis, particularly on the larger ships, spit and polish – both regarding the ship and the sailor's own appearance – and strict discipline were used as a preventative to boredom and mischief. On smaller ships with smaller crews, this was less of a problem, and on the very small ships it often was not an issue at all. Many of the trawlers sent out to the Adriatic and the Aegean, and later Alexandria and Malta, simply kept their pre-war crews, with the addition of a naval officer or warrant officer or two. In these little ships, Royal Navy discipline and procedures made very little headway, and the tough life of the fishermen, in cramped quarters and likely to be thrown around in bad weather, was little different to before the war.

More of a problem to discipline was a new class of crewman: stokers. Up to half or even more of the crews on the larger ships were stokers, whose job it was to feed the furnaces of the massive boilers that drove the ship. They stood apart from the rest of the crew in attitude and routine; for example, their shifts were different and hours were shorter, due to the arduous nature of their work, in the searing heat of the boiler rooms with the air thick with coal dust. They were notorious for their independent attitudes and tendencies towards ill-discipline, and a 'them-and-us' attitude regarding the rest of the crew was a frequent cause of friction.

In recent decades, and particularly since the start of the war, the Royal Navy had been working to reform the conditions of service and pay of their sailors. Whereas sailors traditionally lived as members of a 'mess' who arranged for the preparation and cooking of their own food, the bigger ships now carried more trained cooks to make the rations more palatable. Meanwhile, food was better, and often fresh produce could be obtained from markets onshore. Although the 'fleshpots' of Cairo were usually too far out of reach, a good time could also be had in the bars of Alexandria or Port Said.

The possibility of going ashore was taken to the extreme by the ships off the Smyrna coast, albeit as part of a wider objective. Many within the Royal Navy were convinced that the Ottomans were providing the Germans with secret submarine bases along their coast lines or among the scores of small islands in the Aegean. After the withdrawal from Gallipoli, the Eastern Mediterranean Squadron was maintained largely in the Aegean, partly to prevent the Ottoman Navy, and particularly the *Yavuz Sultan Selim* (SMS *Goeben* as was), from breaking out. The squadron was also tasked with patrolling the coast and the islands (many of which came under Greek or Italian control) down the western seaboard of Anatolia. While looking for submarine bases, it also became apparent that large flocks of sheep and cattle were being driven through these areas, on their way to Constantinople. Here, they were being loaded and transported to Germany for use as food and raw materials (Zeppelin airships, for example, relied heavily on cow-gut). While patrols of this complicated and intricate area of coastline and islands continued throughout the war, with raids being mounted against military targets where appropriate, over the spring and summer of 1916 the Royal Navy also branched out into sheep-rustling. Using Greek irregular volunteers, from March 1916 numerous raids were launched, sweeping up many thousands of head of livestock, principally sheep, but also cows, oxen, goats and horse (*see* Appendix E).

The cattle raids tailed off in September 1916 after strenuous protests by the Ottomans over the use of the Greek irregulars, and the legitimacy of the actions under international law. In October, the cattle raids were stopped entirely, although the Greeks were used for a few more weeks for attacks on purely military targets. In November these too were dropped but the patrols – that 'tedious and soul-destroying task' – were maintained. Without the excitement of the moonlit landings, 'the work, though, arduous and important, was monotonous and largely devoid of picturesque incident'.[456]

A close watch was also maintained for any sign that these villages, or their boats, were being used to supply submarines. In the intricate coastlines, full of tiny islands and narrow harbours, there was no shortage of hiding places for any potential sources of supply, and searching them was an exacting and wearisome job. The British mined the mouths of many harbours and inlets, and the whole area was regularly patrolled. This could also be a dangerous business, as even destroyers had relatively weak protection against close range small arms fire, while the commandeered trawlers and other small ships could be easily torn to pieces. An officer on HMS *Scorpion*, under Commander (later Admiral of the Fleet and First Sea Lord) Andrew Cunningham, recalled:

> In the case of villages with bottle-neck harbours, the usual enemy plan was to allow the destroyer to enter without opposition, and to open a heavy rifle fire upon her as she came through the narrows. Some of the narrow harbours were strenuously defended, both on our entry and withdrawal ... It was soon discovered that the protective mattresses round our bridges were no resistance to close range rifle fire. We were therefore supplied with ½-inch loop-holed steel plates ... which were fitted round the bridge whenever we made a raid.[457]

These plates cut down visibility drastically and also made the ships' compasses useless. Fire could be returned by the destroyer's own guns, although working on the open deck was a risky business. Sometimes, the only return fire that could be made was with rifles, through the loop-holes in the plates around the bridge, and through the scuttles on the mess deck.[458] Commander Cunningham would recall how on one occasion:

> On arriving within about 600 yards of the entrance [of the harbour of Gumishlu we were] greeted with heavy rifle fire and had three men of the 4inch gun crew wounded. I considered that the reason for this obstinate defence needed investigation, so we withdrew a little and rigged the steel plates around the bridge. Then, with the upper deck cleared of men, and riflemen manning the bridge loop-holes and mess-deck scuttles, we again steamed for the entrance ... A great battle with rifles took place as we moved through the entrance. Particularly heavy fire came from a small rocky promontory on our starboard side. Our sailors, who could see the Turks dodging and lying behind rocks and bushes replied with vigour at ranges of fifty yards and less. Bullets whizzed through the air and banged incessantly on the bridge plating ... Nothing was found in the harbour to justify this resistance,

though we heard later that at the time of our visit a party of Turkish troops were in the village collecting taxes in kind.[459]

These efforts, based on an erroneous assumption as they were, had no effect in the wider war against the submarines. In March 1916 the situation in the Mediterranean was so bad that it was decided that delays were now preferable to the increasing losses. Orders were issued that all ships bound to or from points east of the 110th Meridian – effectively Australia and New Zealand, or east of the Java Sea – were now to sail via the Cape rather than through the Suez Canal. At the same time, troop movements to the eastern Mediterranean now began to flow across land to Marseilles, or even into Italy, to shorten the distances they would need to cover by sea.[460] In December 1916 the rules were tightened further, and ships bound to or from anywhere east of Ceylon (Sri Lanka) were now routed via the Cape.[461]

Only slowly would the tide be turned against the submarines in 1917 with the introduction of escorted convoys, the improvement of the Otranto Barrage, and an increasing problem for the Germans in maintaining and supplying their ships. Through attrition the Entente would finally gain the upper hand in 1918, but not until a vastly disproportionate amount of effort had been laid against the handful of submarines

Men of the Queen's Own Worcestershire Hussars (Yeomanry) being marched into Jerusalem after their capture at Katia. (Trustees QOWH)

Ottoman troops marching into Constantinople before the war. The Ottoman military was generally looked down upon by the Western powers.

The officers of SMS *Breslau*, after their arrival at Constantinople in 1914.

A British warship escorting a merchantman in the Mediterranean. The smoke would later make it very easy for German submarines to find their targets.

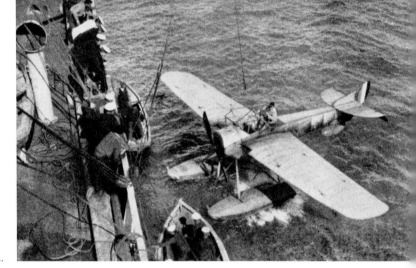

A French seaplane being winched aboard HMS *Anne* after returning from a flight over Palestine or Syria.

British troops undergoing desert training in Egypt. (Trustees QOWH)

Indian troops formed the backbone of the British defences in Egypt during 1914 and 1915.

A *sowar* of the Bikaner Camel Corps.

Moving horses by rail. The Egyptian State Railway played an important role in the defence of Egypt.

The Pyramids at Giza, and site of the ANZAC Depot at Mena Camp.

An Ottoman infantry regiment marching to war behind a band.

A ferry taking British troops across the Suez Canal.

Indian troops in action during the attack on the Suez Canal, February 1915.

RIMS *Hardinge* during the battle for the Suez Canal, February 1915, showing damage inflicted on her funnels by an Ottoman shell.

Two of the small boats used by the Ottomans in their attempt to cross the Canal, on display in Cairo.

Ottoman prisoners, captured after their attempt to cross the Suez Canal in February 1915.

The Heliopolis Palace Hotel, Cairo, was one of the most modern hotels in the city, and was used as a hospital (note the ambulances by the front doors).

Colonel Kress von Kressenstein and his staff, outside Gaza.

Ottoman howitzer firing from a prepared position.

British troops sightseeing in Egypt. For the vast majority this was their first time overseas. (Trustees QOWH)

HMS *Ben-My-Chree*. Originally an Isle of Man ferry, it was converted to operate seaplanes, with a hanger being built on the rear deck.

Signallers (with their flags) relaxing outside a blockhouse.

Rolls-Royce Armoured Car. Such cars could achieve unprecedented speeds, as long as the ground was not too rough.

Ottoman lancers scouting in the Sinai.

Kantara. In 1914 it had been a small hamlet, but by the end of 1916 it was a massive, sprawling logistical hub. Today it remains a major town.

A gun team on the move in Egypt. Over the soft sands of the Sinai most wheeled vehicles were fitted with 'pedrails'. These wooden spats were attached around the wheel to increase the surface area of the rims.

A parade in Egypt. These were regular occurrences, mostly for reasons of discipline although many soldiers believed they were also aimed at impressing the locals, to discourage civil unrest.

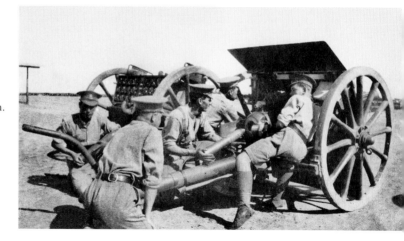

A gun team exercising in a staged photograph. In action, the limber (carrying the ammunition) would be much further away, in case an enemy round set the waiting shells off.

A field bivouac, using a rifle as a prop for the shelter.

Infantry collecting their rations in camp in Egypt.

A shelter for Yeomanry horses in Egypt. These at least provided a respite from the direct heat of the sun. (Trustees QOWH)

The Officers Mess of the QOWH. Open sided shelters allowed breezes in, while the loose foliage roof kept the sun off. (Trustees QOWH)

Members of the Norfolk Yeomanry digging a trench. In the soft Sinai sand, the trenches needed to be dug several times wider than necessary. A wooden framework would then be built, and then the outer sections back-filled with sand.

Laying barbed wire in the deserts. Wire entanglements tended to be less dense but still proved useful in slowing an attacking force or inhibiting the enemy's movements. (Trustees QOWH)

Thomas E. Lawrence, the popular face of the First World War in the Middle East, was only just starting to make his mark by the end of 1916.

A member of the QOWH in light order, ready for a patrol. (Trustees QOWH)

Members of the New Zealand Mounted Rifles. (Trustees QOWH)

An Egyptian lancer. Despite British concerns over their loyalty and willingness to fight fellow-Muslims, the Egyptian Army saw service on the Suez Canal, in the Sudan, in the Western Desert and in the Arabian peninsula.

The Australian Light Horse proved invaluable in the Sinai campaign of 1916. (Trustees QOWH)

The Camel Transport Corps gave the British forces the capability to operate large numbers of troops deep into the desert.

Sikh pioneers building a road in the central Sinai Desert.

A British cavalry patrol talking to the local population, sometimes a useful source of information. (Trustees QOWH)

A Field Ambulance in the Sinai Desert. These units provided basic first aid to the wounded or sick, before evacuating them in ambulances or on camels. (Trustees QOWH)

Ottoman prisoners in a temporary holding area, probably after the Battle of Romani judging by the Scottish infantry behind them. (Trustees QOWH)

Ottoman officers, at least one of them (*front left*) a Gallipoli veteran, and two (*front left and front right*) with German decorations. (Trustees QOWH)

British Yeomen resting on a patrol in the Sinai. (Trustees QOWH)

Anti-aircraft defences on the Suez Canal.

The mouth of the Wadi El Arish, where British ships would bring supplies ashore in late 1916.

11

THE EGYPTIAN EXPEDITIONARY FORCE

In the early months of 1916, the Mediterranean Expeditionary Force was reconstituted in Egypt. While the decision to withdraw from Gallipoli was being debated, it was suggested that a face-saving gesture was needed to reassert Britain's status in the region (and, one imagines, the morale of the troops involved). The idea of landing a force in Ayas Bay, perhaps at or near Alexandretta on the Syrian coast or Adana on the Anatolian, had been studied by the Admiralty and the War Office before the war and in 1914 and 1915 (with an outline plan being prepared by Lieutenant Harry Pirie-Gordon RN, former intelligence officer on HMS *Doris*).[462] More recently it had been extensively discussed at Cabinet level.[463] Estimates had varied between needing 12,000 men or the entire evacuated force from the Dardanelles (potentially over 50,000 men, perhaps landed directly upon being lifted from the beaches at Gallipoli, without any chance to rest or refit), who could push inland and cut the single railway line that connected Constantinople with Syria, Palestine, Mesopotamia and the Hedjaz. In the end, calmer heads, and the RN's doubts about their ability to keep such a landing supplied, won out and the idea was finally dropped in November 1915.[464]

At the same time, concern grew for the safety of Egypt. With the withdrawal from Gallipoli, it would not be long before the Ottomans could turn their attention, and the forces previously employed in the Dardanelles, back towards the Suez Canal. Reports confirmed a growing Ottoman railway network in southern Palestine and the area of the Egyptian border, which could be used to support a large invasion force.[465] In November 1915 it was estimated that the Ottomans had 47,000 men in Palestine available for an attack south, and it was expected that this would rise to 300,000 before long.[466] These were both grossly exaggerated estimates, as were those supposing that the British would need between 200,000 and 500,000 men to defend the Canal,[467] but it did not alter the facts that, at that time (mid-November 1915) the garrison in Egypt was still dangerously small. Of the 80,500 men in the country, only the 16,200 men from the Indian Expeditionary Force were actually guarding the Suez Canal, although 12,000 British troops were en route from the UK having been urgently ordered out by the War Committee of the Cabinet.[468] Even so, for an 80–100-mile front, the defences were dangerously thin.

In early 1916, after the failure of the Gallipoli expedition and the abandonment of the Alexandretta plan, the focus came squarely on the Sinai Desert, and for the first time the resources were potentially on hand to see the plans through. Between those withdrawn from Gallipoli and those under training, Egypt now contained the equivalent of fourteen infantry divisions, on top of the existing Indian Army garrison on the Canal.[469] It had been clear for a long time that a defensive system based on using the Canal itself as a barrier was simply not practical; General Maxwell, Sir Henry McMahon and Lord Kitchener had all warned London of such.[470] What was needed was a more forward posture, and preferably one that included the cluster of wells around Katia. From here, a relatively small force could dominate the centre of the Sinai Desert, and with support from the Royal Navy offshore, cover the most likely routes for any future attacks against the Canal. From December 1915 it was being suggested by the War Office that Katia should be seized.[471]

With the arrival of the troops from Gallipoli came a new commander. Lieutenant General Sir Archibald Murray had stepped down as Chief of the Imperial General Staff, and requested a field command instead. He was sent to Egypt, arriving in early January to replace General Munro as commander of the Mediterranean Expeditionary Force.[472] With him came orders to take direct command of the Canal defences, the MEF in Egypt, and to have 'supervision' of the administration of the Salonika force, while leaving Maxwell to command the forces in the Western Desert and in central Egypt. Murray was an excellent administrator and organiser (although he had very little experience of battlefield command) and immediately began to overhaul the MEF from his headquarters at Ismailia. Fresh equipment was issued, specialist schools established, and a broad training programme introduced to retrain the men from Gallipoli in modern techniques.

Some of those recently arrived from Gallipoli were less than impressed with the leadership of General Maxwell, and indeed the idea of replacing him had even been discussed at the War Council in November 1915.[473] Perhaps typical of Maxwell's critics was Sir Arthur Lynden-Bell, who had gone out to Gallipoli from the UK in October 1915 as Chief of Staff to General Munro when he had relieved General Hamilton. In a series of, at times vitriolic, letters (some written while still at Gallipoli) to the Director of Military Operations at the War Office, Lynden-Bell was highly critical of the situation in Egypt and of Maxwell in particular. These unfairly criticised Maxwell's intelligence system, his concerns about the Senussi, and general atmosphere at his headquarters.[474] However, some criticisms were close to the truth, including Lynden-Bell's opinion that not enough had been done to collect camels for the army.[475]

This is perhaps part of the greater truth that the forces in Egypt had fallen into a defensive frame of mind, although there were mitigating circumstances. Not least among these was the shortage of troops and resources to launch major offensive operations; indeed, even the limited defensive operations against the Senussi had been a struggle to support. There was also the oft-overlooked fact that Maxwell was effectively responsible for the civil administration of Egypt, which took considerable time and effort, and which he performed very well. This was the main difference between

Maxwell and some of the newcomers. The bulk of the army viewed Egypt as an area of land from which to launch military operations, with little concern for the local population, economy, politics or administration. After spending most of his career in Egypt and the Sudan, Maxwell on the other hand had a wealth of experience and a feel for the country and its people. Sir Ronald Storrs, a pre-war civil servant in the Egyptian administration and nobody's fool, wrote in his memoirs that:

> I keep a clear memory of Sir John Maxwell, the General Officer Commanding the Troops. During the previous decade he had been employed in administrative rather than on active service, but for those initiatory days of transition he proved exactly what was required; knowing and liking, known and liked by, Egyptians for the past thirty years. Sitting tunicless in his office he would see every applicant and read most petitions personally, dealing out a summary justice which expressed itself by speech or by a stub of the blue pencil in a brief convincing expletive. It was no good bluffing, for 'Conkey' had your life-history – whether you were a Pasha or a dragoman, a Sephardi Banker or a Greek cotton broker, a British official or a Syrian Consul-General for a Baltic State; but this patriarchal militarism provided a satisfaction, a finality, very seldom afforded by the Mixed Court of Appeal.[476]

For the first year or more of the war, this had been exactly what was needed. Now, though, the situation was different and the military side of his duties were becoming increasingly muddled. The different commands and headquarters in Egypt confused everyone up to and including the War Office, and both Maxwell and Murray applied to London for clarification of the system, even if at the cost of their own jobs.[477] On 10 March 1916 the answer arrived from London: Murray was to take command of all of the forces in Egypt, and Maxwell was to return to the UK.

Some officers, such as Lynden-Bell, positively gloated over Maxwell's dismissal;[478] Storrs on the other hand recorded that 'the recall of Maxwell evoked one of the most spontaneous outbursts of general regret that I have seen during twelve years' residence here'.[479] His role at the time was often misunderstood, or at least the breadth of his responsibilities not fully grasped, and he has subsequently perhaps not received the recognition that he deserved. Partly this is because shortly after his return to the UK Maxwell was despatched as Commander-in-Chief to Ireland, where the Easter Rising of April 1916 had broken out. He is now better remembered for his controversial handling of the Rising and its aftermath, during which he exercised the wide powers bestowed on him by the government, imposing martial law and executing nationalist leaders after the minimum of legal processes.

Field Marshal Edmund Allenby, who would replace Murray in 1917 and go on to conquer Palestine and Syria, would write in his final despatch that his victory owed its foundations to Murray for his work on the laying the pipeline that 'brought the waters of the Nile to the borders of Palestine' and building a 'standard gauge railway to the gates of Gaza'.[480] While Murray certainly saw both of these projects to fruition, it was Maxwell who had begun them, as well as beginning the recruitment of the men and animals of the Egyptian Labour Corps and Camel Transport Corps, whose sweat and muscle would carry the army across the Sinai. His deft handling of martial law and the civil administration in Egypt provided a secure base for the army, but are now overshadowed by the later events that have tarnished his reputation.

Now that the whole of the British forces in Egypt were under his command, Murray set about following his second set of instructions from London. Once the units from Gallipoli had begun refitting and reorganising, they were to be considered the Imperial Strategic Reserve, ready for despatch to other fronts as the need arose. Soon, orders were indeed flowing in for more troops to be sent to elsewhere (*see* Appendix G): one division to Mesopotamia, where the siege of the British and Indian garrison at Kut al Amara would soon end in disaster, and nine other divisions to France, where forces were being gathered for the offensive planned for the Somme area that summer. In all, not including any sick or wounded personnel who were evacuated, some 232,000 men left Egypt in the first six months of 1916.[481] This included 11,000 men from the Indian forces on the Canal, where the 10th and 11th Indian Division had been officially disbanded, leaving a number of independent brigades. By July Murray would be left with just four 'weak' infantry divisions, plus two 'weak' Indian brigades on the Canal, the Australian and New Zealand (A&NZ) Mounted Division and the 5th Mounted Brigade as an independent brigade of yeomanry.[482] In March 1916 the forces under his command were officially designated the Egyptian Expeditionary Force (EEF).[483]

While training continued and divisions were stripped away, a steady advance into the Sinai was begun. The railway from Kantara, where an immense supply depot had been amassed, was now well underway, although the pipeline still awaited pipes to arrive from America. A second, 2ft 6in-gauge line was also started, running east along the shore of the Mediterranean from Port Said.[484] Over the coming months, patrols ranging in size from a few dozen men to entire brigades spread out through the desert, probing enemy outposts, plotting and sometimes destroying wells and oases, and skirmishing with enemy patrols. Perhaps most impressive of these patrols was the squadron-sized unit drawn from the 8th and 9th Australian Light Horse (ALH) and the Bikaner Camel Corps, which, between 11 and 15 April 1916 conducted a round trip of over 100 miles to Jifjafa, catching the Ottoman garrison by surprise. Jifjafa stood on the central route across the Sinai, and had been used during the first attack on the Suez Canal in early 1915. Now, five Ottoman soldiers were killed and more than thirty captured, including an Austrian engineers officer, and the wells they had been digging for the past five months, and the equipment used, destroyed.[485] Two months later, a raid on the oasis at Moiya Harab, again on the central route and used during the previous campaign, was carried out by the 9th and 10th ALH, with Bikaner Camel Corps support. The ancient stone cisterns here were emptied and sabotaged to stop them refilling during the next rainy season, with around 5 million gallons (23 million litres) of water being pumped into the desert. With this, the central route across the Sinai was essentially denied to any large bodies of Ottoman troops.[486]

For the Ottomans, the year was starting slowly. It had been intended to launch a new attack against the Suez Canal in February, to discourage the British from moving too many divisions from Egypt to more active fronts.[487] This would take advantage of the Ottoman's own railway network, which had been extended to Beersheba in November 1915, and would proceed south to El Auja, just on the border into Egypt, by May 1916. This expedition was to be based around Kress von Kressenstein's Desert Force, supplemented by troops reassigned from Gallipoli and a large body of support and specialist German and Austrian troops, collectively known as 'Pasha' force. This force consisted of machine guns, artillery and flying units, but delay followed delay both in Germany and on the long route south through the Ottoman Empire. By early April, only the aircraft (FA300 – see Chapter 7) and some Austrian artillery had arrived, and indeed some units, such at the 605th Machine Gun Company, only left Germany in late March.[488] This unit did not reach Adana, in Ayas Bay, until early May, and entered Palestine in early June.

In the meantime, Kress von Kressenstein had launched what he described as a 'reconnaissance in force' but could equally be described as a spoiling attack, hoping to upset British plans to move troops to France and scare them into keeping them in Egypt, while the main force was gathered. In April this struck at the British garrisons at Katia and Dueidar (see Prologue). Although Katia was temporarily taken, it was at a heavy cost, while the assault on Dueidar was repulsed. While he passed it off as a reconnaissance in his memoirs, there is little doubt that he would have garrisoned and held Katia himself given the chance.[489] Although Kress von Kressenstein achieved his aim of mapping the British defences, his losses and the robust British response were such that he was forced to fall back across the Sinai without having achieved any permanent gain, and the movement of British divisions to France continued unchanged.

The heat of the summer now descended on the Sinai, although this only impaired operations rather than stopping them entirely. In early May, Murray ordered Major General the Honourable Herbert Lawrence, commander of No. 3 Canal Section (the northernmost sector of the Canal defences) to push forward into the desert. Lawrence's own unit, the 52nd (Lowland) Division (temporarily placed under the command of General W.EB. Smith) occupied the area of Romani, an area that covered many wells or 'hods' (small clusters of palms around a well) stretching over some miles, and surrounded to the east and south by large, steep sand dunes.[490] They were soon joined by elements of the A&NZ Mounted Division (also placed under Lawrence's command), which ranged far and wide on patrol. One of their duties at this time was to round up Bedouin tribes from the areas over which the army was operating. Both sides were convinced that these Arabs spied for the enemy and preyed on the wounded.[491] In truth, they did scavenge from the armies that were crossing their homeland, including from the dead and wounded, and sold information to both sides. Now, they were rounded up where found, and passed back to camps in the Canal Zone.[492]

By the middle of the month, the heat was becoming a serious problem. On 16 May, patrols of both the 5th ALH and the Canterbury Mounted Rifles ran into severe difficulties as, with the *khamsin* blowing, temperatures rose to 51–54°C (125–129°F) in the shade. In both cases, field ambulances had to be despatched to bring the suffering units home, and dozens of men and hundreds of horses were hospitalised.[493] One of the major problems was simply lack of water. The existing wells were never intended to supply such large numbers of men and horses, and much of that which could be brought out of wells or found by digging was too brackish for British or ANZAC troops to drink (although the Ottomans managed to stomach it); boiled up it 'made the most atrocious tea, but passable coffee'.[494] Initially, even horses refused to drink it, although necessity soon overcame their reluctance. It also took a considerable time to haul water up from wells in sufficient quantities to serve hundreds of thirsty horses at a time, even assuming that half a day did not have to be spent digging the well in the first place. This problem was eventually overcome by the 'spearpoint pump'. A device commonly used in Australia, it consisted of a long tube that could be thrust deep into the ground, avoiding the need to dig. Once water was found, it was a simple matter to pump water up the tube and into the collapsible wood-and-canvas troughs that cavalry units carried. Initially the device was introduced by Lieutenant Colonel Wilson of the 5th ALH, and met with resistance from the British commissariat authorities. A few weeks' experience in the Sinai soon convinced them otherwise, and this life-saving tool was issued across the EEF.[495]

The Germans newly arrived in Palestine also suffered and had to learn to deal with desert conditions. The men of the 605th Machine Gun Company had to discover how 'the tents have to be dug out about 4'6" [deep] (137cm), first in order to be cooler, and secondly for protection against the awful sand drifts'.[496] The company initially only consisted of a training cadre of around thirty Germans, and once in Palestine an Ottoman officer and seventy-five men were added who had to be trained from scratch. The German instructors did their best, as their British counterparts did, to avoid the heat of the day; on a typical day 'on account of the great heat we drill from 6–8 am, instruction from 9–11 am, instruction 3–4 pm and drill from 5–6 pm', although a high rate of sickness was still suffered.[497] When the time came to move into the Sinai, camels with Arab drivers were assigned to carry the guns and their ammunition.[498]

This advance into the Sinai began in July 1916, although the motives and objectives of the operation still remain unclear. The original intention seems to have been to establish a strong outpost within artillery range of the Canal, from where long-range shelling could make the waterway too dangerous to use.[499] However, Kress von Kressenstein's attack in April had alerted the British defenders and led to a renewed effort to move a large force into the desert to interdict any further attempts. It was well known from aerial reconnaissance that an infantry division, augmented by cavalry, was positioned at Romani, and it was also clear that the Ottoman logistics would not allow more than an augmented infantry division of their own to cross into the desert. To send a force to attack an essentially equally sized enemy that were backed up by (comparatively) excellent logistics and in prepared positions was militarily madness, and yet the expedition was mounted anyway. Kress von Kressenstein maintained that the plan went ahead at Djemal Pasha's insistence, while Djemal was equally insistent that it was his German subordinate's idea. Liman von Sanders was under the impression that the orders came from Constantinople.[500]

The expedition was to come under Kress von Kressenstein's command, and consist primarily of the 3rd (OT) Infantry Division, which itself was formed of the 31st, 32nd and 39th (OT) Regiments. These men were dismissed by von Sanders as 'only moderately trained and poorly equipped'[501] but while they undoubtedly suffered from the equipment shortages common to all Ottoman troops, they were actually hardened and combat-experienced, having performed with distinction at Gallipoli.[502] Supporting them, thanks to the 'Pasha' force, would be a higher than usual proportion of machine guns and artillery, although these were indeed green troops in as far as the Ottomans had only received a few weeks' training on their weapons and the Germans and Austrians were new to desert operations.

Kress von Kressenstein's force set out from Bir el Mazar, just over 40 miles east of Romani, on 16 July 1916. The force marched in several staggered columns so as not to overload the local water sources, and at night, in an attempt to avoid observation. Marching over the soft sand was hard work. The *Mehmetçik* were likely to sink up to their ankles at every step, and tracks had to be laid for the movement of guns and other wheeled vehicles. Scrub was cut and either laid into crude roadways or packed into parallel ruts dug at the right width to provide a solid surface for the wheels.[503] At around 16,000 men, of whom 11,000–12,000 were front-line troops, plus 2,000 camels and nearly as many horses, their progress could not remain hidden for long, while a sharp increase in enemy air activity also aroused suspicions.[504] However, it was still something of a surprise to the British high command when, on 19 July a large body of men was spotted by a reconnaissance flight carrying Brigadier General Edward Chaytor, commander of the New Zealand Mounted Rifles Brigade, at Bir Bayud, less than 20 miles east of Romani.[505] The following day the RFC picked them up again, at Mageibra, about 15 miles south-east of Romani, and at a base being established at Bir el Abd, north of Bir Bayud.[506]

The discovery of a large Ottoman force so close to Romani galvanised the British preparations. Murray temporarily transferred 158th Brigade from 53rd Division to 52nd (Lowland) Division on 20 July, despatching them immediately to the front by train, and began preparations to move 42nd Division into a supporting position as well. Meanwhile, Major General Harry Chauvel's A&NZ Mounted Division was also reorganised. While the 1st and 2nd ALH Brigades remained at Et Maler, just south of Romani, the 3rd ALH Brigade (General John Antill) was detached and sent south to join No. 2 Canal Section. Here, along with a mixed Mobile Column of ALH, Camel Corps and Yeomanry under Lieutenant Colonel Clement Smith VC,* they would stand ready to attack north into the flank of any Ottoman attack. The New Zealand Mounted Rifles Brigade temporarily exchanged one unit with the 2nd ALH Brigade,** and was posted with the still under-strength 5th Mounted Brigade to Hill 70, to the south-west of Romani, where the two brigades were designated as the Sector Mounted Troops.

While strong in cavalry and infantry (Lawrence would have about 14,000 fighting men to command, excluding the 42nd Division), the British were relatively weak in artillery. A single battery of heavy 60pdrs, two batteries of 4.5in howitzers, four 18pdr batteries and two light batteries of the Royal Horse Artillery were sent to

---

*   11th ALH Regt, City of London Yeomanry, 4th, 6th and 9th Companies Imperial Camel Corps.
★★   The Wellington Mounted Rifles were exchanged with the 5th ALH Regt.

Romani.[507] Given the length of frontage expected to be protected, this was light coverage, although RN monitors offshore were able to reach the northern areas with their guns, and indeed were able to shell some of the Ottoman camps in the days running up to the battle.[508]

The new organisation was a bold move to make so soon before a major engagement, as unit cohesion was compromised and lines of command changed. Perhaps more crucially, Lawrence declined to move his headquarters from Kantara, 23 miles to the west of Romani. While Murray continued to leave the arrangements for the defence of Romani and command of the forthcoming action to Lawrence, he did not approve of his subordinate being so far from the front lines. Fearing that it would leave Lawrence out of touch and unable to exercise effective control of his troops, Murray suggested that Lawrence move further east, but Lawrence refused.[509]

For the two ALH brigades remaining at Et Maler, a new, intense routine was instigated. Each morning one of the brigades would leave camp at 2 a.m., marching to a spot near Katia where they would make camp and wait for dawn. As the sun rose, at around 4 or 4.30 a.m., the brigade would spread out and advance to contact with the Ottoman advance guards. The day would be spent skirmishing with the Ottomans, ambushing patrols and making hit-and-run attacks on outposts, delaying them wherever possible while avoiding getting into a serious fight.[510] A few deliberate strikes were also made, such as by the Wellington Mounted Rifles with RHA support against the Ottoman 31st Regiment at Hod um Ugba, just 5–6 miles east of Romani, on 28 July.[511] The brigade would return to Romani after dark, and sometimes not long before midnight, and be ready again an hour before dawn to stand-to in case of Ottoman attack.

However, the last thing that Murray and Lawrence wanted at this point was to stop the enemy advance. Quite the opposite, both wanted Kress von Kressenstein to continue. At Romani they were preparing fixed defences along 52nd Division's front, which faced east towards the enemy. A series of strong redoubts was dug along the ridges of sand dunes, with machine guns and barbed wire waiting to ensnare the advancing Ottoman infantry. Despite these preparations, Murray did not believe that a serious attack would be made on the Lowlanders. Instead, he expected the Ottomans to make a demonstration on this northern flank to hold the infantry in place, and then swing their main force around the southern flank, through an area that contained a maze of sand dunes, in an attempt to sweep into the rear of the Romani positions. Here, they could not only potentially surround and destroy the British force, but also cut the railway and pipeline, and advance directly towards the Canal.

With this in mind, Chauvel's horsemen were ordered to scout and plan positions that would extend the southern flank of the army for another 4 miles, towards Hod el Enna. This would place them along the edge of the area of the sand dunes. Their left flank would meet the Lowland infantry at Katib Gannit, and the centre of the Australian position would rest on a high, prominent sand dune dubbed Mount Meredith, after Lieutenant Colonel John Meredith, temporary commander of the 1st ALH Brigade.[512] Upon being pressed, the Australians and New Zealanders would only fight a holding action, moving back slowly through the sand dunes. This would delay the Ottomans and also, due to the ground, hopefully break up their cohesion and spread the attackers out. The pivot point would be Katib Gannit, with the final position running from another high sand dune – Wellington Ridge, which ran north-west from just behind Katib Gannit – to the west. On the western flank, it was hoped that Mount Royston, named for the commander of the 2nd ALH Brigade, Colonel John Royston,[513] would form a final barrier to the attacking Ottomans. After all, if the enemy captured Mount Royston or broke through either side of it, only the smaller rise of Canterbury Hill (garrisoned by a single squadron of the Royal Gloucestershire Hussars) lay between the Ottomans and the railway line which 42nd Division would be using. Once the flank had withdrawn to right angles to the infantry, the Sector Mounted Troops would attack into the open Ottoman flank, while the mounted troops in No. 2 Canal Section would swing in behind them.[514] Meanwhile, 42nd Division were being kept in reserve near the Canal, ready either to move up by rail to support the forces at Romani, or to deploy into the desert to intercept any Ottoman force that had slipped past the cavalry.

This attack was expected on 3 August at the earliest, and probably a few days after that. The A&NZ Mounted Division was to carry on its exhausting routine until then, and was not allowed to make any preparations that may give away the intended first line of defence. No trenches or redoubts could be dug, and no sand bags or barbed wire put in place. The only concession was that telephone lines could be laid under the sand. After discussions from the War Office, who were keen to retake the offensive, Murray agreed that should no Ottoman attack occur by 13 August 1916, he would launch an attack himself, although obviously having the enemy attack his own prepared positions was clearly preferable. In the event, he did not have long to wait.

12

THE BATTLE OF ROMANI

The Battle of Romani is one of those rarest of events in British military history: a battle that went almost entirely to plan. That is not to say that things went smoothly or that near disaster did not threaten at least once, and sadly the follow-up to the victory fell to pieces almost at once. It is also unusual as a First World War battle won principally by cavalry, albeit ones who used their horses to gain superior mobility before fighting on foot, and it is distinguished as being a primarily Australian victory.

On 3 August 1916 the 2nd ALH Brigade moved out of camp as usual before dawn and spent the day skirmishing with Ottoman forces a few miles from Romani. The 1st ALH Brigade, after being out on patrol until after dark the previous day and standing-to at dawn, spent the day in rest and the usual routine of military life. Major General Harry Chauvel, commander of the A&NZ Mounted Division, considered 4 August to be the earliest day that the Ottomans would be able launch an attack, and so before dusk he deployed the 1st ALH Brigade (his old command) along the planned line running south from Katib Gannit. On his left flank, joining up with the infantry and covering the area south to (and including) Mount Meredith, was the 3rd ALH Regiment, covering a front of about 1½ miles. South of them was the 2nd ALH Regiment, with a front of 2½ miles. Both units were understrength, at around 400 men. Two squadrons from each were placed in the front line, with the third squadrons held in reserve. In each case, the front-line squadrons had to leave a quarter of their men behind the lines to hold and care for the horses, further depleting their front-line strength and leaving about 400 men to hold a 4-mile front. Not that a true line was formed; each squadron split into piquets of four to eight men, spread 100yd or so from their neighbours. This was judged enough to detect any advance, and put up a token resistance to slow an enemy force down. The third unit in the brigade, the 1st ALH Regiment, was held under Lieutenant Colonel Meredith's control in reserve.[515]

Colonel John Royston's 2nd ALH Brigade returned after dusk, and slowly filtered through the 1st Brigade's piquets. Starting from around 8.30 p.m. it was not until probably 9.30 p.m. or later that the final rearguard piquets passed through the line.* Sometime thereafter, sporadic shots began to be exchanged by the piquet posts with what were taken to be Ottoman patrols, barely visible in the dim moonlight. (Interestingly, the sand around Romani had a slightly phosphorescent quality and gave off a very slight glow. This was only visible from a few inches, and did not allow figures to be silhouetted at a distance, but it did cause a sparking effect when bullets hit the sand.)

By midnight, it was clear that more than just patrols were involved, with heavier firing sporadically flaring up along the line. It would later be established that several very large columns of Ottoman troops had advanced on the Australian line, which happened to have been drawn up in the same area that had been designated as the forming up point for the Ottoman attack. After midnight the fighting had become general along the line, although at 1 a.m. the Ottomans fell back to reform. On both sides, the fighting in the darkness had seriously affected communications and co-ordination. In the desert the British usually passed information with signals flags and heliographs (flashing mirrors), neither of which worked at night, and some of the prelaid telephone lines had been damaged or cut. The 2nd ALH Regiment had called for reinforcements before their telephones had stopped working, but elements of the 1st ALH Regiment did not begin to arrive for another two and a half hours.[516] In the meantime, the moon had set soon after 2 a.m. and the Ottoman's renewed their attacks with vigour. Outnumbered by as many as ten-to-one, cut off from their higher formations, and spread dangerously thin, the lighthorsemen fought on in the darkness. It became a troop- and squadron-level battle, with NCOs and junior officers leading their men the best they could. The 2nd and 3rd ALH Regiments had both committed their reserve squadrons and could now only hold on as long as possible.[517]

At around 3 a.m., Mount Meredith was overrun. With the front line pierced and their flank turned, word rippled through the 1st ALH Brigade to fall back to the next designated line. The horses were brought forward and the lighthorsemen ran back to mount up. The Ottoman line, which had stalled only as little as 50yd away, surged forward as the Australian fire slackened. Many of the *Mehmetçik*, as was common with the poorly supplied Ottoman Army, were without boots, but this time it may have been intentional. Bare feet allowed them to move faster over the soft sand than the heavy boots and puttees of the Australians, and several piquets were completely over-run before they could reach their horses. Some of the retreating Australians were encumbered by wounded comrades, and so intense was the dark that at least one lighthorseman hauled a wounded comrade onto his horse, only to find he had picked up a *Mehmetçik* by mistake.[518]

The Australians now conducted one of the most difficult manoeuvres in the military drill book: a controlled and steady fighting retreat, made even more difficult by the extreme dark. It would have been incredibly easy for order to break down, and

---

*   This raises a significant point. The different war diaries and personal accounts of Romani can give times for the same event that differ by some hours. For the early action this is largely due to it being fought in the dark, which is confusing at the best of times, and makes it difficult to consult watches. It was also, obviously, an extremely busy time for those involved, and accurate record keeping was not high on the list of priorities.

the men either intentionally (after several hours heavy fighting against huge odds) or unintentionally (in the darkness) missed commands to dismount and reform, and instead continued to race back to the safety of the rest of the army. Lieutenant Colonel G. Bourne, commander of the 2nd ALH Regiment, was intensely aware of the precarious position:

> Which of us will forget the scamper away? How so many did get away is a marvel. The bullets were making little spurts of flame all round and among us, on strik-ing the sand. Here we experienced for the first time, the moral effect of turning our backs on the enemy, and the question arose in our minds as we rode, 'Can we reform?' The order 'Sections about – Action front' was given as we reached the posi-tion, and was splendidly carried out.[519]

The Australian line deployed back into place without hesitation, and over the next hour or more a succession of short withdrawals were carried out, demonstrating remarkable levels of courage and discipline. On the left of the Australian line, after taking Mount Meredith, the Ottoman 31st Regiment had paused to take stock, but in the centre and on the right the pressure continued. The Ottoman 32nd and 39th Regiments continued to swing around this southern flank, pushing not only north against the Australian line, but also creeping westwards in an attempt to pass around behind them. At dawn, shortly before 4.30 a.m., this became clear to Chauvel. He had allowed the 2nd ALH Brigade to rest for a few hours after their day's exertions before standing them to at 3.20 a.m., and he now sent them into the line.

Chauvel had two basic options on where to send his reinforcements. He could deploy them to the right flank, where the Australian and Ottoman lines continued to extend toward Mount Royston, or to his left flank, near where his line met that of General Smith's 52nd Division. Here his men were being forced slowly back up the slopes of Wellington Ridge. Far off on the right there were other cavalry reinforce-ments that could be used, and he hoped to gain infantry support on the left, but in the short term at least he judged the most urgent need to be bolstering Wellington Ridge. If this fell, the enemy would have a direct line into the heart of the British posi-tion and be able to fire directly into the camps at Et Maler and Romani. Therefore, 6th and 7th ALH Regiments were sent to Wellington Ridge, while the Wellington Mounted Rifles were held in reserve.[520]

Soon after dawn the German Air Force made its contribution, with aircraft from FA300 bombing and strafing the camp at Romani. At about the same time the Ottomans managed to get some artillery in place on Mount Meredith and opened fire on Wellington Ridge. An infantry attack followed and by 6 a.m. the Australians were being pushed back along the crest towards the north-western end. At 6.15 a.m., Chauvel was forced to order the troops on the ridge to fall back before they were overrun.[521] Thankfully, the pursuing Ottoman troops did not press hard and remained behind the crest of the ridge to regroup rather than pressing forward down the north-western slope. Even so, parts of the Ottoman 31st Regiment were now just

700yd (640m) from the A&NZ Mounted Division camp at Et Maler. At the foot of the slopes below them the men of the different ALH Regiments, now mixed up together, dug in.

Some of the infantry from 156th Brigade of 52nd (Lowland) Division swung around slightly to bolster the flank of the Australians, although no large-scale redeployment was made. The rest of the Ottoman 31st Regiment had begun a frontal attack on the Lowlanders' positions, supported by heavy artillery. This was intended to pin the British infantry in place, and worked admirably even though only a few half-hearted Ottoman advances were made.[522] Instead, concentrated artillery was used to hammer several of the redoubts, and whether under fire or not, the Lowlanders were forced to stay in place and accept the discomforts. The 5th Highland Light Infantry (HLI) discovered that:

> Little or no news filtered through to us, and the redoubt companies spent a hot day in their trenches, which were but ill suited for permanent occupation, while the reduction in the water issue, made necessary by the fear of future difficulties in refilling the storage tanks, started a thirst which was not appeased for many days.[523]

When, in the mid-morning, Chauvel made a formal appeal to General Smith to divert some of 52nd Division's men to help hold the southern flank, Smith informed him that he had been ordered to hold his men in readiness for a counter-attack, and none could be spared.[524] In the meantime, the Ottomans, who had moved infantry and machine guns to the crest of Wellington Ridge at around 8.30 a.m., had a free rein to fire into the ALH below. Artillery fire came from Mount Meredith behind, and although the high explosive shells tended to bury themselves too deep in the soft sand to do much damage, the shrapnel shells were more effective. The Australians could only dig in and endure, although the proximity to their camp did at least allow their cooks to bring hot tea to the forward positions.[525] The stubborn resistance of the lighthorsemen, ably assisted by the Ayr Battery of the Royal Horse Artillery, discouraged the Ottomans from advancing any further:

> The Ayrshire battery in particular won the whole-souled admiration of the Anzacs [*sic*]. Every time a likely target showed up the Lowlanders smashed it instantly. Once some German machine guns, cleverly posted, were inflicting considerable damage on the Australians. The Ayrshires vouchsafed the Huns three shells, which landed precisely on the spot, wrecking the guns and slaughtering the teams.[526]

While the left of the Australian line held at the foot of Wellington Ridge, the whole British position was in danger of being flanked in the west. Ottoman forces continued to move around that flank through the morning, and captured the position on Mount Royston. Back in Kantara, the information being passed to General Lawrence was often delayed and at times interrupted – when the direct line was broken in the early morning, the telephone calls had to be routed via Port Said for a time[527] – but even he had seen the danger. At about 5.30 a.m. he had ordered the 5th Mounted Brigade* to move up towards Mount Royston from their position on Hill 70. As the seriousness of the situation continued to increase, at 7.30 a.m. Brigadier General Edward Chaytor's New Zealand Mounted Rifles (NZMR) Brigade was also ordered to move up from Hill 70, albeit via Dueidar where its Auckland Mounted Rifles were positioned. At the same time, the 3rd ALH Brigade at Ballybunion was ordered to take the New Zealanders' place.[528] At around the same time, 127th Brigade from 42nd Division was ordered to move up to Pelusium Station by train.

These movements took time, and it was not until after 10 a.m. that the Composite Regiment of the 5th Mounted Brigade reached the right area. By then the Ottoman advance on this flank had been halted by the quick thinking of another of the brigade's units, Major Charles Turners' 'D' Squadron RGH. Posted to guard Pelusium Station, Turner had seen the Ottoman movement in the distance and, without orders, rushed south to a new position about a mile north of Mount Royston. His quick thinking checked the Ottoman advance long enough for the Composite Regiment to arrive and join up on their flank.[529]

A pause now descended over the battlefield. The shelling, sniping and machine-gun fire continued but no serious attempts were made on either side to advance further. The Australians were exhausted after their long night's fighting, while the bulk of the British and New Zealand forces were either still moving into position or being held in readiness for a counter-attack. The Ottoman forces were also exhausted. Their attack had begun much earlier than anticipated, thanks to the ALH piquet line and had lasted much longer. For most of this time the average *Mehmetçik* had gone without food or, most importantly, water.

The pause around Wellington Ridge would continue for many hours but at Mount Royston the arrival of the NZMR Brigade (minus the 5th ALH Regiment, still en route) sparked a British counter-attack. At 11.30 a.m., the NZMR and 5th Mounted Brigades began to advance across the mile or so of open ground before the sand dune, with covering fire from the Somerset Battery RHA. Behind them, 127th Brigade had detrained and begun to form up at Pelusium Station, and would advance in support. It took over two hours to close with the Ottoman positions, and there the advance slowed to a crawl until 5 p.m., when Colonel Ralph Yorke led the one squadron of RGH and two troops of QOWH in a mounted charge onto the southern slopes. Once safely lodged, they covered the advance of the New Zealanders and by 6 p.m. Mount Royston was back in British hands.[530] Shortly before 7 p.m. the cavalry were relieved by 127th Brigade, and withdrew to Pelusium Station to water their horses. The Ottoman forces also withdrew.

For 'D' Squadron RGH it had been a trying day, from their first deployment to hold the line under the direct view of the Ottomans on Mount Royston to the last dash to recapture that dune. Lieutenant E.T. Cripps was one of them:

---

*   At this time the 5th Mounted Brigade was still understrength from the action at Katia in April and consisted of a single Composite Regiment of two squadrons of the Royal Gloucestershire Hussars (RGH) and one squadron of Queen's Own Worcestershire Hussars (QOWH). A further squadron of the RGH was detached at Pelusium Station.

I and three other troops were told to hold a line of sand, which we did from 9 till 3 [*sic*] in the blazing sun – fired at the whole time and no target to shoot at within range. We lay in the boiling hot sand and every now and then fired volleys at a stump where there was a sniper ... I hated it – nothing to do and being shot at the whole time. But after that we had the show of the war! We were called in, allowed a suck at our bottles, and then off to a flank, to a high sky line. Got shrapnelled on the way ... We got on the ridge, which was like a razor back and which the Turks evacuated as we advanced. And down below us in the plain such a scene! ... We gave them hell! About 500 surrendered and four guns to us. It was brilliant.[531]

Back on Wellington Ridge the fighting resumed at 5.30 p.m. when the Ottomans made a renewed attack down the north-eastern slope. This assault was quickly broken up, principally by artillery fire. Chauvel now ordered a counter-attack, for which 156th Brigade** had been loaned to him. The infantry went forward at 6.45 p.m. but co-ordination with the Australian Light Horse was difficult. Eventually the 1/7th and 1/8th Scottish Rifles managed to advance to within 100yd (90m) of the crest of the ridge but there the line stopped and the Scots dug in for the night.[532]

It had been a long hard day but the actions of the Ottomans and the British had gone almost exactly as General Murray had anticipated. For all of that, it had been touch and go on more than one occasion, and only the staunch determination and discipline of the Australians, and of the British and New Zealanders in the west, had saved the line from being broken. Much of the credit for the performance of the ALH must go to their leaders. Chauvel played a steady hand, holding back his reinforcements until daylight showed where they could be of most use. Throughout he stayed calm and kept control of his units. Closer to the front, Colonel John 'Galloping Jack' Royston had proven to be an absolute dynamo in action. Fifty-six years old and heavy set, this South African had seen service as a trooper in the Zulu War (1879), as a senior NCO and later officer in the Boer War (1899–1902), where he had eventually been appointed to command an Australian contingent, and in the Zulu Rebellion (1906). Despite his age and bulk, he was on the move all day, constantly exhorting his men to 'Keep your heads down, lads! Stick to it! Stick to it! You are making history today.' To one troop he cried: 'We are winning now. They are retreating in their hundreds.' 'And' said one of the light horsemen afterwards, 'I poked my head over the top, and there were the blighters coming on in thousands.'[533] His indomitable spirit was passed on to his men. He reportedly ran fourteen horses into exhaustion during the day, and even when wounded would not slow down.[534] At 3 p.m., Chauvel had to personally chase Royston down and order him to have his wound dressed,[535] and even after that he would be seen riding along the front line with blood-stained bandages flapping out behind.[536]

The ALH's casualties were heavy. The 1st and 2nd ALH Brigades lost four officers and fifty-seven men killed, and fifty-one officers and 312 men wounded. Overnight the wounded were patched and sent back either to Pelusium Station or north to

---

**   1/4th Royal Scots, 1/7th Royal Scots, 1/7th Scottish Rifles, 1/8th Scottish Rifles, plus the 1/5th Royal Welch Fusiliers attached from 158th Brigade.

Mahemdia Station on the coast. Here the field ambulances, where basic treatment was given, were soon overwhelmed.[537] The wounded were to be evacuated by train back to the Canal Zone – either to No. 31 General Hospital at Port Said on the coastal line or on the main line to No. 26 Casualty Clearing Station at Kantara before being despatched to the hospitals in Cairo. However, no special ambulance trains or facilities were provided and the wounded had to wait for a space in the open trucks of a returning train. Oskar Teichman, the Medical Officer of the QOWH and who had broken a leg, was disgusted by the facilities:

> This 'hospital train' consisted of one engine and a number of open trucks, the latter containing nothing – not even straw … The stretcher cases were placed on the floor of these trucks, while the walking cases sat on the sides. When we started off there was the usual 'bump, bump, bump' which one hears from a goods train, and pitiful groans escaped from the badly wounded and fracture cases.[538]

As the wounded were slowly sent back, so the 42nd Division was brought forward.[539] The intention was to take the offensive in the morning, pushing south and east; after all, the 52nd Division was further east, and thus closer to the Ottoman base at Katia, than the bulk of the Ottoman force.[540]

Overnight, the troops who had endured all day regrouped, ate, drank, replenished their ammunition and rested. For the Australians, this meant collapsing into their camp at Et Maler, which was now:

> In a terrible mess, blankets and mess tins and dirty dishes all over the place, the tents were full of bullet holes and bomb holes on the ground. On the horse lines there were still a few horses, some dead from shell fire, the others done from the work they'd been doing.[541]

On the British side, water was strictly limited, just in case the Ottomans managed to cut the supply lines back the Canal. On the Ottoman side, the water supply appears to have been almost non-existent. The battle had started sooner and lasted longer than the Ottomans had expected, and their supply lines, at least as far as the fighting troops were concerned, had effectively broken down. This would have a significant impact the following morning.

General Lawrence gave orders that the British counter-attack should begin at 4 a.m. on 5 August. The plan was that the A&NZ Mounted Division, supported by the NZMR Brigade and 5th Mounted Brigade, would swing back south and east through to their old positions, while the 156th Brigade retook Wellington Ridge and Mount Meredith. At the same time, 42nd Division, with the 3rd ALH Brigade, would advance to the south-east, and 52nd Division directly east. This would push the Ottomans back in all sectors, and once they were in retreat the cavalry would pursue them while the infantry came up behind, ready to break up any points of heavy resistance.[542] The advance would continue until the heat of the day struck, and then pause and resume in the afternoon.[543]

This plan fell apart almost immediately, for two reasons. Firstly, after a furious but brief resistance, the Ottoman line crumbled much earlier than expected. Wellington Ridge and Mount Meredith were retaken by 5 a.m. with around 2,500 Ottoman prisoners, taking everyone by surprise.[544] The rest of Kress von Kressenstein's force began a general retreat east towards Katia. The cavalry were not expecting to be needed yet and were still watering their horses. It was not until 6.30 a.m. that Chauvel, now commanding all three ALH Brigades, the NZMR Brigade and the 5th Mounted Brigade, was able to start his pursuit. His forces found groups of Ottoman stragglers, in a desperate state from thirty-six hours hard marching and fighting without water, scattered all along the line of retreat.

The second reason was the simple unpreparedness of the infantry for desert operations. The 125th Brigade of 42nd Division had been travelling all night, and only arrived at Pelusium Station after dawn. Both it and the 127th Brigade experienced problems in collecting water, and in loading and preparing their baggage camels, which they had never had to co-operate with before. By 9.30 a.m., 127th Brigade had only marched the few miles to Hod el Enna, where they stopped exhausted. Even over that short distance, some 800 men had fallen out of the march. It would be two hours before 125th Brigade joined them, and both were incapable of any further movement that day.[545] The Lowlanders were more acclimatised than 42nd Division but they also encountered significant delays due to problems with both water and their camels. They were unable to start their advance until noon, the hottest part of the day, and hours after the opposing Ottomans had retreated. They too made little progress over the rough ground. The historian of the 5th HLI recorded that his company:

> Left the Battalion moving off S.E. from the camp for the Brigade rendezvous. Here we received orders to attack a 'hod' named Abu Hamrah, which lay between us and Katia. The distance was not great, hardly six miles as the crow flies, but we were not crows and had to adopt less direct as well as more laborious methods. The Battalion was on the right in support to the 7th HLI, and the march continued with but short halts until 4 p.m., when we had a somewhat longer pause, and a chance to reinforce our early breakfasts. Few men, however, can eat either bully beef or biscuit when they are thirsty, and that was all we had.[546]

After dark, he candidly admits that 'the Brigade had become somewhat disintegrated', and only:

> After superhuman efforts on the part of various exalted personages, things were straightened out, pickets detailed and posted, and the men, too tired even to swear, dropped where they were, and rapidly cooled down in the chilly dew. It was now nearly eleven o'clock, and a half bottle of water was issued, enough merely to whet the consuming thirst that gripped everybody.[547]

The cavalry meanwhile followed close on the heels of the retreating Ottomans, rounding up prisoners as they went; by the end of the day, approximately 4,000

Ottoman or German troops had surrendered, on top of the estimated 1,250 bodies found on the battlefield.[548] As the sun rose, the advancing cavalry made an impressive sight. Trooper Ion Idriess of the 5th ALH Regiment recorded:

> Dawn came with a crimson sky. From a ridge we gazed behind at a grand sight all lit up in pink and grey and khaki stretching right back past the redoubts of Dueidar, a winding column of New Zealand and Australian mounted troops. The sun blazed at Bir el Nuss where we watered the horses and waited a hard and expectant two hours, while up rolled more Australians, more New Zealanders and finally the helmeted Yeomanry. And then came the Somerset and Leicestershire Batteries of the Royal Horse Artillery, all chirpy and spoiling for a fight, the spare battery horses prancing and fat. Regiment after regiment, brigade after brigade ... the oasis was surrounded by a dark brown cloth of horses and men. But the faces of the [1st and 2nd Brigade] men who had been fighting day and night were haggard, their eyes stary, their horses very tired.[549]

The pursuit met with mixed success. At Hamisah, the 3rd ALH Brigade (supported by the Inverness Battery RHA) charged in close to the Ottoman rearguard, dismounted and stormed their position, capturing over 400 men and seven machine guns.[550] Elsewhere, Kress von Kressenstein had carefully prepared defensive positions at key points as he had advanced, and these now provided an effective rearguard for his shattered forces. At Katia, the rest of Chauvel's force ran into one such position and was stoutly rebuffed. In the mid-afternoon, while the 5th Mounted Brigade moved around the flank, the other three Australian and New Zealand brigades had charged in on horseback with fixed bayonets, until boggy ground forced them to dismount. Despite support from the Ayr and Somerset Batteries RHA, the ANZACs could make little progress against the well-positioned and dug-in Ottoman infantry and German machine guns, and at dusk the attack was called off. That night, the 1st and 2nd ALH Brigades, some of whose horses had not been watered for sixty hours and whose men were in the last stages of exhaustion, were withdrawn from the line for rest.[551]

That same evening Kress von Kressenstein withdrew his own forces from Katia, back to Oghratina. On 6 August the British advance resumed, with the 42nd and 52nd Divisions again only making slow progress across the sand. The remaining British cavalry scouted Oghratina on 6 and 7 August, but the position was judged too strong to assault without infantry support. On 8 August, it was found to be deserted, and contact with the Ottomans was finally re-established at Bir el Abd, where the fresh troops of the 81st Regiment appear to have been waiting. Chauvel, by this time with the 1st and 2nd ALH Brigades restored to him (albeit still greatly under strength) determined to make a night march to surround the Ottoman rearguard, and at dawn on 9 August his division attacked Bir el Abd from all sides. The Ottoman defenders held, even making several small counter-attacks, and the fighting flowed backwards and forwards throughout the day.

However, Chauvel had orders not to get tied down into a slogging match.[552] His cavalry were lightly equipped compared to infantry units, and their main advantage was the mobility gained from their horses. A drawn out fight could easily lead to his force running out of water or ammunition, and becoming dangerously vulnerable to a counter-attack. Just as their horses gave them the advantage of mobility, they could also be a considerable handicap; too long without water and they would become uncontrollable, and then seriously ill, inhibiting future operations. At 5.30 p.m. Chauvel was forced to abandon the attack, and begin the march back to Oghratina. The operation had cost eight officers and sixty-five other ranks killed and over 230 wounded.[553]

On 12 August 1916 the Ottomans also abandoned Bir el Abd, falling back to Bir el Mazar, their original starting point. It would be a month until the British attempted to evict them from here, too. On the night of 16–17 September, the 2nd and 3rd ALH Brigades, supported by No. 1 Battalion Imperial Camel Corps Brigade and the Ayr and Inverness Batteries RHA, surrounded the Ottoman base, and attacked at dawn. Again, an attack from all sides met with only small success, with some of the Ottoman forward trenches being taken. Once more, due to lack of water, the action had to be broken off at dusk and the British forces retreated, although, also true to the established pattern, the Ottomans abandoned Bir el Mazar a few days later.[554] Their forward positions now lay just a few miles west of El Arish.

The British pursuit had been largely thwarted, and Kress von Kressenstein had been able to extract most of his surviving force in good order. However, this surviving force had been soundly beaten, losing perhaps half its number killed or taken prisoner, and not counting those who were wounded. There was little doubt now that the British controlled the Sinai Desert, although a few small pockets of Ottoman forces still needed to be cleared. Over the next few months, the Ottoman garrisons were driven out of Bir el Tawal (about 30 miles west of El Kubri) and Gebel Bishr (about 30 miles south-east of Suez), and an unsuccessful attack was made on Bir el Maghara (about 50 miles south-east of Romani).[555] Meanwhile, the air forces on both sides conducted active bombing campaigns, with the RFC and RNAS increasingly working in conjunction with the forces on the ground. During the advance on Bir el Mazar on 16 September the RFC intensively patrolled the area in an attempt to stop German aircraft spotting the attacking force. With their outdated machines outclassed by the German aircraft, they failed: one aircraft was shot down (a Martinsyde Elephant flow by commander of No. 14 Squadron, Major E.J. Ballantyne, who survived[556]) and another forced to land with engine problems, leaving a gap for the Germans to exploit. On the day of the attack, the RNAS bombed the aerodrome at El Arish and the road from there to Bir el Mazar from HMS *Ben-My-Chree*, while also directing gunfire from the sloop HMS *Espiègle* and the Monitors *M15* and *M31*. Again, the aircraft in use were outclassed by the enemy, who shot down two Sopwith Babys, while another was badly damaged by ground fire.[557]

While these further operations to clear up isolated Ottoman posts were carried out, the British continued their relentless progress across the Sinai. Through the last months of 1916 there was some debate both in the War Cabinet and in Egypt, and between the two, as to what the future of the campaign would be. The biggest question was whether to pour more resources into the army in Egypt, giving them the strength either to move into southern Palestine or more actively support the campaign in the Hedjaz, or whether to restrict operations to the static guarding of the Egyptian border. This debate was tied into the larger disagreement in London about the ultimate direction of the war. In early December 1916 the Prime Minister, Herbert Asquith, had resigned due to growing criticism in Parliament and the Press over his leadership of the war. Asquith was a 'Westerner', someone who believed that Germany could and would only be defeated on the Western Front. He was replaced by David Lloyd George, who was an 'Easterner', believing that other fronts could be exploited to drain German resources, knock her allies out of the war, and weaken her to the point of surrender without the need for long, bloody battles in France and Belgium. By mid-December the answer settled on the defensive plan, although this was to change in early 1917.[558]

For the time being it almost did not matter, as either course of action relied upon the British occupation of El Arish. From here, the British could strike at and push back the remaining Ottoman garrisons along the Egyptian border, and easily intercept any further Ottoman attacks into the Sinai Peninsula. The British were already, by late September, in possession of Bir el Mazar but advancing the final 20 miles or so to El Arish would be difficult. Water was much scarcer east of Bir el Mazar and even underground sources would be difficult to detect or exploit. The main water pipeline from the Canal Zone was only begun in mid-September, due to pipe shortages, and even by 1 December had only reached as far as Bir el Abd. In the meantime, most of the water for the troops was being brought up to the forward areas by train, but after the Battle of Romani the railhead had been left far behind. Only in early December would the railway line reach Bir el Mazar and until then water had to be transported by convoys from the Camel Transport Corps (CTC), carried in tin tanks on the camels' backs.[559]

While the logistics system caught up with the forward areas, the EEF itself was reorganised to better fit the new situation. With the immediate threat to the Canal gone, on 23 October 1916 General Murray moved his headquarters from Ismailia to Cairo. This led to a certain amount of discontent among the soldiers in the Sinai, who saw their commander as losing touch with them and conditions in the field. However, Murray was responsible not only for the Sinai campaign, but also operations in the Western Desert, various parts of the forces in Salonika, and of course the administration of martial law within Egypt. There was no question that these tasks could be carried out much more efficiently from Cairo.[560]

Murray now prepared a series of changes to his forces, starting (also on 23 October) with the formation of the Eastern Frontier Force, usually known (as it will be here) as Eastern Force. This gathered all of the forces in the Sinai, the Suez Canal Zone, and as far west as the Nile Delta under the command of Lieutenant General Sir Charles Dobell. In effect, Eastern Force became a separate army corps within the EEF, and as such Murray was relieved of much of the routine administration of its divisions, allowing him to concentrate more on his other duties.[561] Dobell and Murray now rearranged the command structure and physical locations of their forces, to mirror the change in the strategic picture. Through November and into early December 1916, the old Nos. 1, 2 and 3 Sections of the Canal Defences were abolished. The southern end of the Canal was now extremely unlikely to come under attack, and Nos. 1 and 2 were merged to become the Southern Canal Section. The garrison was stripped of 53rd Division, leaving only the independent Indian brigades for defence. No. 3 Section, in the north, was split into the Northern Canal Section, while the mobile forces (A&NZ Mounted Division, 5th Mounted Brigade, 42nd Division and 52nd Division) were formed into the Desert Column under Lieutenant General Sir Philip Chetwode.

By the first week in December, the redeployments were complete. The Desert Column was now responsible for forward operations east of Romani: the A&NZ Mounted Division (plus elements of 42nd Division) were at the head of the railway, now 5 miles east of Bir el Mazar. At Bir el Mazar was 42nd Division and most of 52nd Division, with one brigade of the latter division retained to guard the lines of communications back to Romani. At Romani, most of 53rd Division protected the railway line back to the Canal, where one brigade remained. The railway line had now caught up with the advance troops, and each division had been allocated 3,000 camels for the carrying of supplies and water, not including further CTC units stationed along the lines of communications.[562] Everything was now set for the final advance to El Arish.

13

ADVANCE TO PALESTINE

In the last few months of 1916, the forces of the British Empire moved further east towards the border with Palestine. The sand in this region was soft, making movement difficult, and water was scarce. With the railway (and even more so pipeline) trailing far behind, supplies were at a premium. Rations were kept to basic foodstuffs, and strictly limited at that. The animals of the Camel Transport Corps were widely used, but a large part of the burden still had to be carried by the men themselves. Lieutenant A. Briscoe Moore of the New Zealand Mounted Rifles recorded his average burden in late 1916:

The load carried by a Mounted Rifleman's horse in the field is considerable, and may be described here in some detail, to give the reader some idea of what is required of these horses in endurance. The description given is of the minimum load … consisting of bare essentials only.

The Mounted Rifleman wore, on his person, a leather bandolier containing 150 rounds of ammunition, bayonet, service rifle, and haversack, the latter usually stuffed with tins of the inevitable 'bully' beef and army biscuits. The saddlery on his mount consisted of headstall and bridle, headrope, picketing rope, saddle and blanket. In addition to this the horse carried, slung around his neck, a leather sand muzzle, which was slipped on in place of the nosebag when he had finished his meagre feed, to prevent him eating sand and dirt; this being a bad habit quickly indulged in by many horses when hungry.

In this sand-muzzle the trooper often carried his mess-tin, or 'billy' for cooking or making tea, and his dandy brush for grooming. The next item was the horse bandolier, slung around the horse's neck and containing an additional 90 rounds of ammunition. Strapped on the front of the saddle were two leather wallets, probably containing towel, soap, spare shirt, socks, and what rations the rider could not get into his haversack; strapped on top of these again would be the greatcoat and one blanket.

The men usually set out with forty-eight hours' rations and an iron ration, while the horse ration for three days (27 lbs) would be carried. This horsefeed would be distributed between two nosebags, tied to the side of the saddle, and a sandbag, round which might be rolled a ground or bivouac sheet, strapped across the rear of the saddle. Also slung to the side of the saddle would be the canvas water-bucket which served the soldier for the watering of his horse and his own ablutions, and his water-bottle. When the Desert was behind them, and our troops were in Palestine, where a sufficiency of water was usually obtainable, two or three water-bottles would be carried by each man.[563]

The infantry were also heavily festooned with pack, haversack, rifle, bayonet, waterbottle, entrenching tool, ammunition and other accoutrements: 'a wonderful assortment of articles that bristle out from him like the quills of a porcupine'.[564] In the desert conditions, a soldierly appearance was impossible to maintain, and a practical approach adopted:

> We were allowed a good deal of latitude in the matter of the tunic and a man might choose whether he would increase the warmth of his body by wearing it, or the load on his back by putting it in his pack. Water sterilisers were part of each man's kit – in order that in the event of his having to drink unauthorised well water he should be able to kill off some of the more ferocious bacilli likely to be found therein. They were contained in glass bottles, which were easily broken in the pack, and the little tablets, especially when damp, showed the most extraordinary power of eating holes in the kit, and even of making their way through the pack itself, till it looked as if it had been partially burnt. As damaged articles could not be quickly replaced, a ragged pack often added to the bizarre aspect of the British soldier, with his dew-whitened helmet, squashed out of all decent shape, shirt of varied hue rolled back from sunburnt chest and arms usually marked by a dirty grey bandage or two, drill shorts stained, blackened and often torn, bare knees, puttees and rather disreputable boots.[565]

This basic existence could occasionally be augmented by unexpected windfalls. The 5th Highland Light Infantry were lucky enough to come across a camp abandoned by horsemen ordered to make a raid:

> The Australian light horseman has the bump of acquisitiveness even better developed than the Lowland infantryman, and having a horse on which he can hang his trophies he can give this penchant greater scope. But when he is going into action – or believes himself to be – he unhesitantly sacrificed all that will incommode him in the serious business of war. In consequence the ground recently vacated appeared at dawn to our astonished eyes covered with a litter of discarded possessions. When *we* moved camp it was our honourable custom to pick up and burn or bury every tin, every fragment of paper and every match and cigarette end and to leave the desert swept and garnished as we found it – or better. So our first thought was one of scandalised amazement at the extreme untidiness of the business. Our next was less disinterested. We were on mobile rations, bully, biscuit, milk and jam. Vegetables and the 'wee piece ham' had disappeared. Surely Australians did not live like that. Nor

were we disappointed. Foraging parties returned laden with sides of bacon, cheese, bread, Maconochies,* sacks of onions and desiccated vegetables ... all the things which stand for wealth among such a primitive tribe as we were then.[566]

Although the terrible heat of the summer had faded, the temperature remained a problem. Now temperatures fell drastically at night, making a dreadful contrast with the day. Where once the troops needed to dig into the ground and build bivouacs to avoid the heat while sleeping, now they had to do so to find it. Gunner Anthony Bluett recorded that sleeping soldiers would wrap up in:

Our blankets, of which we had two, together with a greatcoat, cardigan-waistcoat, and a cap-comforter or balaclava helmet, this last a very stout bulwark against the cold blast. The first business was to dig a shallow, coffin-shaped trench large enough to contain two; it was much better for two men to bivouac together, since by putting one blanket only to sleep on, we had three with which to cover ourselves, besides our greatcoats. Nobody took any clothes off, with the exception of boots and putties ... The pillow universally used was a nosebag filled with the next day's feed, and very comfortable it was ... Then with our cap-comforters on, and perhaps the spare shirt wrapped round the head, we were snug for the night.[567]

During the day the temperatures were more comfortable, although the soft sand made movement hard work anyway. Corporal Victor Godrich of the Queen's Own Worcestershire Hussars (Yeomanry) recorded that it was hard going for both horses and men:

The going was terrible for the horses as the poor beasts always went in over the fetlocks, frequently as deep as their knees and hocks. It had the same effect on men, everybody walked with a long, slow stride, like the plough-boy at home. In fact when we went to Cairo for a few days leave, we all suffered with stiff legs and backs due to walking on the hard pavements![568]

For the infantry at least, the hard going over the sand was alleviated by the laying of an ad hoc road across the Sinai. It was impossible to build a metalled road with the resources available, and there was not enough timber or scrub to lay a surface that way. Instead, a crude but effective technique was mastered, using rabbit- or chicken-wire, which:

Consisted in cutting [and removing] scrub [that was in the way] and flattening out a track at a reasonable gradient. On this long rows of ordinary rabbit wire netting were pegged down four abreast and the result was a 'road' which very greatly increased the pace and extent of infantry marching. The wire prevented a man from sinking into the sand and was comfortable enough to walk on, if one was careful not to catch one's toes.[569]

---

*   A popular brand of tinned stew.

Through early December, Eastern Force prepared to once again take the offensive. Troops, camels and large stocks of water had been amassed at Bir el Mazar, ready to advance the 20 miles to El Arish. Water grew increasingly scarcer on this side of the Sinai. There were fewer wells, and it was considerably harder to find underlying water in the desert. The principal water sources were ranged along the Wadi El Arish, which ran south from the Mediterranean. The Ottoman positions at the town of El Arish (about 2 miles inland), at El Magdhaba (about 25 miles to the southeast), and in the area of Abu Aweigila (about 15 miles further south, and covering the Ottoman railhead at El Kossaima) all stood along the banks of the Wadi, and between them controlled the most abundant water sources along its course. In early December several patrols were sent out by the A&NZ Mounted Division with engineers to prospect for water along the Wadi to the south of the town, to act as a forward supply, but none could be found.[570] Any attack on the garrison at El Arish (which British intelligence reported to be an infantry division of 6,000–7,000 men, but actually stood at two battalions, about 1,600 men) would have to be quick and direct.[571]

By 20 December 1916 the A&NZ Mounted Division, 52nd (Lowland) Division and the Imperial Camel Corps (ICC) Brigade were poised to make a night march against El Arish. On the same day, an RFC patrol reported that the Ottoman positions around the town appeared to be empty. The A&NZ Mounted Division and the ICC Brigade were immediately despatched to investigate, marching through the night and surrounding the town at dawn on 21 December. The Ottomans had indeed withdrawn their garrison on the 17 or 18 December, and once the news was confirmed the British began moving up to secure the area.[572] On 22 December 52nd Division began to arrive on foot, while General Chetwode arrived on the coast by ship. Once the mouth of the Wadi El Arish had been swept for mines, work began on building a pier, and on 23 December supplies began to arrive for the advance troops by sea.

The bloodless capture of the town was not the only good news for the troops. To approach the town they had to cross wide, firm mud flats on either bank of the Wadi. For the first time in half a year, they moved out of the soft, shifting sand and onto solid ground. Lieutenant Colonel Charles Cox, commanding the 1st ALH Brigade, recorded:

> That night will always seem to me the most wonderful of the whole campaign. The hard going for the horses seemed almost miraculous after the months of sand; and, as the shoes of the horses struck fire on the stones in the bed of the wadi, the men laughed with delight. The Sinai was behind them.[573]

Actually, the Sinai was not quite behind them yet. Although El Arish had been successfully taken, the two Ottoman garrisons to the south and Rafah to the northeast remained.

On 22 December Chauvel was ordered to send some of the ICC Brigade to keep the garrison at Rafah pinned down, while taking the rest of his A&NZ Mounted Division south to attack El Magdhaba and Abu Aweigila. However, the RFC again provided vital information. A force of ten BE2c aircraft from No. 1 Squadron AFC plus three more from No. 14 Squadron RFC staged a raid on the garrison during the day, dropping over 100 bombs and encountering heavy ground fire.[574] They reported that the forces present at El Magdhaba were far greater than had been expected, and so it was decided to concentrate the available forces against them. Chetwode now ordered Chauvel to take his division* and the ICC Brigade on a night march to El Magdhaba, where they arrived at 4 a.m., shortly before dawn. While his men made tea and breakfast and recovered from the 23-mile ride through the freezing night, Chauvel rode with his staff to view the Ottoman position.[575]

As the sun began to rise, smoke from the camp fires of the Ottoman garrison obscured their positions. Only at 6.30 a.m. was a clear picture of the defences gained when more British aeroplanes arrived to attack the garrison again. The ground fire that met each attacking aircraft showed up the Ottoman positions, strung along both banks of the Wadi El Arish. The A&NZ Division had marched south-east down the Wadi, and here it meandered more towards the east. The Ottomans had dug their defences on a 2-mile stretch on both banks, with two large redoubts on the northern bank and three on the southern.[576] Held by the 2nd and 3rd Battalions of the 80th Regiment under the command of Khadir Bey, the redoubts were well placed to dominate the low, rolling scrubland around them, and to give fire in support of each other. Between the redoubts were systems of connecting and supporting trenches. At around 8 a.m. reports began to arrive from the aircraft, confirming the layout and strength of the position. They also confirmed that no significant Ottoman forces could be seen within at least an 8–10-mile radius. This meant that the only time factor involved in the attack would be the division's finite water supply, although this was already causing concern.[577]

Chauvel set about deploying his forces, and mindful of the state of their waterbottles, gave orders that each attack should commence as soon as it was in place, as there was no time to wait to make a co-ordinated attack. Chauvel decided to keep his main force on the northern bank of the Wadi, where the ground was firmer and movement would be quicker. He ordered the ICC Brigade to attack parallel to the northern bank of the Wadi against the closest Ottoman position, designated No. 1 Redoubt. The cameliers were a heavier force than the cavalry; their battalions were half the size again of a cavalry regiment, and they carried more ammunition. Against this superior size and firepower was the fact that they moved slower, partly because the camels could not be ridden in close to the enemy before dismounting, as the horses could. Instead, the attack would have to be made on foot from a greater distance. As the ICC Brigade deployed, Brigadier General Chaytor was sent around to the north of the Ottoman position with the 3rd ALH Brigade and the NZMR Brigade. He immediately sent the NZMR to assault the eastern end of the Ottoman positions, centred around Redoubt No. 4. The Wellington and Canterbury Mounted Rifles carried out the main attack, while the Auckland Mounted Rifles were held in reserve. The bulk of the 3rd ALH Brigade was also held back, although the 10th ALH Regiment was sent on a fast ride around the eastern end of the Ottoman line, crossing the Wadi

---

*   Apart from 2nd ALH Brigade and the Ayr and Leicester Batteries RHA, which were left
     behind.

(in which they captured a party of 300 *Mehmetçik*) and taking up position to the south of El Magdhaba.[578]

At 10 a.m., before the cameliers had even begun their attack, an aeroplane landed near Chauvel's headquarters and reported that a large body of Ottoman troops had been seen leaving El Magdhaba towards the south. Afraid that the garrison was slipping away, Chauvel immediately threw his divisional reserve – General Cox's 1st ALH Brigade – straight down the northern bank of the Wadi. Cox formed his men and began to trot directly towards No. 1 Redoubt, but after a mile or so they came under fire from Ottoman mountain guns. Shaking out into artillery formation, with larger gaps between each horse, Cox spurred his brigade into a gallop, but half a mile later rifle and machine-gun fire opened up on them from Redoubt No. 1 and, beyond it on the southern bank, Redoubt No. 2. It was clear that the garrison was still very much in place; in fact it later transpired that the Ottoman forces seen escaping to the south were a large party of Arab deserters. Still over a mile from the nearest redoubt, Cox wheeled his force into the Wadi itself, where they dismounted and began a slow advance on foot.[579]

By noon, the position was quite static. Most of Chauvel's forces were now deployed, with the 3rd ALH Brigade moving into the line to support the New Zealanders in the north, and all were making agonisingly slow progress as they crossed ground largely devoid of any cover, and staunchly defended by well-sited Ottoman positions. At 1 p.m. the news reached Chauvel that the parties of engineers who had been sent out to scout for water as far as 14 miles away could find none; as none of the horses had been watered since the beginning to the march the previous evening (and some not for many hours before that), this was critical news. The whole operation was, as one New Zealand officer put it, 'a race against darkness and water', and it now began to look as if the ANZACs were going to lose that race.[580]

After conferring with Chetwode via a telegraph, Chauvel reluctantly decided to call off the attack. Just before 2 p.m., he issued an order to his brigade commanders, telling them to disengage as best they could and withdraw. One of these messages was taken to General Cox, whose 1st ALH Brigade was still slowly advancing up the Wadi El Arish. His advance unit, the 3rd ALH Regiment under Lieutenant Colonel Fulton, had now made their way to within 100yd (90m) of No. 1 Redoubt, and were in touch with the ICC Brigade on their left. Arrangements were being made to rush the redoubt, and Cox thrust the order from Chauvel back to the messenger, declaring 'Take that damned thing away, and let me see it for the first time in half-an-hour.'[581] Within minutes the 3rd ALH Regiment surged forward with fixed bayonets, joined by Nos. 1 and 11 (Australian) Companies of the ICC Brigade on their left. They met with an initial burst of heavy fire but as the Australians poured in from two sides resistance crumbled. Nearly 100 Ottoman troops surrendered, and No. 1 Redoubt was captured.[582]

Chauvel immediately rescinded his previous order and telephoned Chetwode to tell him of his certainty that El Magdhaba would fall. The attack was now pressed with renewed vigour, and the 10th ALH Regiment started their assault from the south. Although the ground was softer and more sandy to the south, it was also more broken and the 10th managed to get in close to No. 4 Redoubt, furthest east; one party of thirty to forty Australians even managed to ride over and through No. 3 Redoubt (in the centre of the southern line and with a garrison of 300–400 *Mehmetçik*) to do so. At 4 p.m., with covering fire coming from the Australians in No. 1 Redoubt, the 1st ALH Brigade swarmed into No. 2 Redoubt, capturing among others Khadir Bey, the Ottoman commander. Soon afterwards, the New Zealanders and the 3rd ALH Brigade captured No. 5 Redoubt and the other northern defences, and entered El Magdhaba itself.[583]

The garrison now surrendered en masse, totalling almost 1,300 troops. The French military attaché, Captain Count St Quentin, who had ridden with Chauvel, was also briefly interred by the lighthorsemen in a case of mistaken identity.[584] Chauvel's force had suffered five officers and seventeen men killed, and seven officers and 117 men wounded. The various field ambulances had been doing their best all day to pick up the wounded from the field, but the efforts to recover them all continued until long after dark. For the men who had lay untreated all day under the hot sun, the one small consolation was that the garrison at El Magdhaba had its own hospital. Corporal Patrick Hamilton served with the 4th Australian Light Horse Field Ambulance:

> We kept moving forward all day from place to place, looking for and collecting wounded under fire. We continued to pick up wounded till dark ... Finally, we took all our wounded to a Turkish hospital, a brick building, with one very large bare hall. Here 85 wounded were assembled in two long lines on the cement floor. Four of us, with Captain Evans, worked along these lines, dressing the wounded for four hours until 10 p.m. We then took night shifts in turn ... We then loaded our patients onto sand carts and camels till 11.30 a.m. Very heavy, hard physical work. On the move by midday.[585]

While the medical staff worked to collect the wounded, assisted and guarded by the Auckland Mounted Rifles, the rest of Chauvel's force began to march back to El Arish. Along the way, they were met by a column sent out by Chetwode, bearing water and rations. Even with this support, it was a long hard march:

> To pass one night without sleep is trying; two nights is absolutely painful; but the third night without sleep, after heavy fighting with all the added strain and excitement, is almost an impossibility. Men and horses were dropping off at the oddest times. The dust was intense, and to the lightly clad men bereft of their overcoats, the cold seemed to penetrate to the bone.[586]

Many of the exhausted men experienced hallucinations or waking-dreams as they rode; even Chauvel himself at one point galloped off away from the column with one of his staff officers, returning later and admitting that they thought they had been on a hunt and had sighted a fox.[587]

For the wounded, the ordeal was, regrettably, only beginning. After the long, uncomfortable ride back to El Arish on 24 December, instructions were given to prepare them for evacuation by sea. However, the weather had now turned and the winter rains arrived. Wind and rain buffeted the area, and no ships were able to approach the pier at El Arish. For the men stationed there it meant a cold and miserable Christmas with only basic rations and whatever impromptu celebrations they could muster from within themselves. For the wounded it meant an agonising delay until 28 December, when it was finally decided to give up waiting and despatch them back to the hospitals in Egypt by rail.[588]

On the day before the wounded were finally sent for proper care, General Murray made a rare visit to the front. News was coming in that the remaining Ottoman garrisons in the Sinai were being withdrawn, for fear that they too would be cut off and destroyed as El Magdhaba had been. Indeed, by New Year's Day, the Sinai Peninsula was, for the first time in over two years, completely clear of Ottoman troops.[589] All that remained was a garrison of around two battalions at El Magruntein, a mile or two south of Rafah, on the border with Palestine. Both Murray and Chetwode agreed that they should press their current advantage, and launch a similar attack on Rafah as had taken El Magdhaba.

While by rights this would be the last action of the 1916 campaign, preparations had to be made and it was not until early January 1917 that all was set. In the meantime, supplies had been stockpiled at El Arish (where the 52nd Division were busy digging in), the troops had been rested, and several large-scale reconnaissances had been made up the road to Rafah. These confirmed that the road was clear and safe to use, that there were no other Ottoman outposts in the area, and, most importantly, that there was water at the village of Sheikh Zowaiid, about 20 miles from El Arish and 10 miles short of the Ottoman positions.[590]

The attacking force left El Arish at 4 p.m. on 8 January 1917, under the overall command of General Chetwode. The 5th Mounted Brigade (which remained under Chetwode's personal control) led the way, followed by the bulk of the A&NZ Mounted Division (the 2nd ALH Brigade was again left behind), the Imperial Camel Corps Brigade, and No. 7 Light Car Patrol (of four armoured cars and three store-cars), all under the command of Chauvel. As they marched, the RFC patrolled overhead to keep away German patrols. The 5th Mounted Brigade moved ahead of the main force, and enveloped Sheikh Zowaiid at around 10 p.m., making sure that no Bedouin could escape to warn the Ottoman garrison of the British arrival. Soon after, the entire column made camp just west of the village.[591]

After a short rest, the column began to move out again at 1 a.m., leaving their wheeled transport (except artillery) at Sheikh Zowaiid under guard. This included all of the supply wagons, carrying among other things the force's reserve ammunition. Only half a mile outside of Sheikh Zowaiid, the advance guard ran across an Arab camel patrol, which was captured, and by 3.30 a.m. the main force was less than 5 miles south of El Magruntein. After a brief pause the NZMR Brigade pushed on to the east and circled around south of the Ottoman positions, and just after 5 a.m. surrounded the Arab villages at Karm Ibn Musleh and Shokh es Sufi, on the Egyptian border. Again the plan was to prevent any of the locals warning the Ottoman garrison of the proximity of the British but upon being rounded up the women of the villages began an ululation that was clearly heard over some miles in the still dawn air. In at El Magruntein, around 2,000 Ottoman troops from two battalions of the 31st Regiment were roused and stood-to, to man the defences.[592]

Just over an hour later, the Auckland Mounted Rifles marched north to take up position to the north-east of the Ottoman positions, cutting their line of retreat, and the line that any help from Shallal or Khan Yunis may take. As they did so, they crossed the border into Palestine and stepped from Africa into Asia.[593]

Chauvel, in consultation with Chetwode, now deployed his troops as the dawn broke on 9 January. By 7 a.m., the ICC Brigade was in position to the south of El Magruntein, with the 1st and 3rd ALH Brigades on the right, just over the border near Shock es Sufi. The New Zealanders were stretching around to the east and north of the garrison, capturing the Ottoman police post at Rafah and a convoy with around forty-five Ottoman, German and Bedouin troops in the process. The 5th Mounted Brigade were placed to the west and north-west of El Magruntein, and it would not be until early afternoon that the Yeomen and the New Zealanders met up to the north of the position, completing the encirclement.[594]

In the light of dawn, the troops could take proper stock of their surroundings. Having marched the previous evening across the barren sand of the desert, they now found themselves in rolling grassland:

> The country had completely changed during out night-ride; much of it here was in crop, and everywhere the grass grew luxuriantly. What a relief the green was from the glare of the sand, and how greedily the horses cropped the sweet grass and young corn.[595]

There were even signs of cultivation, with fields of young barley growing up to about 9in (23cm) tall. Unfortunately, while pleasant on the eye, these crops also constituted almost the only cover available in an otherwise flat, open landscape.[596] The Ottoman position at El Magruntein was formidable. One of the New Zealand officers recalled:

> The centre redoubt crowned a conical hill some two hundred feet above the surrounding plain, which was bare of cover and as smooth as a lawn. Spread out fanwise from the central redoubt were a cleverly sited series of trenches, invisible in the grass.[597]

The central redoubt, also known as 'The Reduit' or 'Point 255', was based upon the remains of an old and substantial keep, although further trenches had been dug to reinforce it. It was certainly the strongest part of the defences, but although generally referred to as being 'central' it was in fact on the northern face of the position. Spread out to the south-east, south and south-west were three further trench systems, forming distinct but interconnected positions. They lacked barbed wire but were in every other way formidable. Due to the flat, sloping ground around them, they could dominate the ground for up to 2,000yd (1,800m) in every direction. The one weakness was that, as at El Magdhaba, it would only need one of the four systems to be captured to fatally compromise the others.

The attack began at 9.30 a.m. The various mounted units (less the 3rd ALH and 5th Mounted Brigades, kept for now in reserve) rode up to around 2,000yd (1,800m) from the Ottoman positions, dismounted, and began to advance on foot. As they did so, covering fire was provided by the various brigade and divisional artillery detachments: the Leicester, Inverness and Somerset Batteries RHA for the A&NZ Mounted Division, the Hong Kong and Singapore Battery for the ICC Brigade, and 'B' Battery, Honourable Artillery Company, for the 5th Mounted Brigade. Each of these units would keep up a steady fire into the afternoon, until stocks of ammunition began to run out.[598] For the first time in Egypt artillery fire would be directly targeted by aeroplanes, communicating with the ground via wireless sets. Two aeroplanes were maintained over Rafah all day (using separate frequencies) and communicated with five wireless stations on the ground; four attached to artillery batteries and one with the headquarters.[599] This allowed an unprecedented accuracy for the artillery fire, which was sadly negated by the depth and strength of the Ottoman positions.

Ammunition would be a problem for all of the forces through the day. The Ottomans were well sited and well dug in. With the lack of natural cover the only way to make any serious advances was to lay down enough covering fire from rifles, machine guns and artillery to temporarily keep the enemy's heads down. When enough fire was brought to bear, small rushes could be made to cover the ground:

> The advance was slow but steady, the men advancing on foot as though they were carrying out manoeuvres. Everything worked like clockwork. A troop would rise from the ground and, covered by the fire of their comrades on either flank, dash forward a few yards, the men throwing themselves down, and bringing fire to bear on the trench in front of them till the remaining troops had come into line.[600]

However, the attacking force was stretched very thinly, and it was difficult to concentrate enough fire on any one spot for long enough. The use of the armoured cars as mobile machine-gun posts between the 5th Mounted Brigade and the NZMR Brigade helped, as did the British artillery, but keeping both (and the machine guns sections with the dismounted troops) supplied was difficult, especially as ammunition had to be brought up from the dump at Sheikh Zowaiid, 10 miles away. By 1.30 p.m., four of the machine guns of the NZMR Brigade were out of action, due to lack of ammunition.[601]

By noon, the NZMR were still 600yd (550m) from the Ottoman redoubt. In the south, the Australians were 400yd (365m) from the Ottoman positions, and between 1 p.m. and 2 p.m. managed to capture a few of the outlying trenches, although they soon became pinned down and were even forced to abandon one.[602] At 3.30 p.m. the Inverness Battery RHA had to withdraw due to shortages of ammunition[603] and overall the situation was looking bleak. At 4 p.m. news arrived from both the RFC and piquets to the north-east that large bodies of Ottoman troops – probably some 2,500 in all – were advancing from Shallal and Khan Yunis.[604]

Dusk was now approaching and Chetwode's position was grim. Although the British force would outnumber the reinforcements several times over on paper, once casualties and the loss of one-quarter of the force as horse-holders was taken into account, these odds shortened drastically. More seriously, the British forces were thinly spread over a wide area, exhausted from marching most of the night and fighting all day, and dangerously short of ammunition and water. The reserves had all been deployed and no fresh troops were available. In these conditions, it would be all too easy for the Ottoman forces to set about overwhelming and destroying the various regiments and brigades piecemeal. At 4.30 p.m. Chetwode gave the order to withdraw. The closest troops, the 5th Mounted Brigade, under his own command, began to fall back at once. For Lieutenant E.T. Cripps of the Royal Gloucestershire Hussars, this was a blow as, after six hours spent getting within attacking range of the enemy, his squadron found itself alone:

> We got to within 200 yards of the fort as it was getting dusk - five bounds. The men were simply splendid. My troop were up the moment I gave the word, and rushed in a beautiful line and dropped down absolutely in line, keeping their extension ... When we got [orders] for the final assault we found the troops on the right had orders to retire and were 200 yards in rear of us and the others on the left very slow. 'A' Squadron was up by itself. I crawled to Tom and told him it must be done now or never, as the light were nearly gone. He wisely ordered a retirement.[605]

But the order to the rest of the brigades had to go via Chauvel and had further to travel. This was just as well. At the moment that the order to withdraw was going out, both the NZMR Brigade and the ICC Brigade were separately gathering themselves for final efforts. Under a concentrated artillery barrage, which kicked up billows of smoke that helped to mask the advance, the New Zealanders swept in from the north, while the cameliers attacked from the south. The smoke and panic helped confuse the aim of the *Mehmetçik* and although both charges suffered casualties, the speed of their advance carried them through and into the Ottoman trenches. As the British troops poured into the redoubt and the southern trenches, the surviving garrison began to surrender. Meanwhile, seeing the charges, the Australian Light Horse joined the assault, and the Yeomanry of the 5th Mounted Brigade also turned back. These swept into the eastern and western trench systems and Ottoman resistance collapsed.

The fight at El Magruntein, generally known as the Action at Rafah, was a close-run thing. British casualties amounted to seventy-one officers and men killed, and over 400 hundred wounded, many of whom still lay out on the battlefield. The Ottomans had lost about 200 men killed and over 1,600 surrendered. Darkness was now falling but there was much to be done, and decisions to be made. On the one hand, the wounded needed to be collected, but on the other the force was low on water and ammunition and needed to reach its supplies at Sheikh Zowaiid as quickly as possible. In the end, the various brigade field ambulances were left behind, with the 8th ALH Regiment to guard them. The rest of the force marched to Sheikh Zowaiid, arriving around 10 p.m., where they resupplied and briefly rested. The bulk then set out for El Arish at 1 a.m. on 10 January, although the armoured cars and detachments of the Australian Light Horse returned to Rafah to help out.

For those marching home, it was a long night. As after the attack on Magdhaba, many men reported having hallucinations:

The darkness plays strange tricks with the eyes of tired men riding through the night, and many and various were the hallucinations of the riders, fortunately unshared by the mounts. Many went frankly to sleep in the saddle but others rode through limitless forests, rows and rows of tents, up steep mountain sides, over sheer precipices, and many other forms of illusion, differing according to the individual concerned. The Colonel said afterwards that he rode in his imagination past an endless succession of public-houses, the contents of which lay in the roadway. He called them 'cafes' but his meaning was understood, and he received a full measure of sympathy.[606]

The columns staggered into El Arish throughout the morning, to be met by volunteers of the 52nd (Lowland) Division, who turned out to guide them in and to pump water for their horses, a gesture that was greatly appreciated. Back at El Magruntein, though, the work went on. Soon after dawn on 10 January, a light skirmish was fought between the 8th ALH Regiment and the Ottoman reinforcements, who soon retreated once it was confirmed that the garrison had fallen.[607] The field ambulances had worked all night to collect the scattered wounded in the darkness. At least one, the 5th Mounted Brigade, had lit a beacon at their position, to help guide the stretcher bearers in to the right place.[608] It was not until nearly noon that the work was finally completed, and the last ambulance (and escort) began the long march back to El Arish. Patrick Hamilton's unit did not arrive there until late in the evening:

We collected all our own Brigade wounded and moved them back a few miles to the 1st LH Field Ambulance Casualty Clearing Station, temporarily established for the purpose, by about 4 a.m. on 10 January. We buried nine who had died of wounds. After the wounded had been redressed and fed, we loaded up the sand carts again and travelled steadily back some 20 miles to the Anzac Casualty Clearing Station at El Arish which we reached by about 9 p.m. There we cleared our wounded and returned to our own camp to turn in about 1 a.m. on January 11, after 65 hours without any sleep – except once when I fell off my horse asleep and woke up on the ground![609]

Although the British had withdrawn, the Ottomans did not reoccupy Rafah. They had finally learned that isolated garrisons were, while no easy pickings, still far too vulnerable to attack by the British mounted forces. With their withdrawal back to Khan Yunis, Shallal, Gaza and Beersheba, the Ottomans had ceded the Sinai Peninsula and for the first time adopted a purely defensive posture. For the British, Egypt was finally secured. Now all that remained would be to push the Ottomans out of Palestine too.

EPILOGUE

EGYPT 1917–18

By the end of 1916, Egypt was safe. While the Senussi were still occupying large parts of the Western Desert, there had been no popular uprisings in their support. The fighting along the coast had cost them heavily in men and equipment; at the same time a new level of Anglo-Italian co-operation was also inhibiting their operations. While they would remain a concern for some months into 1917, they were not a great danger. Equally, the spectre of an Islamic uprising across Egypt and Sudan, inspired either by the Ottomans or the Senussi, had failed to materialise. After the campaign in the Darfur, apart from a few tribal or border disputes unrelated to the war, the Sudan remained peaceful.

The threat of invasion had passed. The campaign in the Sinai had been an arduous ordeal for all involved – British, Ottoman and Bedouin. For the common soldiers it had meant months of toil in a hostile environment, plagued by the dust and flies, always short on water and poorly fed, and in searing heat. Now, however, the British were safely in place at El Arish, with a solid logistics network to back them up. The Ottomans, already fighting active campaigns in the Caucasus, the Balkans, Mesopotamia and the Hedjaz, would not be able to spare the men to evict such a strongly positioned force. Instead, they would reinforce the line between Gaza and Beersheba. For the British, the deteriorating situation in the wider war through late 1916 and 1917 led to a desire to push the Ottomans back further, into Palestine, in order to achieve any kind of victory to boost morale at home. Two attempts would be made against Gaza in early 1917 and both would be bloodily repulsed. Despite the use of the most modern weapons of war – tanks and poison gas – Gaza would hold. These defeats saw the replacement of Sir Archibald Murray in June 1917 by General Sir Edmund Allenby. With him would come reinforcements and a new offensive spirit, but even so, only in late October would this line finally be pierced, by one of the oldest weapons of war – cavalry – and the British able to start the hard push north to occupy Jerusalem.

Egypt had remained calm, or as calm as it could be, given the massive increase in the number of soldiers in the country. Martial law was generally imposed with a light hand, while some positive moves had been made to sweep away archaic laws.

At the same time, while there had been some controls over agriculture, the economy had benefited from the army's presence. The army as an entity and as a collection of individuals had created markets for Egyptian goods and services, and created jobs not only in catering to these markets but also in working directly for the army as labourers or cameliers. At this stage in the war, the Egyptian Labour Corps (ELC) and Camel Transport Corps (CTC) were an attractive proposition, providing fairly well-paid but short-term contracts, allowing Egyptians to serve a few months and then return home with their accumulated back pay. Over the next two years, the situation would change. Food shortages would begin to occur and prices would rise. As the fighting moved further from Egypt's borders and the direct threat declined, so did support for the war. The nationalists gained ground, helped in no small way by Britain's own carelessness.

Sir John Maxwell had known, and been known by, Egypt and the Egyptians, and had been fully aware of his responsibilities to the government and people. After he returned to the UK in early 1916, no one of a similar calibre came forward to take his place. General Sir Archibald Murray, and later General Sir Edmund Allenby, were more concerned with military matters than the domestic or political situation in Egypt. In January 1917 Sir Henry McMahon would be replaced as the British High Commissioner in Egypt by Sir Reginald Wingate (who himself was replaced as Governor General of the Sudan by Sir Lee Stack). Wingate had performed very well in the Sudan but would find working in Egypt much harder, and his actions would become increasingly controversial towards the end of the war.

The country began to feel neglected, and became dissatisfied as Britain placed more obligations on the Egyptian people, despite the 1914 promise that they would not be required to shoulder any of the war effort. For example, when it was discovered that the greatly extended supply lines of 1917 needed an increased number of labourers and cameliers to keep them flowing, the three-month enlistment period of the ELC and CTC were arbitrarily extended to six months. This was a much less appealing proposition, not least for those already serving. Later still, the *corvée*, a system whereby village elders were obliged to produce set quotas of men for government service, had to be introduced to keep the ELC and CTC up to strength. Such measures increasingly caused discontent among the common people and led in 1919 to open revolt against British rule. This was followed in 1922 with independence for Egypt, albeit with caveats covering British interests (such as the Suez Canal) in the country.

The Suez Canal remained important to the British war effort even as the level of traffic was reduced: between 1915 and 1917 the tonnage of British shipping passing through the Canal dropped by nearly 50 per cent.[610] The German submarine threat was a serious blow to British and Entente shipping but would slowly be overcome in the Mediterranean. In the meantime, although some shipping began to be sent via South Africa instead of through the Suez Canal, the eastern Mediterranean remained an important theatre. All supplies and reinforcements for the British forces in Salonika continued to arrive by sea, and a good deal of support for the forces fighting in Mesopotamia, where Britain was slowly seizing the strategically important oil fields.

Egypt and the Sudan were also the natural places to use to support the Arab Revolt, which expanded throughout 1917 and 1918 into a major problem for the Ottoman Empire. This ever-fluctuating alliance of local tribes grew with British arms, funding, support and leadership (by the inspired Thomas Lawrence) to become an army, capable of acting in conjunction with the EEF in late 1917 and in 1918 to drive the Ottomans up through Palestine and into Syria. From being local rebels in 1916, they became a serious player in the region, indeed one that Britain would later regret encouraging during the post-war peace settlements. The tangled maze of alliances and agreements made by the British with the Entente powers and the Arabs would come back to haunt them, and would lead directly to many of the problems that still plague the region today.

These problems lay in the future. At the end of 1916 Britain could look back at a job well done. Today the failed campaign in Gallipoli and the romantic adventures, and personal enigma, of Lawrence of Arabia and his Arabs dominate the popular view of the war in the Middle East. In fact, working at times with very few men and little resources, the British had achieved several notable victories and secured a strategically vital area for the war effort. The troops in Egypt felt themselves to be neglected during the war, and they have remained so since. The popular image of the day, of their lazy sojourn in the sun and sand of Egypt, was as unfair and inaccurate as could be. Theirs had been an arduous and hard-fought war, and over the coming year it would not get significantly easier. In 1917 they would discover that Palestine's reputation for being the 'land of milk and honey' would be as misguided as Egypt's for being the land of 'pyramids and fleshpots'.

APPENDIX A

BRITISH MEDITERRANEAN FLEET, 1914

Commander-in-Chief: Admiral Sir Berkeley Milne Bt GCVO KCB
Chief of Staff: Commodore Richard Phillmore CB MVO

2nd Battle Cruiser Squadron:

HMS *Inflexible*, (Flagship of C-in-C) Captain Arthur Loxley (8 x 12in guns)
HMS *Indefatigable*, Captain Charles Sowerby (8 x 12in guns)
HMS *Indomitable*, Captain Francis Kennedy (8 x 12in guns)

1st Cruiser Squadron:
Rear Admiral Ernest Troubridge CB CMG MVO

HMS *Defence*, (Flagship) Captain Fawcet Wray (4 x 9.2in and 10 x 7.5in guns)
HMS *Black Prince*, Captain Frederick Gilpin-Brown (6 x 9.2in and 10 x 6in guns)
HMS *Duke of Edinburgh*, Captain Henry Blackett (6 x 9.2in and 10 x 6in guns)
HMS *Warrior*, Captain George Borrett (6 x 9.2in and 4 x 7.5in guns)

Light Cruisers:

HMS *Chatham*, Captain Sidney Drury-Lowe (8 x 6in guns)
HMS *Dublin*, Captain John Kelly (8 x 6in guns)
HMS *Gloucester*, Captain W.A. Howard Kelly MVO (2 x 6in and 10 x 4in guns)
HMS *Weymouth*, Captain William Church (8 x 6in guns)

Destroyer Flotilla:

Sixteen destroyers

APPENDIX B

NOTE ON THE ORGANISATION OF BRITISH AND IMPERIAL FORCES

It is interesting that, for the period covered in this book, the white forces involved in the campaigns in Egypt were almost entirely amateurs. The Indian forces sent out in 1914 were mostly regulars, but the British, Australian, New Zealand and (later) South African troops were a mixture of various types of Territorial forces – part-time soldiers – or wartime volunteers, leavened by small numbers of regular officers and NCOs. On the outbreak of war the British and Indian armies mobilised as complete units; for the British at least, this meant that the various Territorial and later volunteer units tended to maintain the distinctive local character of the areas in which they were recruited. In New Zealand, South Africa and Australia, the volunteers were taken from the existing Territorial units and formed into new battalions and brigades for overseas service.

The question of conscription was a thorny issue across the British Empire. In Britain, after the flow of volunteers began to tail off in late 1915, the Military Service Act was introduced in England, Wales and Scotland in January 1916. This initially made all single men aged 18–41 eligible for conscription, and was expanded in May 1916 to married men. (Later, in April 1918, the age limit was raised to 51.) Conscription was also introduced in New Zealand in August 1916, although 75 per cent of their soldiers remained volunteers. In Australia two fiercely contested national referendums were held on the issue, and conscription was rejected by the electorate (which included the forces deployed overseas) both times. In South Africa, as in Ireland, the political situation made any kind of conscription too contentious, although neither country faced any great shortage of volunteers.

The relatively low casualty rates of the forces engaged in Egypt in 1916 meant that few replacements were needed, and so even after the introduction of conscription in Britain, relatively few of these men were deployed to the country. There were certain exceptions: the heavy casualties suffered by the 5th Mounted Brigade in April 1916 led to a large influx of replacements for outside the traditional recruiting area of the units involved. However, for the most part the Territorial and volunteer units kept their local character and close-knit nature. Only after the high casualty rates of the Battles of Gaza in early 1917, when conscripted men were posted to wherever they were needed, regardless of county or city of origin, did their character begin to become diluted.

The basic infantry unit of the British and Imperial forces was the battalion (under a colonel or lieutenant colonel). For the British and ANZACs, this consisted of just over 1,000 officers and men, divided into four companies (under a major or captain) of just over 200 men, plus a battalion headquarters. Each company was divided into four platoons (under a lieutenant), each of which was divided into four sections (under a sergeant or corporal). Each battalion had small sections of specialist troops attached: medical staff, signallers (and later, wireless operators) and from late 1915 members of the Machine Gun Corps with heavy machine guns (before then, they had been members of the battalion).

Indian units were smaller, being just over 700 officers and men. Until recently they had been organised into eight companies, but by 1914 had only four. As these were twice the size of the old ones, they were often referred to as 'double-companies'. Officers commanding companies and above were British, and platoon-level officers were Indian. Companies were usually organised on a racial basis, with each one being formed from a particular caste, region or section of society. Despite the nominal titles used ('Rajput', 'Punjab' etc), battalions usually had companies from highly diverse areas, each with its own character and culture. This led to problems with languages and also in supplying the correct types of food to each company.[611]

The basic infantry weapon was the .303in calibre Short Magazine Lee Enfield (SMLE) rifle, which was rugged and accurate and came with a bayonet. Machine guns were also issued. The 'heavy' types, initially the Maxim but later the Vickers machine gun with a four-man crew, were used by battalion level units who could be moved around to where they were needed. Increasingly, each company, and then platoon had its own 'light' machine guns with two-man crews, either Lewis guns or the French Hotchkiss gun. Both of these lighter types had magazines with open sections that easily became clogged and jammed in sandy conditions.

Battalions were usually numbered as part of a larger regiment, although this latter was a largely administrative designation. As a rule, the 1st and 2nd battalions of a regiment were the regular troops, the 3rd and 4th battalions the part-time soldiers of the Territorial Army, and the 5th and 6th battalions the nominal formations of the Reserves (soldiers who had served as regulars and were bound to act as a reserve force for a set number of years). With the massive expansion of the army in 1914, many new battalions were established. The Territorial Army was meant only for home defence and not obliged to serve overseas, but the vast majority volunteered anyway. As a result, a 'second line' of battalions was established to take their place. The original units, with a '1/' prefix, were despatched to the war, while battalions with a '2/' prefix were raised at home. Many of these units, once fully trained, were despatched too, and a 'third line' ('3/') were raised in their place. Some of these third-line units would be sent to the front later in the war, and a fourth line established at home. The Indian, Australian and New Zealand forces had a straightforward numerical system of units, and the above system should not be confused with the Gurkha system of having multi-battalion regiments. For example, the 2/7th Gurkha Rifles refers to the 2nd Battalion of the 7th Regiment.

On active service, the regiment was (for infantry) a largely irrelevant concept. Instead, three or four battalions were grouped together to form brigades. Above that, three or four brigades were grouped into divisions, and two to four divisions would make up a corps. Brigades, divisions and corps had additional support troops attached, ranging from artillery and cavalry to signals, medical and administrative units.

The artillery was split into several groups, each prefixed in the British service with the title 'Royal'. Horse Artillery units were fast moving, with lighter guns, used for close support to attacks. Field Artillery units had heavier guns for harder pounding, positioned in rear of the front lines. Garrison Artillery units operated the big guns, mostly used in static positions such as coastal defences or fortresses, although they also operated some of the larger battlefield guns and mortars. The Indian forces also had Mountain Artillery, which were light guns (sometimes known as 'screw guns') that could be dismantled and carried to otherwise inaccessible areas on the backs of elephants, camels or mules. Artillery forces were usually organised into batteries of six guns, which could be further split into sections.

Unlike in the infantry, the regiment in the cavalry was a battlefield unit. As a note on terminology, technically the British, Australian and New Zealand cavalry were actually 'mounted rifles', who were to ride into battle and then fight on foot, although they would act like traditional cavalry when it came to scouting before and after battle. On occasion they would fight mounted.

In peacetime, cavalry units did not have separate equivalents to battalions, although some formed second-line units after the outbreak of the war. A regiment consisted of just over 500 officers and men, divided into three squadrons of 150 men plus a headquarters and a machine-gun section. Each squadron was sub-divided into four troops, and each troop into sections of four men. These men would ride four abreast on the march. As, in the vast majority of cases, the cavalry were supposed to only ride into action, and then fight on foot, one of those four would lead the horses of the other three to safety in battle. Obviously, this greatly weakened the fighting strength of the unit.

Armed with the same rifles as infantrymen for when they fought on foot, British and Indian cavalry also carried swords or (in the case of some of the latter) lances. Operating in very different conditions to the Western Front, the cavalry in Egypt and Palestine often had the opportunity to charge into an enemy with sword and lance, and, although they had only bayonets to use up until then, in 1918 the Australian and New Zealand cavalry were issued with swords as well.

Cavalry could be grouped together in brigades and divisions, and would be in Egypt and Palestine, but could also be attached as individual regiments to infantry divisions or corps. Here, they would be on hand to act as scouts or messengers for the different headquarters, or as a highly mobile reserve that could be despatched quickly to a point of danger or opportunity.

The Egyptian Army was in fact largely Sudanese and based in the Sudan. In 1914 it consisted of eight Egyptian, seven Sudanese, one South Sudanese and Bedouin Sudanese infantry battalions, several mounted infantry companies, the elite Camel Corps, and various support units of engineers and artillerymen. It amounted to about 18,000 men, of which about 14,000 were garrisoned in the Sudan. The army had been disbanded and re-raised in 1883 after the revolt against the *Khedive*, but continued to be organised largely along Ottoman lines and with Ottoman ranks. It now contained many British officers, and the men had British-style equipment and outdated British arms – the single-shot Martini-Henry rifle was in common use until late in the war. Soldiers were required to serve a number of years in the Regular Army, followed by a set number of years in the Army Reserve.

In 1914 the Egyptians were promised that they would not be required to fight the Ottomans but several artillery and engineering units were used for the defence of the Suez Canal in 1915 and during the Western Desert campaigns. On 20 January 1916 the Reserve was called up and put to fairly menial tasks such as the care of horses. This led to considerable unrest.

A further part of the Egyptian forces that saw extensive service was the Coastguard. This paramilitary force, also with many British officers, was split into a Sea Service and a Land Service. The former operated motor cruisers along the coast, while the Land Service patrolled the shorelines and borders of the country. They were largely concerned with stopping smuggling – which could be a dangerous business – therefore it had its own Camel Corps, mounted on distinctive white camels. They would see service in the Western Desert, the Sinai Desert and the Sinai Peninsula, and suffered a far higher desertion and defection rate than the Egyptian Army.

APPENDIX C

CANAL DEFENCES ORDER OF BATTLE, FEBRUARY 1915

GOC, Canal Defences: Major General A. Wilson

Sector I: Port Tewfik to Geneffe
HQ: Suez

30th Brigade (24th and 76th Punjabis, 126th Baluchis, 2/7th Gurkha Rifles)
1 Squadron Imperial Service Cavalry
1 Company Bikaner Camel Corps
½ Company Sappers and Miners
1 Battery Royal Field Artillery (Territorial)
1 Indian Field Ambulance
HMS *Ocean*
HMS *Himalaya*
HMS *Minerva*

Sector II: Deversoir to El Ferdan
HQ: Ismailia

22nd Brigade (62nd and 92nd Punjabis, 2/10th Gurkha Rifles, less 3rd Brahmins detached)
28th Field Force Brigade (51st and 53rd Sikhs, 56th Punjabis (1/5th Gurkha Rifles)
1 Squadron Imperial Service Cavalry
Bikaner Camel Corps (less 3½ Companies detached)
MG Section of Egyptian Camel Corps
1 Brigade Royal Field Artillery (Territorial)
1 Battery Indian Mountain Artillery
2 Field Ambulances
French warship *D'Entrecasteaux*
French warship *Requin*
RIMS *Hardinge*

Sector III: North of El Ferdan to Port Said
HQ: Kantara

29th Brigade (14th Sikhs, 69th and 89th Punjabis, 1/6th Gurkha Rifles)
3rd Brahmins (detached from 22nd Brigade)
1 Squadron Imperial Service Cavalry
2 Companies Bikaner Camel Corps
2 Batteries Royal Field Artillery (Territorial)
26th Battery Indian Mountain Artillery
Armoured Train with ½ Company of Indian infantry
Wireless Section (Territorial)
Indian Field Ambulance
Detachment Royal Army Medical Corps (Territorial)
HMS *Swiftsure*
HMS *Clio*

Advanced Depot: Zagazig

1 Battalion 32nd (Imperial Service) Brigade

Defence of Railway and Sweet Water Canal

1 Troop Imperial Service Cavalry
½ Company Bikaner Camel Corps
½ Company Indian infantry

General Reserve Camp: Moascar

31st Brigade (2nd Queen Victoria's Own Rajput Light Infantry, 27th Punjabis, 93rd Burma Infantry, 128th Pioneers)
32nd (Imperial Service) Brigade (less one battalion detached to Zagazig) (33rd Punjabis, Alwar, Gwalior and Patiala Infantry)
Imperial Service Cavalry Brigade (less 3 squadrons and 1 troop detached)
1 Egyptian Royal Engineers Section (Camels)
1 Egyptian Mountain Battery
2 Sections Field Artillery (attached to Cavalry Brigade)
3 Indian Field Ambulances

APPENDIX D

BRITISH FLYING SERVICES ORDER OF BATTLE, DECEMBER 1915

5th Wing, Royal Flying Corps
Lieutenant Colonel W.G.L. Salmond
HQ: Heliopolis
Aircraft Depot: Abbassia

14 Squadron: 2 Flights Ismailia
½ Flight Mersa Matruh
½ Flight Fayoum

17 Squadron: 2 Flights Suez
½ Flight El Hammam
½ Flight Heliopolis

Royal Naval Air Service

East Indies Fleet:
HMS *Ben-My-Chree*
HMS *Empress*

Eastern Mediterranean Station:
HMS *Ark Royal*

Seaplane Carriers (joint command):
HMS *Anne*
HMS *Raven II*

APPENDIX E

CATTLE RUSTLERS OF THE AEGEAN

The commander of the Eastern Mediterranean Squadron, Rear Admiral John de Robeck RN,[612] applied to the Admiralty in March 1916 for the Royal Naval Division (RND), surplus after the withdrawal from the Dardanelles, to be assigned to him to allow him to make raids against the Turkish coastline, with the twin aims of seeking out and destroying submarine bases or enemy stores and interdicting the supply of cattle (the RN used the term in its oldest sense, to mean all livestock) to Ottoman and German forces.[613] The request was refused as the RND was being sent to France, and a request for troops from Egypt was also turned down.[614] In the absence of any other possibilities, the Royal Navy in the Aegean now turned pirate.

The islands that are scattered along the western Anatolian coast of Asia Minor were in a mix of Greek and Italian[615] ownership, and several were occupied as bases by the Entente powers. The most notable were Lemnos, which was just to the north of the region and which included the major base at Mudros, and the island of Rhodes in the south. In the centre of this stretch of coast was the Gulf of Smyrna, and this whole coastline was known generically as Smyrna. Bases were established on several islands to facilitate the close blockade of the coast, including at Gaidaro, just south of the island of Samos, at Port Laki on the island of Leros just off the Gulf of Mendelyah, at Port Iero on the island of Mytilene, and Long Island within the Gulf of Smyrna itself. The main purposes of the bases were to prevent coastal traffic and seek out submarine bases, but de Robeck believed in maintaining an aggressive posture, trying 'to impress on my fellows that they must be at the Turk everyday'.[616] His policies included using his smaller ships – trawlers, gunboats and ketches, supported by destroyers and monitors (shallow-draft floating gun platforms) – to enter and search harbours and bays and where necessary destroy local craft or Ottoman defensive structures. As an extension to this, he thought that livestock, which he believed had been commandeered by the Ottoman government for their own uses or export to Germany, and other military stores should also be destroyed, as part of the wider blockade.[617] However, to do a proper job in this he needed landing parties, but the ships under his command simply had too small crews to spare men to go ashore.

The solution was to recruit Greek Irregulars – some were inhabitants of the islands and others ethnic Greeks who had been living in Anatolia but had fled Ottoman oppression since the start of the war. In March 1916 a small number were engaged on a trial basis, and orders were given to Captain Frank Larken RN of HMS *Doris*, who himself had gained considerable experience in operating landing parties in late 1914 and early 1915, and who now commanded the 6th Detached Squadron. Larken tasked one of his subordinates, Lieutenant Commander Bertram Drake RNR, captain of the minesweeper HMS *Whitby Abbey*, to conduct a landing in Lebedos Bay, just north of Skala Nova (modern-day Kusadasi). Under his command, apart from his own ship, was Trawler 1844 (formerly the trawler *St. Clair*) and six Greek caiques (small local fishing boats). On board these were thirty armed and six unarmed Greek Irregulars.

Landing at 2 a.m. on 22 March, the Irregulars immediately spread out and began rounding up the local livestock, seizing or chasing off the shepherds. At dawn, an Ottoman patrol emerged from the nearest village but the Irregulars ambushed them, capturing six and killing or wounding several more. By now, sheep, oxen and goats were being ferried by the caiques out to HMS *Whitby Abbey*, and penned on deck. At 11 a.m., Ottoman reinforcements arrived and took up positions overlooking the bay where the livestock was being loaded; shrapnel shells from HMS *Whitby Abbey* dispersed them but Drake decided not to push his luck, especially as the weather was turning bad. The last men and animals were collected and loaded (apart from two camels, which were left behind), and sailed for Long Island. Here the spoils were counted and divided. Of the 600 sheep, fifty goats, thirty oxen and five horses collected, the Greeks took 278 sheep, thirty goats and ten oxen.[618]

The raid had been a complete success, and within weeks other such forces were being arranged. The 6th Detached Squadron was joined by the 1st and 4th Detached Squadrons, and the coastline divided between them. They would take the bulk of the strain, although other units, including the 5th Destroyer Flotilla or French and Italian units were drafted in when necessary.[619]

As naval preparations were made, the needed infantry were gathered from throughout the islands. One officer drafted in to help with this, and who was placed in charge of the 1st Detached Squadron, was the unlikely figure of Lieutenant Commander John Myres RNVR.[620] A pre-war Oxford professor of classics, Myres knew the area and the languages and had been employed since late 1915 in running intelligence gathering operations among the Greek islands and the Anatolian coast out of Athens (under the cover of the 'British Refugee Relief Office'). Now he proved to be an enthusiastic raider, dubbed by his officers 'the Blackbeard of the Aegean' for his many successful cattle raids.[621] His contacts and local knowledge were used to raise volunteers, who, he recalled:

> Were partly professional cattle thieves (an ancient profession and well organised), and partly main-land peasants avoiding Turkish military service ... They were paraded in squads of ten under a 'dekanos' grouped by villages, and I gave them gay printed head kerchiefs of which they were very proud. The threat 'I will take away

your kerchief' was a severe one. They had no superior officers except the contractors who recruited them.[622]

In fact, discipline was not found to be that easy on the whole, and it would become an increasing issue as the summer dragged on. For now, though, there was no choice, and, besides, they had showed considerable promise during the first raid. Drake would report that:

> In the particular work of this occasion, no better men could have been found than the Irregulars, they acted with promptitude and pluck, obeying the orders given them … I am of the opinion that Irregulars could be more extensively made use of. There should be no lack of Volunteers for such work as this, up to some hundreds in Samos alone. There was considerable competition to be allowed to take part in this raid.[623]

Volunteers joined under a one-month contract and received training and a Mauser rifle. They received rations but had to pay for their own cartridges, as this was the 'only way to check promiscuous firing'.[624] Apart from the *dekanos*, leadership was provided by a small number of particularly gifted Greeks. One, called Asfalia but generally known as 'Longshanks', was recommended by Lieutenant Commander Gerald Hodson RN to Larken, as:

> undoubtedly a most able general on a small scale, [and] it would not be possible to find a better man to carry out the business at hand. I submit that it is advisable that he and some of his men should be permanently engaged.[625]

Myres agreed with this assessment, recommending that the navy 'engage all men through Longshanks and use him as C-in-C'.[626]

The three basic objectives of the force, as reiterated by Vice Admiral Sir Cecil Thursby RN when he replaced de Robeck, were:

- Capture or destruction of enemy guns
- Destruction of Ottoman lookout posts
- Removal or destruction of herds and flocks etc etc[627]

Only livestock and 'military stores' (which later included stocks of timber) were to be destroyed or brought off, and buildings being used by Ottoman forces, even if they were civilian houses, could be burnt, while Larken recorded after one raid that 'a good many threshing floors were fired, and the countryside was ablaze'.[628] As always, the definition of what was a legitimate target was highly questionable, and stern measures were put in place to try to keep the actions of the Irregulars even vaguely legal. Even so, they were frequently referred to as 'brigands' and de Robeck himself was even given that sobriquet by Sir Francis Elliot, the British Minister in Athens.[629]

Sometimes the Irregulars were searched on returning from an operation, and if anyone was found with personal loot, they were dismissed without pay. All of the official loot was pooled and either sold or a value set upon it. Half of the proceeds would then be evenly divided among the Irregulars (although a *dekanos* would some-times receive several shares[630]), and the other half placed into a reserve fund. This went to funding the operations – boat hire, rations, etc. – and also to provide special bounties. These could be for valorous acts, or for particular items destroyed or recov-ered. Those who captured or destroyed an artillery piece, for example, received £100; those who captured a rifle and bayonet received £4, or if they went one step further and captured the Ottoman soldier as well as his arms, £5.[631] On the other hand, lost equipment had to be paid for, ranging from 100 *francs* for a rifle, down to two *francs* for an oil bottle.[632]

An item on which less of a set value could be placed was refugees. Raiders fre-quently received pleas to bring off ethnic Greeks and their families who wished to escape from the Ottoman Empire. Officially, only men of military age were sup-posed to be rescued, although some leeway was given to 'non-combatants who were in danger of massacre, if left onshore'.[633] In practice, refugees seem to have been accepted wherever possible. During a raid on Asin, on 29 September, for example, farmer Hadji Stephanos and his family were not only allowed to leave with the raid-ers but boats allocated for his 'furniture and stores'.[634] On another occasion, a young Turkish woman and an 18-year-old boy were wounded in the crossfire during a raid and Larken authorised their evacuation (with the girl's parents and sister) so that proper medical treatment could be administered.[635]

During that particular raid, on 24 July 1916, a considerable force had been landed at the mouth of the Tuzla river, at the northern end of the Smyrna coastline. Larken had gathered a force consisting of the destroyer HMS *Renard*, the fleet sweeper HMS *Newmarket*, monitor *M33*, Motor Gunboat *Oomala*, ketches 251, 326, 334, 445, 705 and 706, the motor lighter from Port Iero, and a steamboat, as well as eighteen local craft carrying 172 Irregulars. A small force was landed to cut the telephone wires connecting the local coastal patrol houses, and the main force was put ashore at 2 a.m. on either bank of the river. Spreading out, they swept far inland, destroying coastal patrol posts and other military targets and herding livestock back to the river banks. Here, the smaller craft ferried them out to the larger ships, except for HMS *Renard* and *M33*. These were busy providing covering fire for the Irregulars, at an average range of 7,000yd (7,600m; communications were established with flag signals). After successfully sweeping the area, and under growing pressure from Ottoman infantry and aircraft, Larken pulled his force out at around midday, having collected one camel, forty-seven horses and ten foals, eighty-three donkeys, 267 bullocks and twenty-four calves, and 2,769 sheep and goats.[636] This was the general pattern for all of the raids, across the three detached squadrons. One officer, who was not too sure about using Greek 'Irregulars', recalled:

> We used to land the brigands late at night, the idea being that they surrounded the
> Turkish post and shot it up at dawn...After the Turkish post had been dealt with, the

cattle were raided, and some 2–300 head generally carried off in the trawlers and native craft.[637]

In fact, as with Larken's 24 July raid, often considerably more livestock than that was collected. This in itself could prove a considerable logistical problem. After a raid on 12 May north of Makaronia, Larken reported to de Robeck:

> The *Whitby Abbey* embarked the majority of the cattle, her officers and men working with most remarkable dexterity, slinging on board Camels, Horses, Water buffaloes, Bulls, etc, till the ship was crowded from stem to stern. Some of the Bulls were very fierce and one went mad after being embarked. It was a novel sight.[638]

It is hard to say how much damage these raids did to the enemy. Reports showed that some 6,000 Ottoman infantry were retained to counter the raids,[639] although the quality of those troops is questionable. Liman von Sanders, the German officer who commanded the Ottoman 5th Army, which had responsibility for this coast, records that by late 1916 it consisted 'almost exclusively of recruits and of the unfit'.[640] While von Sanders grinds his fair share of axes in his memoirs, written while a prisoner of the British immediately after the armistice, there is no doubt that by this time the Ottomans had indeed stripped as many home defence units as possible to bolster the forces in the Caucasus, Mesopotamia, the Hedjaz, and Palestine. Nor is there any doubt that many of the recruits would have been poorly armed. However, their forces were strong enough to retake Long Island (known to the Ottomans as Kösten Island), albeit mostly by the use of long-range artillery.[641]

Von Sanders records several other 'small active operations' to counter 'the piratical irruptions into Turkish territory', which he attributed to 'Greek robber bands that 'carried off women, children and herds of cattle, and burned the villages'.[642] He attributed a great reduction in the numbers of raids to these counter-measures, although the only two he gives any specifics on where carried out in September and November 1916. By then, international law was catching up with the Royal Navy.

The use of irregular, non-uniformed troops is always a legal grey area, and in this case it was complicated by Greece still being a neutral country. The Greek and Ottoman government both complained about the raids; the Greeks directly to London, and the Ottomans via the United States.[643] This is surely one of the few cases of those two governments agreeing on anything, and indeed the level of hereditary animosity between the Greeks and the Turks, and the possibility of resulting atrocities, was a major concern for all.[644] At the same time, shortages of small boats was causing problems in maintaining regular anti-shipping and anti-submarine patrols, without their diversion on to cattle raids, and the Royal Navy and French Navy as a whole were being distracted by the operation to seize the Greek fleet. On 26 October 1916 Thursby declared an end to the cattle raids, considering that they:

> Have now served their purpose, and their utility is more than counterbalanced by the difficulty they add to the maintenance of the blockade, the number of craft

employed on them, and the impossibility of controlling the irregular volunteers taking part.

In the case of operations carried out against military objectives, these take place in close proximity to the coast, where irregulars are more easily controlled, and opportunities for looting, etc., do not exist.[645]

The idea was again suggested by the commander on the spot in late 1917, but it received little support and was quietly forgotten again.[646]

APPENDIX F

EGYPTIAN EXPEDITIONARY FORCE ORDER OF BATTLE, APRIL 1916

General Headquarters

Commander-in-Chief: Lieutenant General (temp. General) Sir A.J. Murray, KCB, KCMG, CVO, DSO
Chief of the General Staff: Major General A.L. Lynden-Bell, CB, CMG

Australian and New Zealand Mounted Division

General Officer Commanding: Colonel (temp. Major General) H.G. Chauvel, CB, CMG

1st Australian Light Horse Brigade (Western Force)
Lieutenant Colonel C.F. Cox (acting)
1st, 2nd and 3rd Regiments Light Horse
Attached: 4th Regiment Light Horse

2nd Australian Light Horse Brigade
Colonel (temp. Brigadier General) G. de L Ryrie, CMG
5th, 6th and 7th Regiments Light Horse
Attached: 12th Regiment Light Horse

3rd Australian Light Horse Brigade
Brevet Lieutenant Colonel (temp. General) J.M. Antill, CB
8th, 9th and 10th Regiments Light Horse
Attached: 11th Regiment Light Horse

New Zealand Mounted Rifles Brigade
Brigadier General E.W.C. Chaytor, CB

Auckland, Canterbury and Wellington Mounted Rifles Regiments
Attached: Otago Mounted Rifles Regiment (less 1 sqdn)

Divisional Troops
Artillery:III (T.F.) Brigade, RHA, Leicester and Somerset Batteries
IV (T.F.) Brigade, RHA, Inverness and Ayr Batteries
Engineers: 1st Australian Field Squadron
Signal Service: 1st A & NZ Signal Squadron
ASC: HQ Light Horse Divisional ASC
Light Horse Supply Column (MT)
Medical: 1st, 2nd and 3rd LH Field Ambulances, NZ Mounted Brigade Ambulance

IX Corps

General Officer Commanding: Major General (temp. Lieutenant General) Sir
F.J. Davies, KCB, KCMG

Corps Troops
Colonel (temp. Brigadier General) A.H.M. Taylor, DSO

8th Mounted Brigade
1/1st City of London Yeomanry
1/1st and L/3rd County of London Yeomanry
1/1st London Signal Troop
'B' Battery, HAC
No. 9 Field Troop
1/1st London Mounted Brigade Field Ambulance

Signal Service
'HH' and 'KK' Cable Section
London Pack and Northern Wagon Wireless Sections

42nd (East Lancashire) Division
General Officer Commanding: Major General Sir W. Douglas, KCMG, CB

125th Infantry Brigade
Colonel (temp. Brigadier General) H.C. Frith
1/5th, 1/6th, 1/7th and 1/8th Lancashire Fusiliers
125th Brigade Machine Gun Company

126th Infantry Brigade
Major (temp. Brigadier General) A.W. Tufnell
1/4th and 1/5th East Lancashire Regiment

1/9th and 1/10th Manchester Regiment
126th Brigade Machine Gun Company

127th Infantry Brigade
Lieutenant Colonel (temp. Brigadier General) V.A. Ormsby, CB
1/5th, 1/6th, 1/7th and 1/8th Manchester Regiment
127th Brigade Machine Gun Company

Divisional Troops
Mounted Troops: 1 Sqdn Duke of Lancaster's Yeomanry
13th Cyclist Company
Artillery: 1/1st, 1/2nd and 1/3rd E. Lancashire Brigades, RFA
1/4th E. Lancashire (How.) Brigade, RFA
42nd Divisional Ammunition Column
Engineers: 1/1st and 1/2nd E. Lancashire Field Company, RE
1/2nd W. Lancashire Field Company, RE
Signal Service: 42nd Divisional Signal Company
ASC: 42nd Divisional Train
Medical: 1/1st, 1/2nd and 1/3rd E. Lancashire Field Ambulances

Attached
3rd Dismounted Brigade
Lieutenant Colonel Lord Kensington, DSO

1/1st E. Kent Yeomanry
1/1st W. Kent Yeomanry
1/1st Sussex Yeomanry
1/1st Welsh Horse
1/1st Norfolk Yeomanry
1/1st Suffolk Yeomanry
Machine Gun Company
3rd Dismounted Brigade Signal Troop
1/1st Eastern and 1/1st S. Eastern Mounted Brigade Field Ambulances

54th (East Anglian) Division
General Officer Commanding: Colonel (temp. Major General) S.W. Hare, CB

161st Infantry Brigade
Colonel (temp. Brigadier General) F.F.W. Daniell
1/4th, 1/5th, 1/6th and 1/7th Essex Regiment
161st Brigade Machine Gun Company
162nd Infantry Brigade
Lieutenant Colonel (temp. Brigadier General) A. Mudge
1/5th Bedford Regiment

1/4th Northampton Regiment
1/10th and 1/11th London Regiment
162nd Brigade Machine Gun Company

163rd Infantry Brigade
Major (Hon. Colonel, Temp. Brigadier General) T. Ward
1/4th and 1/5th Norfolk Regiment
1/5th Suffolk Regiment
1/8th Hampshire Regiment
163rd Brigade Machine Gun Company

Divisional Troops
Mounted Troops: 1 Sqdn 1/1st Hertfordshire Yeomanry (with HQ and Machine Gun Section)
Artillery: 1/1st, 1/2nd, 1/3rd and 1/4th E. Anglian Brigades, RFA
54th Divisional Ammunition Column
Engineers: 2/1st E. Anglian Field Company, RE
1/2nd E. Anglian Field Company, RE
1/1st Kent Field Company, RE
Signal Service: 54th Divisional Signal Company
ASC: 54th Divisional Train
Medical: 2/1st, 1/2nd and 1/3rd E. Anglian Field Ambulances.

Attached
20th (Indian) Infantry Brigade
Brigadier General H.D. Watson, CMG
2/3rd Gurkhas
58th Rifles
Alwar Infantry
Gwalior Infantry

29th Indian Infantry Brigade
Colonel (temp. Brigadier General) P.C. Palin
23rd Pioneers
57th Rifles
Patiala Infantry
No. 10 Coy, QO Sappers and Miners
110, 121 and 135 Indian Field Ambulances
7th and 26th Mule Corps

II Australian and New Zealand Army Corps

General Officer Commanding: Major General (temp. Lieutenant General) Sir A.J. Godley, KCMG, CB

Corps Troops
Signal Service: No. 24 Airline Section
'FF' and 'NN' Cable Sections
ASC: 1st Australian Ammunition Park
1st Australian Supply Column
Engineers: Royal Australian Reserve Naval Bridging Train
14th Fortress Company, RE

4th Australian Division
General Officer Commanding: Major General Sir H.V. Cox, KCMG, CB, CIE

4th Australian Infantry Brigade
Colonel (temp. Brigadier General) J. Monash, CB
13th, 14th, 15th and 16th Battalions
4th Machine Gun Company

12th Australian Infantry Brigade
Major (temp. Lieutenant Colonel) D. Glasfurd
45th, 46th, 47th and 48th Battalions
12th Machine Gun Company

13th Australian Infantry Brigade
Lieutenant Colonel D.W. Glasgow, DSO
49th, 50th, 51st and 52nd Battalions
13th Machine Gun Company

Divisional Troops
Mounted Troops: 'B' Sqdn 13th Light Horse Regiment
4th Divisional Cyclist Company
Artillery: X, XI and XII Field Artillery Brigades
XXIV Howitzer Brigade
4th Divisional Ammunition Column
Engineers: 4th, 12th and 13th Field Companies
Signal Service: 4th Divisional Signal Company
Pioneers: 4th Pioneer Battalion
ASC: 7th, 14th, 26th and 27th Coys, AASC
Medical: 4th, 12th and 13th Field Ambulances

5th Australian Division

General Officer Commanding: Colonel (temp. Major General) Hon. J. McCay, CB

8th Australian Infantry Brigade
Colonel (temp. Brigadier General) E. Tivey, DSO
29th, 30th, 31st and 32nd Battalions
8th Machine Gun Company

14th Australian Infantry Brigade
Colonel (temp. Brigadier General) G.G.H. lrving
53rd, 54th, 55th and 56th Battalions
14th Machine Gun Company

15th Australian Infantry Brigade
Lieutenant Colonel (temp. Colonel) H.E. Elliott
57th, 58th, 59th and 60th Battalions
15th Machine Gun Company

Divisional Troops
Mounted Troops: 'C' Sqdn 13th Light Horse Regiment
5th Divisional Cyclist Company
Artillery: XIII, XIV and XV Field Artillery Brigades
XXV Howitzer Brigade
5th Divisional Ammunition Column
Engineers: 8th, 14th and 15th Field Companies
Signal Service: 5th Divisional Signal Company
Pioneers: 5th Pioneer Battalion
ASC: 10th, 18th, 28th and 29th Coys., AASC
Medical Units: 8th, 14th and 15th Field Ambulances

11th Division

General Officer Commanding: Major General E.A. Fanshawe, CB

32nd Infantry Brigade
Brevet Lieutenant Colonel (temp. Brigadier General) T.H.F. Price
9th West Yorkshire Regiment
6th Yorkshire Regiment
8th West Riding Regiment
6th York and Lancaster Regiment
32nd Brigade Machine Gun Company

33rd Infantry Brigade
Colonel (temp. Brigadier General) J.F. Erskine
6th Lincolnshire Regiment

6th Border Regiment
7th South Staffordshire Regiment
9th Notts and Derby Regiment
33rd Brigade Machine Gun Company

34th Infantry Brigade
Colonel (temp. Brigadier General) J. Hill, DSO
8th Northumberland Fusiliers
9th Lancashire Fusiliers
5th Dorsetshire Regiment
11th Manchester Regiment
34th Brigade Machine Gun Company

Divisional Troops
Mounted Troops: 1 Sqdn 1/1st Hertfordshire Yeomanry
11th Cyclist Company
Artillery: LVIII, LIX, LX and CXXXIII Brigades, RFA
Engineers: 67th, 68th and 86th Field Companies, RE
Signal Service: 11th Divisional Signal Company
Pioneers: 6th East Yorkshire Regiment
ASC: 11th Divisional Train
Medical: 33rd, 34th and 35th Field Ambulances

No. 3 Section, Canal Defences
General Officer Commanding etc., as Headquarters, 52nd Division

Corps Troops
Mounted Troops: 5th Mounted Brigade
Colonel (temp. Brigadier General) E.A. Wiggin, DSO
1/1st Warwickshire Yeomanry
1/1st Gloucestershire Yeomanry
1/1st Worcestershire Yeomanry
1/1st S. Midland Signal Troop
'A' Battery, HAC
No. 7 Field Troop
1/1st S. Midland Mounted Brigade Field Ambulance
Engineers: 220th Army Troops Company, RE
Signal Service: No. 21 Airline Section
'WW' Cable Section

52nd (Lowland) Division
General Officer Commanding: Major General Hon. H.A. Lawrence

155th Infantry Brigade
Lieutenant Colonel (temp. Brigadier General) J.B. Pollok-M'Call
1/4th and 1/5th Royal Scots Fusiliers
1/4th and 1/5th King's Own Scottish Borderers
155th Brigade Machine Gun Company

156th Infantry Brigade
Brevet Colonel (temp. Brigadier General) L.C. Koe
1/4th and 1/7th Royal Scots
1/7th and 1/8th Scottish Rifles
156th Brigade Machine Gun Company

157th Infantry Brigade
Brevet Colonel (temp. Brigadier General) H.G. Casson, CMG
1/5th, 1/6th and 1/7th Highland Light Infantry
1/5th Argyll and Sutherland Highlanders
157th Brigade Machine Gun Company

Divisional Troops
Mounted Troops: HQ and 'C' Squadron, Royal Glasgow Yeomanry
52nd Cyclist Company
Artillery: 1/2nd, 1/3rd, 1/4th and 1/5th Lowland Brigades, RFA
52nd Divisional Ammunition Column
Engineers: 2/1st, 2/2nd and 1/2nd Lowland Field Companies, RE
Signal Service: 52nd Divisional Signal Company
ASC: 52nd Divisional Train
Medical Units: 1/1st, 1/2nd, 1/3rd Lowland Field Ambulances

Attached
1st Dismounted Brigade
Temp. Brigadier General the Marquess of Tullibardine, MVO, DSO
1/Lst, 1/2nd and 1/3rd Scottish Horse
1/1st Ayr Yeomanry
1/1st Lanark Yeomanry
Machine Gun Company
1st Dismounted Brigade Signal Troop
1/1st Scottish Horse and 1/1st Lowland Field Ambulances

Western Frontier Force

General Officer Commanding: Major General W.E. Peyton, CVO, CB, DSO

Force Troops
Mounted Troops: 6th Mounted Brigade
Lieutenant Colonel (temp. Brigadier General) Viscount Hampden, CMG
1/1st Buckinghamshire Yeomanry
1/1st Berkshire Yeomanry
1/1st Dorsetshire Yeomanry
1/2nd S. Midland Field Troop Signal
No. 6 Field Troop
1/2nd S. Midland Mounted Brigade Field Ambulance
Attached: 1/2nd County of London Yeomanry
Royal Flying Corps: No. 17 Squadron
Artillery: 1/1st Berkshire Battery, RHA
1/1st Nottinghamshire Battery, RHA
Infantry: 1st, 2nd and 3rd Battalions, British West Indies Regiment
Signal Service: 2nd Mounted Divisional Signal Squadron
No. 42 Airline Section
'UU' Cable Section
No. 6 Pack Wireless Section

North-Western Section
General Officer Commanding, etc., as Headquarters, 53rd Division

53rd (Welsh) Division
General Officer Commanding: Colonel (temp. Major General) A.E. Dallas, CB

158th Infantry Brigade
Major (temp. Brigadier General) S.F. Mott
1/5th, 1/6th and 1/7th Royal Welch Fusiliers
1/1st Herefordshire Regiment
158th Brigade Machine Gun Company
159th Infantry Brigade
Colonel (temp. Brigadier General) J.H. du B. Travers, CB
1/4th and 1/7th Cheshire Regiment
1/4th and 1/5th Welch Regiment
159th Brigade Machine Gun Company
160th Infantry Brigade
Colonel (temp. Brigadier General) W.J.C. Butler
1/4th Royal Sussex Regiment
2/4th Royal West Surrey Regiment
2/4th Royal West Kent Regiment
2/10th Middlesex Regiment
160th Brigade Machine Gun Company

Divisional Troops
Mounted Troops: 1 Sqn 1/1st Hertfordshire Yeomanry
53rd Divisional Cyclist Company
Artillery: 1/1st Cheshire Brigade, RFA
1/1st, 1/2nd and 1/4th Welsh Brigades, RFA
53rd Divisional Ammunition Column
Engineers: 1/1st and 2/1st Welsh Field Companies, RE
2/1st Cheshire Field Company, RE
Signal Service: 53rd Divisional Signal Company
ASC: 53rd Divisional Train
Medical: 1/1st, 1/2nd and 1/3rd Welsh Field Ambulances

Attached
4th Dismounted Brigade
Colonel (temp. Brigadier General) E.A. Herbert, MVO
1/1st Shropshire Yeomanry
1/1st Denbigh Yeomanry
1/1st Cheshire Yeomanry
1/1st Glamorgan Yeomanry
1/1st Montgomery Yeomanry
1/1st Pembroke Yeomanry
Machine Gun Company
4th Dismounted Brigade Signal Troop
1/1st Welsh Border and 1/1st S. Wales Mounted Brigade Field Ambulances
22nd Mounted Brigade
Lieutenant Colonel (temp. Brigadier General) W. Bromley-Davenport, DSO
1/1st Lincolnshire Yeomanry
1/1st Staffordshire Yeomanry
1/1st East Riding Yeomanry
Signal Troop
Mounted Brigade, ASC
Mounted Brigade Field Ambulance

Provisional Infantry Brigade (less Headquarters)
1/6th Royal Scots
2/5th Devonshire Regiment
2/7th and 2/8th Middlesex Regiment
2nd Garrison Battalion, Liverpool Regiment
2 Naval 4in guns
1/2nd Kent Field Company, RE
17th Motor Machine Gun Battery
No.1 Armoured Train

South-Western Section

General Officer Commanding: Colonel (temp. Brigadier General) H.W. Hodgson, CVO

Mounted Troops: 1st Australian Light Horse Brigade
(*See* A & NZ Mounted Division)
1 Sqn Egyptian Army Cavalry
Infantry: 2nd Garrison Battalion, Cheshire Regiment
1 Company and Machine Gun Section, Egyptian Army
Signal Service: Detachment, 2nd Mounted Divisional Signal Sqn
Emergency Sqn, Royal Naval Armoured Car Division
HQ and Nos. 1, 2 and 3 Light Armoured Motor Batteries
No. 2 Armoured Train

General Headquarters Troops

Mounted Troops: Imperial Camel Corps
Bikaner Camel Corps
Royal Flying Corps: 5th Wing Royal Flying Corps
Lieutenant Colonel W.G.H. Salmond

No. 14 Squadron
No. 17 Squadron (with Western Force)
2 Kite Balloon Sections (Naval)
Artillery: Heavy Artillery
XX Brigade, RGA
10th, 15th and 91st Heavy Batteries, RGA
1 Heavy Battery and 1 Section Heavy Battery, Royal Marine Artillery
Stokes Gun, Batteries of:
125th, 126th, 161st and 162nd Brigade Batteries
Anti-Aircraft Artillery:
Nos. 30 and 38 Anti-Aircraft Sections
Mountain Artillery:
4th Highland Mountain Battery, RGA
Armoured Cars:
Nos. 11 and 12 Armoured Motor Batteries
Engineers: 115th, 116th and 276th Railway Companies, RE
Signal Service: GHQ Signal Company
Nos. 14 and 15 Airline Sections
'NA', 'NB' and 'W' Cable Sections
Unallotted:
Southern Motor, W/T Station
No. 5 Pack Wireless Section
ASC: 338th, 493rd and 619th Mechanical Transport Companies, ASC

Transport: Camel Transport Corps
59th, 62nd, 70th and 191st Camel Corps

Lines of Communications Defence Troops

Mounted Troops: Imperial Service Cavalry Brigade
Major (temp. Brigadier General) M.H. Henderson

Mysore Lancers
1st Hyderabad Lancers
Kathiawar Signal Troop
124th Indian Cavalry Field Ambulance
Infantry: 1st Garrison Battalion, Essex Regiment
2nd Garrison Battalion, Royal Welch Fusiliers
1st Garrison Battalion, Devonshire Regiment
1st Garrison Battalion, Royal Scots (less 2 companies)
1st Garrison Battalion, Liverpool Regiment
1st Garrison Battalion, Royal Irish Regiment
19th, 20th, 21st and 22nd Garrison Battalions, Rifle Brigade
1st Garrison Battalion, Royal Warwickshire Regiment (Khartoum)

Alexandria District

Colonel (temp. Brigadier General) R.C. Boyle, CB

Coastal Defence Artillery: 84th Siege Battery, RGA
92nd Company, RGA, Mex Battery
Ras el Tin Battery
Silsileh Battery
'Y' Battery Royal Malta Artillery

Lines of Communication Units

Commandant and Inspector General of Communications: Major General (temp. Lieutenant General) Sir E.A. Altham, KCB, CMG
Infantry: 1st Garrison Battalion, Notts and Derby Regiment
1st Garrison Battalion, Northamptonshire Regiment
2 Companies, 1st Garrison Battalion, Royal Scots (Cyprus)
Signal Service: Nos. 12 and 23 Airline Sections
Engineers: 13th Base Park Company, RE
46th Advanced Park Company, RE
3rd Lancashire Army Troops Company, RE
1/3rd Devon Army Troops Company, RE
No. 5 Siege Company, Royal Anglesea RE

Nos. 2, 3, 4, 5 and 6 Egyptian Works Companies
ASC: 10th Australian Reserve Park
Indian Mule Cart Corps
Labour Companies: Nos. 24 and 27 Egyptian Labour Corps
Depot Units of Supply: Nos. 40, 41, 47, 48, 49, 50, 51, 52, 53, 54, 55, 56, 62, 63, 65, 66, 104, 105, 136, 137, 143, 144, 145, 146, 147, 175, 176, 177, 178, 180, 182, 190, 191, 193, 194, 195, 200, 201, 202, 217, 218, 219, 220, 228, 229, 230, 231, 258, 259, 260, 261, 262, 263, 265, 266, 268, 269, 270, 276, 360, 373, 374, 376, 377. Nos. 16, 17, 18, 19, 20, 21, 22, 23, 24, 25 Australian Railway Supply Detachments: Nos. 17 and 56, 1st and 11th Australian Field Bakeries: 29th, 36th, 40th, 42nd, 50th, 51st, 55th, 71st, 4th and 5th Australian Field Butcheries: 10th, 11th, 29th, 32nd, 40th, 42nd, 51st, 52nd, 4th and 5th Australian 345th and 347th Mechanical Transport Companies, ASC
Royal Naval SAA Column (275th Company, ASC)
No. 6 (Auxiliary) Transport Company ASC
Base Horse Transport Depot (No. 137 Company, ASC)
Base Mechanical Transport Depot (No. 500 Company, ASC)
Medical: Nos. 18, 21, 22, 24, 29, 30, 31, 46, 52, 53, 54, 80, 89, 90, 91 and 93 Sanitary Sections
Nos. 13, 24, 26, 53, 54, and 2nd Australian Casualty Clearing Stations
Nos. 15, 17, 19, 21, 27, 31, 3 Australian & New Zealand General Hospitals
Nos. 16, 17 and 18, 1st and 2nd Australian, 1, 2 and 3 Canadian, and Camel Transport Corps Depot Stationary Hospitals
Ordnance Units: Nos. 11, 16, 26, 27, 31, 32, 38, 39, 47, 55 and 58 Companies, AOC
No. 9 Company, AOC (Egyptian Section)
3 Ordnance Travelling Workshops
Veterinary Units: Nos. 11, 17 and 18 Veterinary Sections
Base Depot Veterinary Stores
Advanced Base Depot Veterinary Stores
Base Veterinary Hospital
Nos. 16, 20, 21 and 22 Veterinary Hospitals
Postal Units: Advanced Base Post Office
1 Base Postal Detachment and 11th Postal Detachment

APPENDIX G

IMPERIAL STRATEGIC RESERVE, 1916

11th Division to France 28 June 1916

13th Division to Mesopotamia 15 February 1916

29th Division to France 15 March 1916

31st Division to France 18 February 1916

42nd Division remained in Egypt

46th Division to France 4 February 1916

52nd Division remained in Egypt

53rd Division remained in Egypt

54th Division remained in Egypt

1st Australian Division to France 22 March 1916

2nd Australian Division to France 16 March 1916

4th Australian Division (formed from ANZAC Depot March 1916) to France 3 June 1916

5th Australian Division (formed from ANZAC Depot March 1916) to France 18 June 1916

New Zealand Division (formed from ANZAC Depot March 1916) to France 6 April 1916

APPENDIX H

BATTLE OF ROMANI ORDERS OF BATTLE, AUGUST 1916

British and Imperial Forces

No. 3 Canal Section

Major General Hon. Herbert Lawrence

Australian and New Zealand Mounted Division
Colonel (temp. Major General) H.G. Chauvel

1st Australian Light Horse Brigade (Western Force)
Lieutenant Colonel John Meredith (vice Lieutenant Colonel Charles Cox)
1st, 2nd and 3rd Regiments Light Horse

2nd Australian Light Horse Brigade
Colonel John Royston (vice Colonel G. de L Ryrie)
6th and 7th Regiments Light Horse
Wellington Mounted Rifles Regiment

42nd Division
Major General Sir W. Douglas

125th Infantry Brigade
Colonel (temp. Brigadier General) H.C. Frith
1/5th, 1/6th, 1/7th and 1/8th Lancashire Fusiliers
125th Brigade Machine Gun Company

126th Infantry Brigade
Major (temp. Brigadier General) A.W. Tufnell
1/4th and 1/5th East Lancashire Regiment

1/9th and 1/10th Manchester Regiment
126th Brigade Machine Gun Company

127th Infantry Brigade
Lieutenant Colonel (temp. Brigadier General) V.A. Ormsby
1/5th, 1/6th, 1/7th and 1/8th Manchester Regiment
1/6th Manchester Regiment
127th Brigade Machine Gun Company

52nd (Lowland) Division
General W.E.B. Smith (vice Major General Lawrence)

155th Infantry Brigade
Lieutenant Colonel (temp. Brigadier General) J.B. Pollok-McCall
1/4th and 1/5th Royal Scots Fusiliers
1/4th and 1/5th King's Own Scottish Borderers
155th Brigade Machine Gun Company

156th Infantry Brigade
Brevet Colonel (temp. Brigadier General) L.C. Koe
1/4th and 1/7th Royal Scots
1/7th and 1/8th Scottish Rifles
156th Brigade Machine Gun Company

157th Infantry Brigade
Brevet Colonel (temp. Brigadier General) H.G. Casson
1/5th, 1/6th and 1/7th Highland Light Infantry
1/5th Argyll and Sutherland Highlanders
157th Brigade Machine Gun Company

158th Infantry Brigade (attached from No. 53 Division)
Major (temp. Brigadier General) S.F. Mott
1/5th, 1/6th and 1/7th Royal Welch Fusiliers
1/1st Herefordshire Regiment
158th Brigade Machine Gun Company

3rd Australian Light Horse Brigade
General John Antill

8th, 9th and 10th Regiments Light Horse

Sector Mounted Troops
Brigadier General E.W.C. Chaytor
New Zealand Mounted Rifles Brigade
Auckland and Canterbury Mounted Rifles Regiments
5th Regiment Light Horse

5th Mounted Brigade
Colonel (temp. Brigadier General) E.A. Wiggin
1/1st Warwickshire Yeomanry
1/1st Gloucestershire Yeomanry
1/1st Worcestershire Yeomanry

Ottoman Forces

Fourth Army

Djemal Pasha

Expeditionary Force

Colonel Kress von Kressenstein

3rd Infantry Division
Colonel Refet Bele

31st Infantry Regiment
Lieutenant Colonel Ismail Hakki Bey
1st, 2nd, 3rd and 4th Battalions

32nd Infantry Regiment
Lieutenant Colonel Hasan Basri Bey (from 5 August Lieutenant Colonel Ibrahim Bey)
1st, 2nd, 3rd and 4th Battalions

39th Infantry Regiment
Lieutenant Colonel Nurettin Bey (from 4 August Major Kamil Bey)
1st, 2nd, 3rd and 4th Battalions
Attached Troops
2nd Independent Camel Company (Lieutenant Colonel Bischof)
2nd Battalion 81st Infantry Regiment
3rd Regiment of Mountain Artillery

32nd Machine Gun Company
1/1st, 4/2nd and 1/5th Engineer Companies
German Units
601st, 602nd, 603rd, 604th, 605th, 606th, 607th and 608th Machine Gun Companies
60th Battalion Heavy Artillery

Austrian Units
No. 9 Mortar Battery
No. 36 Howitzer Battery

APPENDIX J

PRISONERS OF WAR IN TURKEY

At the start of this book we saw Arthur Dabbs and scores of his comrades being captured at Katia. From the point of view of the Egyptian campaign this was the biggest collection of prisoners for the Ottomans, although it pales in comparison to the surrender, at around the same time, of around 13,000 British and Indian troops at Kut El Amara in Mesopotamia. Small numbers would also go 'into the bag' at Gallipoli (including submariners), in Palestine, elsewhere in Mesopotamia, and the odd airman would be rounded up after being shot down.

In all, approximately 16,583 British and Imperial troops would be captured by the Ottomans.[647] Their experiences as prisoners would vary greatly, partly based on their rank (which denoted to some extent their treatment), but also on the whims of their gaolers and the physical geography of their surroundings. The majority of prisoners were taken into the mountainous regions of Anatolia. With the dilapidated state of the Ottoman transport system, simply getting there would prove a challenge. Those captured at Katia, for example, were marched back across the Sinai with only the most basic of kit and rations.

Once in Anatolia, officers and other ranks were separated. The luckier 'other ranks' prisoners would be assigned as orderlies to the officer's camps. The less lucky ones were often put into their own cramped, uncomfortable camps in the mountains. Food was supplied on the same scale as for Ottoman other ranks, and was of poor quality. Clothing, extra food, and other necessities from soap to candles had to be bought by the prisoners themselves, for which they received an allowance in Turkish Pounds (£T). The British government forwarded them £T10 a month from their pay, and the Ottomans offered a further £T1 per week to those willing to work for them. This meant relief from the boredom of camp life and a chance to earn extra money that could make the difference between life and death. Many jumped at the chance, although many others were simply conscripted.

The working parties faced hard work in grim conditions. The most common tasks were building roads and railways through the mountains, working in all weathers with inadequate clothing and tools, often besides Russian prisoners and Ottoman slave labour. As the months passed sickness and death rates soared. Medical care was rudimentary and a man refusing to work was more likely to face a beating or even a flogging than be referred to a doctor.

Being separated into small parties in largely inaccessible areas, there was little the Red Cross could do. At best they could make sure that post and parcels of comforts arrived regularly, but as the Ottoman guards were fed and clothed as poorly as the prisoners themselves these were likely to be stolen. Equally, escape from the working parties was almost unthinkable. In their weakened condition, and with no chance to build-up the supplies needed to support an escape, the mountains were more effective gaolers than the Ottoman guards.

Officer faced betters odds of escape, and just over 1,500 men did during the war. The obstacles involved were considerable. Lieutenant Elias Jones recalled:

> The real sentries were the 350 miles of mountain, rock and desert that lay between us and freedom in every direction. Such a journey under the most favourable conditions is something of an ordeal. I would not like to have to walk it by daylight, in peace-time, buying food at villages as I went. Consider that for the runaway the ground would have to be covered at night, that food for the whole distance would have to be carried, and that the country was infested with brigands who stripped travellers even within gunshot of our camp; add to this that we knew nothing of the language or customs of the people and had no maps.[648]

Officers usually had slightly more means with which to build-up supplies for an escape attempt, and occasionally small groups of officers would make a bid for freedom, exploiting the fact that most of the guards (known as 'gamekeepers') were old men or those who had been rejected from front-line service on health grounds, and whose already low motivation was compounded by boredom every bit as great as their captives'. The usual escape route was to the north, to reach the Russian forces in the Caucusus.

Most escapees were rapidly caught and brutal retribution would be poured onto the offending camp. Lieutenant Jones teamed up with RFC officer Cedric Hill[649] and exploited an act they had worked up to help relieve the boredom in the camp. They had made a Ouija board and had become adept at faking séances. Their highly superstitious camp commandant had heard of their exploits, and in return for better billets and treatment they had agreed to act as intermediaries between him and the spirit world. Eventually, they convinced him that they were in contact with the spirit of an Armenian who knew where a vast treasure had been buried. In April 1918 they convinced the commandant to search for the treasure, and the two officers led a small party off into the mountains. After months of wandering, they arrived in Constantinople in August, and Jones and Hill managed to get themselves committed to hospital. After a further six weeks of incredible hardship, they were declared to be lunatics; as such, they were liable for compassionate repatriation. It almost seems a shame, after all that they had been through, that the war ended before they could sail for home. Theirs remains surely one of the most remarkable escape stories of any war, and both published memoirs that are riveting reads.

The majority of personnel simply resigned themselves to captivity and waited. The lot of the officers was easier in many ways, but still far from comfortable. The permanent 'camps' for the officers usually consisted of a clutch of commandeered houses in an isolated hamlet. Typically, the first intake of officers would be constrained to one house, often crammed in with barely room to sit or lie down, until perimeters could be established and the newly appointed commandant came to terms with his duties. At Yozgad, for example, all of the officers and their orderlies were initially confined to two large houses, with simple holes in the floor of one room to act as latrines (leading to an outbreak of typhus). It was some days before the guards could be persuaded to let the prisoners take it in turns to stand on the doorstep, and longer still until they were allowed to walk the few yards either side of the doorway. Eventually, over the course of some months, a small compound was expanded to include several houses, the lane between them, and then into the fields on either side. The slightest transgression would still see the prisoners reconfined for days on end, and the process of expansion begin again. Meanwhile, each officer had to pay rent for his accommodation.

Unlike the other ranks, officers also had to pay for their food, and so they received a larger allowance: the equivalent of four shillings a day from the Ottoman Government, and £T18 per month from the British. As well as rent, this had to cover the purchase and preparation of their food. Many camps had a designated supplier appointed by the commandant, but this arrangement was wide open to abuse, and inflated prices led to many camps insisting on being able to buy their own food directly from the local markets. Even here, prices soon rose. Most of the hamlets used were isolated, and the local farming primarily operated at subsistence levels. With the arrival of the prisoners scores or hundreds of new mouths had been foisted into the local economy and supply struggled to meet demand. In August 1916 the equivalent of a standard daily British ration (¼lb beef, 1¼lb bread and 8oz potatoes) cost an officer two shillings and sixpence. On top of this he would have had to purchase clothing, candles, fuel for the fire, tea, milk, sugar and anything required to vary this bland diet. By January 1918 the same officer was paying thirty-six shillings for the same ration, and some items, such as tea, had risen in price by over 1,000 per cent.

Under the Geneva Convention, officers were not allowed to work to supplement their wages, and perhaps to compensate for this the Red Cross began to add their own, ever increasing allowance to the pay of the officers. Food parcels could be sent from home but these were often looted by the guards (although the wooden boxes they came in could often be salvaged to build furniture or feed fires). Frequently the only way for officers to survive was with money sent from home or through cashing personal cheques either with local shopkeepers or through various amenable embassies. Indeed, the neutral embassies were in many ways life savers; in the winter of 1916–17 the American Embassy in Constantinople provided cold-weather clothing to prisoners who only had their desert uniforms to wear. The American, Swiss and Netherlands Embassies in particular provided material as well as financial assistance.

Simply passing the time was one of the major problems. The boredom and inactivity, the confinement and privations that they were suffering were never far from their minds, and depression often lurked nearby. Lieutenant George Wright would write home:

> Will it ever end? To walk about here during a beautiful sunny day I often think what an awful waste of time it all is, and what a beautiful day it would be if I were only at home free to go where I liked instead of meeting a sentry at the end of the path with a rifle 'This far shallt thou go and no further'. Oh for peace again, when there will be no more destruction and killing and waste. To be free again, to write a letter without having to think whether I can say this or that without fear of having my letter torn up, to do useful work again and not waste day after day with nothing attempted & nothing done, to eat decent food and drink decent liquid once more; I shall have learnt to appreciate every good thing by the time I get back to it again.[650]

Some men could escape purely in their heads, dreaming of the lavish meals that freedom would bring, or the places they would be able to go. Lieutenant Sir Joseph Napier wrote home:

> I am still planning tours big and small, for my return to England. All prisoners seem filled with the same desire to travel round England on their return, and hunt up old spots.[651]

Others needed more active ways to occupy their minds. Some activities could be found to kill two birds with one stone, passing the time and supplying food; gardening, for example, and husbandry. George Wright would write to his mother how:

> We are rearing young Turkeys and chickens & I have a pair of pigeons which I am trying to induce to breed. We have hatched 16 Turkeys out of 19 eggs so far & there are two more broods to hatch yet.

Other animals were slightly less practical for food, but still passed the time; Wright would later try his hand at caterpillar breeding.

Expert help was often at hand. Prisoners were held from all three armed services and from all over the Empire, and there were men with experience in a staggering range of pursuits. Lectures, classes and debates were a common occurrence. Lieutenant Arthur Holyoake found that the essentially civilian character of the wartime army was a boon in this area:

> Those given by regular army officers were all on technical army subjects, but the Yeomanry and the War time people provided some very interesting & entertaining evenings. Herbert on 'Tea planting', Ward on 'Trapping in Canada', Jones on 'Crime in Burmah' [sic], Highett on 'Bees' etc.[652]

These led to more academic pursuits, with libraries being established in many camps. Initially, prisoners simply shared and then pooled their books, but soon specific

requests and orders were being sent home for manuals and technical books on anything from farming to electrical engineering. In some camps, schools were set up
as men shared their experiences or businesses established. Lieutenant Harry Bishop,
66th Punjabis:

> There were soon two or three well-established firms of carpenters, who did a great
> deal of work and made a lot of furniture. Others took to cobbling, and had plenty to
> do to keep our boots in order. A good many studied various languages, but Turkish
> was not very popular, as no one expected ever to want it again when once they had
> left the country.[653]

To keep the body (as well as the mind) occupied sports abounded where space
could be found, with footballs and other equipment coming in through the neutral
embassies or from home, or being built in the camps. At Yozgad, the Ottoman guards
made hockey-sticks to sell to the prisoners, raising money to supplement their own
wretched rations. In some camps, prisoners could offer their parole (their words as
officers and gentlemen not to try to escape) and could, under escort, walk or even ski
(on improvised equipment made from floorboards) in the mountains.

Meanwhile, food for the soul included the ever popular theatrical and cultural
shows: plays, concerts and pantomimes. Costumes and stage equipment were improvised, and scripts often written in the camps themselves, full of pointed barbs at their
guards or conditions to vent their frustrations. Such occasions could be improved by
the liberal provision of homebrewed alcohol.

By far the highlight of anyone's time was the arrival of mail. Being cut off from
news of home drove many nearly to distraction, and all appreciated the arrival of
anything that provided something new and different to look at and think about.
Although letters were censored, fevered imaginations would try to pull all that they
could from them. Lieutenant Jones:

> Mail Day at Yozgad meant visits. The proper thing to do, after giving everybody
> time to read their letters several times over, was to go from room to room and pick
> up such scraps of war news as had escaped the eye of the censor. Some of us received
> cryptograms, or what we thought were cryptograms, from which we could recon-
> struct the positions on the various fronts (if we had imagination enough), and guess
> the progress of the war. The news that somebody's father's trousers had come down
> was, I remember, the occasion of a very merry evening for it meant that Dad's Bags
> (or Baghdad) had fallen at last.

Support also came from organised groups at home. Government bodies were set up
to organise relief for prisoners, and some organisations such as the Victoria and Albert
Museum offered book supply services. It was not uncommon for the families of the
men in a particular camp to band together and form a committee. Letters would
be pooled and extracts circulated in monthly newsletters to help keep the families
informed of the conditions in the camps, and share intelligence on which shops could

provide the best value or most sturdily constructed food parcels. Some groups went a step further and pooled resources for the relief of their loved ones; the subscribers to the *Kedos Gazette*, for example, grouped together and purchased a gramophone and a box of records, after being forced to give up on their rather more ambitious plan to send the camp a piano.

The war in the Middle East ended rather abruptly. With the surrender of the Ottoman Empire at the end of October 1918 most camps and working parties were simply abandoned by their guards. Slowly, the freed prisoners made their own ways to Constantinople, where the Royal Navy and medical support was waiting for them. Most were shipped to southern France or Italy, and then by train to the Channel coast, and so by ship to Dover. Some 3,290 men were known to have died in captivity, although nearly 4,500 others were known to have been captured but were never heard of again.[654]

GLOSSARY

AFC: Australian Flying Corps
AIF: Australian Imperial Forces
ALH: Australian Light Horse
ANZAC: Australian and New Zealand Army Corps, also nickname for a soldier
    from those countries
A&NZ: Australian and New Zealand (title of a mounted division in Egypt)
Bimbashi: Egyptian Army major
Caique: small Greek fishing boat
CTC: Camel Transport Corps (part of Egyptian Labour Corps)
Corvée: Egyptian system for providing forced labour for government projects
CUP: *Ittihad ve Terakki Cemiyeti* (Committee of Union and Progress), Ottoman
    ruling party
Dekanos: leader of a squad of Greek irregulars
EEF: Egyptian Expeditionary Force
ELC: Egyptian Labour Corps
Emir: Arab governor
ESR: Egyptian State Railway
FA: Flieger Abteilung (German Air Force squadron)
Firman: Ottoman government decree
General Service: usually referred to items of equipment that were of the standard
    army pattern (e.g. GS wagons)
HAC: Honourable Artillery Company (a Territorial artillery unit)
HLI: Highland Light Infantry
Hod: a small clump of palm trees around a well
ICC: Imperial Camel Corps
Jemadar: Indian Army lieutenant
Khamsin/khamaseen: the hot wind from central Africa that blows up through
    Egypt between March and May
Khedive: Viceroy of Egypt
MEF: Mediterranean Expeditionary Force

Mehmetçik: literally 'Mehmet', nickname by Ottoman troops for themselves, equivalent of the British 'Tommy' or Australian 'Digger'

Monitor: shallow-draft ship used as a floating gun-platform

Muhafizia: Senussi regular troops

Mulazim Awal: Egyptian Army lieutenant

NCO: non-commissioned officer

NZMR: New Zealand Mounted Rifles

NZRB: New Zealand Rifle Brigade

Pasha: senior Ottoman military or government official

QOWH: Queen's Own Worcestershire Hussars (Yeomanry)

RA: Royal Artillery

RE: Royal Engineers

RFA: Royal Field Artillery

RFC: Royal Flying Corps

RGH: Royal Gloucestershire Hussars

RHA: Royal Horse Artillery

RIMS: Royal Indian Marine Ship

RN: Royal Navy

RNACD: Royal Naval Armoured Car Division

RNAS: Royal Naval Air Service

RND: Royal Naval Division. An infantry division recruited from the Royal Navy

RNVR: Royal Navy Volunteer Reserve

RWF: Royal Welch Fusiliers

Sepoy: Indian Army infantry private

Sowar: Indian Army cavalry/camel trooper

Subedar: Indian Army captain

Sublime Porte: general term for the government of the Ottoman Empire, akin to 'Westminster' or 'Whitehall' when referring to the British government

USSCC: Universal Suez Ship Canal Company

VD: venereal disease

Wali: governor of an administrative division of the Ottoman Empire

WFF: Western Frontier Force

Wilayah: term for an administrative division of the Ottoman Empire

BIBLIOGRAPHY

Primary Sources

Australian War Memorial

AWM4/1/6 War Diary GHQ EEF
AWN4/1/60 War Diary A&NZ/ANZAC Mounted Division
AWM4/10/1 War Diary 1st Light Horse Brigade
AWM4/10/2 War Diary 2nd Light Horse Brigade
AWM4/11 War Diaries Imperial Camel Corps

Imperial War Museum

10416 Lieutenant E.K. Venables
10440 King Edward VIII
11339 Lady Rochdale
11350 Archibald Ross
11665 Pte H. Henfrey
11765 William Lindsay
12330 S. Natusch
13222 W.R. Bowden
13271 Anon RN Division
13560 Corporal Charles Henry Livingstone DCM
16631 John Taberner
17767 Thomas Huntleywood Burleigh
2792 Thomas Brookes Minshall
3628 V.E. Denby
4684 F.S. Hook
86/43/3 Captain C.J. Radcliffe
87/17/1 R. Loudon
90/1/1 Sir Arthur Lynden-Bell
9879 C.H. Rastall

P354 Captain Alan G.D. Twigg RN
P389 Captain G.H. Warner RN

Museum of the Queen's Own Worcestershire Hussars (Yeomanry)

Dabbs, Corporal A.G., *The Land of Promises*
Holyoake, Lieutenant A.V., *My War*
Bell, Major W., *War Diary*
Wright, 2nd Lieutenant G., *Letters* (includes Yozgad, Broussa and Constantinople Magazine)
Royal Air Force Museum

AC97/127 Collection of Wing Commander Malcolm Begg and Captain John Philpott
(includes Kedos Gazette and Prisoners in Turkey Committee newsletters)

The National Archives

ADM 1/8403/427, Naval operations in Egypt. C-in-C East Indies to take charge and to
retain command of East Indies Station, 1914
ADM 1/8447/27, Salonika/Egypt Line of Communication, 1916
ADM 137/1092, Egypt I, January–June 1915
ADM 137/1147, Egypt and Syria, 1915
ADM 137/1148, Egypt Red Sea and Canal, July–December 1915
ADM 137/1199, Mediterranean, East, March–June 1916
ADM 137/1201, Egypt, various subjects, volume 1, January–June 1916
ADM 137/1230, Egypt: Various Subjects, July 1916–December 1916
ADM 137/334, Egypt Telegrams, January–March 1916
ADM 137/335, Egypt Telegrams, April–August 1916
ADM 137/364, Reports of Proceedings of the Vice Admiral Commanding Eastern
Mediterranean Squadron, 20 February 1916–29 April 1916
ADM 137/365, Reports of Proceedings of the Vice Admiral Commanding Eastern
Mediterranean Squadron, 30 April 1916–17 June 1916
ADM 137/366, Reports of Proceedings of the Vice Admiral Commanding Eastern
Mediterranean Squadron, 18 June 1916–12 August 1916
ADM 137/397, Egypt Telegrams, September–December 1916
ADM 137/545, Letter of Proceedings of the Vice Admiral Commanding Eastern
Mediterranean Squadron, 13 August 1916–30 September 1916
ADM 137/547, Egypt and East Indies, 25 October 1915–14 August 1916
ADM 137/899, Egypt, Reports of Proceedings and other papers, 1914
ADM 137/97, Egypt telegrams, 1 November 1914–18 February 1915
ADM 53/40056, Log of HMS *Doris*, September 1914
ADM 53/40057, Log of HMS *Doris*, October 1914
ADM 53/40058, Log of HMS *Doris*, January 1915
AIR 1/1168/204/5/2589, Reports and operations of RFC 30 Squadron, Egypt detachment,
May–October 1915

AIR 1/117/15/40/35, Move of flight of aeroplanes to Egypt, July 1914–January 1915

AIR 1/1712/204/123/98, Organisation: East Indies and Egypt Area and Stations, January–March 1916

AIR 1/2031/204/326/26, Notes on the RFC/RAF in Egypt and Palestine, November 1915–September 1918

AIR 1/2283/209/75/4, Organisation of RFC in Egypt, December 1915–May 1916

AIR 1/2283/209/75/7, Reports of enemy aircraft and raids on Egypt, February–November 1916

AIR 1/2326/223/55/1, Supplementary report on operations on Western Frontiers, Egypt, and work of administration, February 1915–June 1916

AIR 1/660/17/122/620, A week's summary of operations of Egypt Seaplane Squadron, May 1916

AIR 1/665/17/122/722, Reports of French seaplane flight in Egypt, March 1916

AIR 1/667/17/122/736, Summary of operations, East Indies and Egypt Seaplane Squadron, R.N.A.S., August–September 1916

AIR 1/959/204/5/1040, Strength returns and personnel requirements: RFC in Egypt, December 1915–September 1916

CAB 1/44, Documents collected for the information of the special mission appointed to enquire into the situation in Egypt, 1920

CAB 17/71, Egypt: Defence of in case of attack from the East, 1906

CAB 37/123/7, Egypt: Declaration of British Protectorate: Accession as Sultan of Egypt of Prince Hussein Kamel Pasha, January 1915

CAB 37/138/17, Evacuation of Gallipoli and the defence of Egypt, November, 1915

CAB 37/138/6, Evacuation of Gallipoli and the defence of Egypt, November, 1915

CAB 37/140/7, Military and civil conditions in Egypt, January 1916

CAB 37/148/17, Arrangements for Asia Minor; Capitulations in Egypt, May 1916

CAB 37/83/44, The Right of Egypt to the Sinai Peninsula, April 1906

CAB 38/12/43, Garrison of Egypt; Delay in despatch of reinforcements to Egypt from the United Kingdom; Suez Canal Regulations, July 1906

CAB 38/12/54, Conditions governing an invasion of Egypt from the East, 1906–14

CAB 38/24/23, International status of Egypt when Great Britain is at war, June 1913

CAB 41/35/32, Possible invasion of Egypt by Turkey, August 1914

CAB 41/35/59, Annexation of Egypt, November 1914

CAB 41/35/60, Proclamation of protectorate over Egypt, November 1914

CAB 41/35/61, East Africa; Egypt, November 1914

CAB 42/1/2, Egypt, August 1914

CAB 42/1/35, Despatch of forces to Lemnos, Egypt; Dardanelles, February 1915

CAB 42/1/4, Defence of Egypt, November 1914

CAB 42/23/9, Arab Revolt; High Commission in Egypt, November 1916

CAB 42/5/3, The defence of Egypt; The situation at the Dardanelles; Possible evacuation of Gallipoli, November 1915

CAB 42/6/14, Garrison of Egypt, December 1915

CAB 42/6/8, Salonika and Egypt; Shipping transport for the East, December 1915

CAB 44/14, Relations between Great Britain, Italy and the Senussi, 1912–24

CAB37/124/13, Report from Captain Larken, HMS *Doris*, December 1914

CO 323/646/102, Prize court proceedings: extracts from the *London Gazette* of 27 October 1914 and Lloyd's List of 26 October 1914

CO 323/709/113, Regulations with regard to the admission of British subjects and aliens into Egypt, February – March 1916

FO 141/448/6, Senussi establishments and brethren in Tripolitania, an historical account of the Senussi movement and biographical notes on the living members of the Senussi family, 1918–28

FO 141/464/7, Arab Movement in Egypt, Pan-Islamic and Arab propaganda, 1915–28

FO 141/468/1, Activities of Sayyid Mustafa Idrisi, intermediary between the British Residency at Aden and the Idrisi, 1915–29

FO 141/469/2, Egyptians executed, deported, interned or imprisoned or invited to leave Egypt on political grounds, 1915–17

FO 141/472/5, Senussi prisoners of war (British and Italian), 1915–19

FO 141/473/2, Intelligence on the Turkish expedition against Egypt, 1915–18

FO 141/484/1, The Political and Constitutional situation in Egypt, 1884–1927

FO 141/524/1, Aden and the Yemen: general political situation, and military operations, 1917–22

FO 141/567/4, Political status of Egypt after declaration of war by Turkey in 1914, 1914–26

FO 141/610/6, Arab and Red Sea policy: spheres of political control of Cairo and Aden, 1915–16

FO 141/629/4, Ministerial and political situation in Egypt, 1914–22

FO 141/634/1, Western frontier of Egypt: situation reports and surveys; with maps, 1907–20

FO 141/636/1, Trading with the enemy: draft proclamation by GOC, Egypt, as to policy to be adopted in the event of European war, 1915

FO 141/651/1, Italian position in Cyrenaica and negotiations of the Anglo-Italian Mission for an agreement with Idris Senoussi, 1916–17

FO 141/653/1, Situation in Cyrenaica: Italy and The Senussi, 1914–16

FO 141/734/1, Correspondence on the development of British policy on Arab independence and resistance to Turkish domination during the First World War, 1915–18

FO 141/735/2, Policy memoranda and intelligence reports on military operations against Turkey, 1914–19

FO 141/736/1, Intelligence reports from the Arab Bureau on the Arab Revolt against Turkish rule in Hedjaz and elsewhere, 1916–1917

FO 141/825/2, The conduct of British Troops and their relations with the indigenous population, 1915–29

FO 195/2452, Defence of eastern frontier of Egypt, 1913

FO 195/2456, Aden frontiers, 1914

FO 195/2459, Haushabi, frontier of Aden Protectorate, 1914

FO 633/98, Memorandum by Lord Cromer on present situation in Egypt, 1906

FO 881/10517, Turkey: Convention. Aden Boundary (with maps), March 9, 1914

FO 891/12, Proclamation of British Protectorate over Egypt: message to Prince Hussein Kamel, 1914

FO 891/14, War with Turkey: proclamation of martial law in Egypt, 1914

MT 23/313, Conveyance of Troops, 1914

MT 23/322, Coaling, Watering and Repairing Transports in Egypt, 1914

MT 23/327, Copy of Proceedings of a Court of Enquiry on mortality among horses of the East Lancashire Division (T.F.) on voyage, 1914

MT 23/403, Wounded, conveyed from Egypt by returning Transports, 1915

MT 23/442, Necessity of evacuating sick and wounded from Malta and Egypt, 1915

MT 23/465, Evacuation of Sulva and Anzac, 1915

MT 23/468, Despatch of troops from Egypt and France to Basra, 1915

MT 23/468, Moves of Indian divisions to Mesopotamia via Egypt, 1915

MT 23/498, S.S. *Highland Laird*. Shipment of horses from Buenos Aires to Egypt; fittings, rates and delay, 1916

MT 23/539, Conveyance of Horses, 1916

MT 23/550, Naval Transport Work, Egypt. Report of proceedings, February 1916

MT 23/556, Troop move from Egypt to France, 1916

MT 23/586, Transports and store-ships taking fresh water to Salonika, from Egypt, 1916

MT 23/659, Ships employed in maintaining British forces in Egypt and Salonika, 1916

MT 23/661, Queries raised by Vice Admiral Commanding Eastern Mediterranean regarding organisation of transport in Mediterranean, 1916

MT 23/667, Ferry service for personnel between Alexandria and Salonika, 1916

MT 23/669, Report on inefficiency of Transports in Egypt, during July, 1916

MT 23/671, Control of sea transport work, Egypt, 1916

MUN 4/2124, Egypt: List of articles the export of which is prohibited or restricted,

OS1/17/2, Palestine Exploration Fund, 1901–27

PRO 30/57/43, English occupation of Egypt, July 1912

PRO 30/57/45, Egypt 1914: Miscellaneous correspondence

PRO 30/57/46, Egypt 1914: Reports and correspondence

PRO 30/57/47, Egypt 1915: Miscellaneous correspondence

PRO 30/57/48, Egypt 1916: Miscellaneous correspondence

PRO 30/57/51, Correspondence with Major General Sir Henry Rawlinson, 1914–16

PRO 30/57/52, Correspondence regarding Indian troops, 1914–16

PRO 30/57/55, Correspondence with Lieutenant General Sir William Robertson, 1915–16

PRO 30/57/64, Dardanelles expedition, 1915–16

PRO 30/57/69, India and miscellaneous correspondence, 1914–16

PRO 30/57/72, Admiralty correspondence, 1914–15

PRO 30/57/77, Cabinet correspondence, 1911–16

T 1/11809, War Office. Acquisition of hospital accommodation in Egypt, 1915

WO 106/1542, Forces required for defence of Egypt: General Staff estimates, December 1915

WO 106/42, Defence of the Suez Canal, Eastern Frontier, and, Upper Egypt, 1910–15

WO 106/43, Defence of the Eastern frontier of Egypt and proposals for the invasion of Syria, February 1914

WO 106/43, Troops transport required for Egypt, February 1914

WO 106/56, His Excellency General Sir C.C. Monro, GCMG, KCB, on minor military operations undertaken from March 1916 to March 1917

WO 106/710, Military Report on Western Desert of Egypt, 1915

WO 106/713, Numbers necessary for the Defence of Egypt, 1916

WO 106/714, Criticism on Turkish attack on Egypt, January 1916

WO 106/715, Proposed Operations: Force necessary for the Defence of Egypt, 1916

WO 106/742, North West Frontier, elsewhere in the Indian Empire and Aden: Despatch on the minor military operations by General Sir B. Duff, 1916

WO 107/22, Mediterranean Expeditionary Force, Egypt and Salonika, January 1916

WO 158/624, Arab Forces: Historical documents: Summary, 1914–16

WO 158/625, Arab Forces: Supply of arms and ammunition etc to the Sherif of Mecca, 1916–17

WO 158/626, Arab Forces: Co-operation with Arab Tribes, 1916

WO 158/891, Egypt and [Suez] Canal defence: Proceedings of conference, January 1916

WO 158/974, Correspondence between HQ Aden Brigade and Royal Garrison Artillery, July–December 1914

WO 32/7085, Organisation of a force for Egypt, 1909–13

WO 33/796, Despatches from Lieut-General Sir J.G. Maxwell, Commanding the Forces in Egypt, 1915

WO 79/64, Papers of Sir Archibald Murray: Egypt, November–December 1915

WO 95/4293, 2nd Mounted Division, 1914–22

WO 95/4428, Suez Canal Defences, 1914–16

WO 95/4437, Western Frontier Force, November 1915–October 1916

WO 95/4441, Western Frontier Force, 1916–17

WO 95/4520, Australian and New Zealand Mounted Division, 1916–19

WO 95/4539-4543, Australian and New Zealand Mounted Division, 1916–19

WO 95/4591-4595, 42nd (East Lancashire) Division, 1915–17

WO 95/4601, 52nd Division, 1915–18

WO 95/4607-4612, 52nd Division, 1916–18

Published Sources

Books

Aaronsohn, A., *With the Turks in Palestine*, Atlantic Monthly (1916)

Ahmed, M. (ed.), *Egypt in the 20th Century*, MegaZette Press, Middlesex (2003)

Aksakal, M., *The Ottoman Road to War in 1914*, Cambridge University Press, Cambridge (2008)

Anglesey, Marques, *A History of the British Cavalry 1816–1919 Vol. 5: Egypt, Palestine and Syria 1914 to 1919*, Leo Cooper, London (1994)

Anon., *The Fifth Battalion Highland Light Infantry in the War, 1914–1918*, MacLehose, Jackson & Co., Glasgow (1921)

Anon., *History of the 5th Royal Gurkha Rifles (Frontier Force) 1858 to 1928*, Gale & Polden Ltd, Aldershot (1930)

Arthur, Sir G., *Life of Lord Kitchener*, Macmillan & Co. Ltd, London (1920)

Asher, M., *Lawrence: The Uncrowned King of Arabia*, Penguin Books Ltd, London (1999)

Aspinall-Oglander, C., *Roger Keyes*, The Hogarth Press, London (1951)

Baly, L., *Horseman, Pass By: The Australian Light Horse in World War I*, Spellmount, Staplehurst (2004)

Barr, J., *Setting the Desert on Fire: T. E. Lawrence and Britain's Secret War in Arabia, 1916–18*, Bloomsbury, London (2006)

Bean, C.E.W., *Official History of Australia in the War of 1914–18: Vol. 1: The Story of ANZAC: The First Phase*, Angus and Robertson Ltd, Sydney (1921)

Bean, C.E.W., *Official History of Australia in the War of 1914–18: Vol. 3: The Australian Imperial Force in France*, Angus and Robertson Ltd, Sydney (1941)

Behrend, A., *Make Me a Soldier*, Eyre & Spottiswoode, London (1961)

Benn, Captain W.W., DSO DFC, *In the Side Shows*, P.S. Chapman, Auckland (2010)

Bishop, H.C.W., *A Kut Prisoner*, The Bodley Head (1920)

Bluett, A., *A Gunner's Crusade*, Leonaur Ltd (2007)

Bourne, Lieutenant Colonel G.H., *History of the 2nd Light Horse Regiment AIF*, Northern Daily Leader, Tamworth (1926)

Bower, J.G., *Dead Reckoning: The Story of Our Submarines*, Rich & Cowan, London (1933)

Brownlie, Major W.S., *The Proud Trooper: The History of the Ayrshire (Earl of Carrick's Own) Yeomanry*, Wm. Collins, Sons & Co., London (1964)

Bruce, A., *The Last Crusade: The Palestine Campaign in the First World War*, John Murray Ltd, London (2002)

Burns, I.M., *Ben-My-Chree: Woman of my Heart, Isle of Man Packet Steamer and Seaplane Carrier*, Colin Huston, Leicester (2008)

Butler, Colonel A.G., DSO, *The Australian Army Medical Services in the War of 1914–18: Vol. 1*, Australian War Memorial, Melbourne (1930)

'C', *The Yeomanry Cavalry of Worcestershire, 1914–1922*, Mark & Moody Ltd, Stourbridge (1926)

Carver, FM Lord, *The National Army Museum Book of the Turkish Front, 1914–18*, Pan Books, London (2004)

Clifford, R., *The Royal Gloucestershire Hussars*, Alan Sutton Publishing Co., Stroud (1991)

Compton-Hall, R., *Submarines and the War at Sea, 1914–18*, MacMillan Ltd, London (1991)

Corbett, Sir J.S., *History of the Great War: Naval Operations Vol. 1*, HMSO (1920)

Corbett, Sir J.S., *History of the Great War: Naval Operations Vol. 2*, HMSO (1921)

Corbett, Sir J.S., *History of the Great War: Naval Operations Vol. 3*, HMSO (1923)

Cunningham of Hyndhope, Viscount, *A Sailor's Odyssey: The Autobiography of Admiral of the Fleet Viscount Cunningham of Hyndhope KT GCB OM DSO*, Hutchinson & Co. Ltd, London (1951)

Cutlack, F.M., *Official History of Australia in the War of 1914–18: Vol. 8: The Australian Flying Corps*, Angus and Robertson Ltd, Sydney (1923)

d'Enno, D., *Fishermen against the Kaiser: Shockwaves of War Vol. 1: 1914–15*, Pen & Sword Maritime, Barnsley (2010)

Daley, P., *Beersheba: A Journey Through Australia's Forgotten War*, Melbourne University Press (2009)

Djemal Pasha, *Memories of a Turkish Statesman, 1913–19*, Hutchinson & Co., London (1922)

Domville-Fife, C.W., *Submarine Warfare of To-day: How the Submarine Menace was Met and Vanquished*, Seeley, Service & Co. Ltd, London (1920)

Dorling, Captain T., DSO, 'Taffrail', *Endless Story*, Hodder and Stoughton Ltd, London (1931)

Doyle, P., *Gallipoli 1915*, Spellmount, Stroud (2011)

Dudley Ward, Major C.H., DSO MC, *Regimental Records of the Royal Welch Fusiliers Vol. IV: Turkey–Bulgaria–Austria*, Foster Groom & Co. Ltd, (1921)

Dudley Ward, Major C.H., DSO MC, *The 74th (Yeomanry) Division in Syria and France*, John Murray, London (1922)

Duff, R.E.B., *100 Years of the Suez Canal*, Clifton Books, Brighton (1969)

Edwards, B., *War under the Red Ensign 1914–1918*, Pen and Sword Maritime, Barnsley (2010)

Elgood, Lieutenant Colonel P.G., CMG, *Egypt and the Army*, Oxford University Press, Oxford (1924)

Elliot, Captain W.R., MC, *The Second Twentieth: Being the History of the 2/20th Bn. London Regiment*, Gale & Polden Ltd, Aldershot (1920)

Erickson, Lieutenant Colonel E.J. (Retd), *Ordered to Die: A History of the Ottoman Army in the First World War*, Greenwood Press, London (2001)

Erickson, Lieutenant Colonel E.J. (Retd), *Ottoman Army Effectiveness in World War I: A Comparative Study*, Routledge, Abingdon (2007)

Erickson, Lieutenant Colonel E.J. (Retd), *Gallipoli and the Middle East, 1914–1918*, Amber Books Ltd, London (2008)

Fayle, C.E., *History of the Great War: Seaborne Trade Vol. 1*, HMSO (1920)

Fayle, C.E., *History of the Great War: Seaborne Trade Vol. 2*, HMSO (1923)

Fayle, C.E., *History of the Great War: Seaborne Trade Vol. 3*, HMSO (1924)

Finkel, C., *Osman's Dream: The Story of the Ottoman Empire 1300–1923*, John Murray, London (2005)

Ford, R., *Eden to Armageddon: World War I in the Middle East*, Phoenix, London (2010)

General Staff, *Handbook of the Turkish Army*, HMSO (1916)

Godrich, V., *Mountains of Moab: The Diary of a Cavalryman with the Queen's Own Worcestershire Hussars, 1908–1919*, Dr John Godrich (2011)

Grainger, J.D., *The Battle for Palestine 1917*, The Boydell Press, Woodbridge (2006)

Gullett, H.S., *Official History of Australia in the War of 1914–18: Vol. 7: The AIF in Sinai and Palestine, 1914–18*, Angus and Robertson Ltd, Sydney (1923)

Gwatkin-Williams, Captain R.S., CMG, *Prisoners of the Red Desert*, Thornton Butterworth Ltd, London (1919)

Haig, A.B., *War Records of the 24th Punjabis (4th Battalion 14th Punjab Regiment) 1914–20*, Gale & Polden Ltd, Aldershot (1934)

Halpern, Dr P.G., *The Naval War in the Mediterranean 1914–18*, Unwin Hyman Ltd, London (1987)

Halpern, Dr P.G., *The Battle of the Otranto Straits*, Indiana University Press (2004)

Halpern, Dr P.G. (ed.), *The Royal Navy in the Mediterranean 1915–18*, Navy Records Society (1987)

Hamilton, A.S., MM, *The City of London Yeomanry (Roughriders)*, The Hamilton Press Ltd, London (1936)

Hamilton, General Sir I., *Listening for the Drums*, Faber & Faber Ltd, London (1944)

Hamilton, P.M., OBE, *Riders of Destiny: The 4th Australian Light Horse Field Ambulance 1917–18*, Mostly Unsung Military History, Gardenvale (1995)

Hamlin, J.F., *Flat Out: The Story of 30 Squadron*, Air Britain Historians Ltd (2001)

Hatton, S.F., *The Yarn of a Yeoman*, Naval & Military Press Ltd, Uckfield (1930)

Haythornthwaite, P.J., *The World War One Sourcebook*, Brockhampton Press, London (1998)

Hill, Gp Captain C.W., *The Spook and the Commandant*, William Kimber & Co. Ltd, London (1975)

Historical Section, Foreign Office *Handbook No. 46: Turkey in Europe*, HMSO (1918)

Historical Section, Foreign Office *Handbook No. 107: Anglo-Egyptian Sudan*, HMSO (1919)

Hogue, O., *The Cameliers*, Leonaur Ltd (2008)

Holland, R., *Blue-water Empire: The British in the Mediterranean Since 1800*, Allen Lane, London (2012)

Hopkirk, P., *On Secret Service east of Constantinople: The Plot to Bring Down the British Empire*, John Murray, London (1994)

Horner, D.M. (ed.), *The Commanders: Australian Military Leadership in the Twentieth Century*, Allen & Unwin Pty Ltd, Sydney (1984)

Hynes, J.P., *Lawrence of Arabia's Secret Air Force*, Pen & Sword Aviation, Barnsley (2010)

Inchbald, G., *With the Imperial Camel Corps in the Great War*, Leanaur Ltd (2005)

Jones, Captain H.A., *The War in the Air Vol. 5*, Oxford University Press, Oxford (1935)

Keyes, Sir R., *The Naval Memoirs of Admiral of the Fleet Sir Roger Keyes: Scapa Flow to the Dover Straits, 1916–18*, Thornton Butterworth Ltd, London (1935)

Keyes, Sir R., *Adventures Ashore & Afloat*, George G. Harrap & Co. Ltd, London (1939)

Kingsford, A.R., *Night Raiders of the Air*, John Hamilton Ltd, London (1931)

Knight, J., *The Civil Service Rifles in the Great War: 'All Bloody Gentlemen'*, Pen and Sword Military, Barnsley (2005)

Knightly, P. and Simpson, C., *The Secret Lives of Lawrence of Arabia*, Thomas Nelson & Sons Ltd, London (1969)

Lavery, B., *Able Seamen: The Lower Decks of the Royal Navy, 1850–1939*, Conway, London (2011)

Lawrence, T.E., *Seven Pillars of Wisdom*, Penguin Books Ltd, London (1979)

Lloyd, M., *The London Scottish in the Great War*, Leo Cooper, Barnsley (2001)

Mackay, Colonel J.N., DSO, *History of the 7th Duke of Edinburgh's Own Gurkha Rifles*, William Blackwood & Sons Ltd, London (1962)

Mackenzie, C., *Aegean Memories*, Chatto and Windus, London (1940)

MacMunn, Lieutenant General Sir G., KCB KCSI DSO, *The History of the Sikh Pioneers (23rd, 32nd, 34th)*, Sampson Low, Marston & Co. Ltd, London (1932)

MacMunn, Lieutenant General Sir G., KCB KCSI DSO & Falls, Captain C., *Military Operations: Egypt and Palestine Vol. 1*, HMSO (1928)

Magnus, P., *Kitchener: Portrait of an Imperialist*, John Murray, London (1958)

Mason, P., *A Matter of Honour: An Account of the Indian Army, its Officers and Men*, Jonathon Cape Ltd, London (1974)

Maxwell, R., *Desperate Encounters: Stories of the 5th Royal Gurkha Rifles of the Punjab Frontier Force*, The Pentland Press, Edinburgh (1986)

McGreal, S., *The War on the Hospital Ships*, Pen & Sword Maritime Ltd, Barnsley (2008)

McGuirk, R., *The Sanusi's Little War*, Arabian Publishing, London (2007)

McMeekin, S., *The Berlin–Baghdad Express: The Ottoman Empire and Germany's Bid for World Power, 1898–1918*, Penguin Books, London (2011)

Meinertzhagen, Colonel R., CBE DSO, *Army Diary*, Oliver & Boyd, Edinburgh (1960)

Mitchell, Major T.J., & Smith, G.M., Medical Services: Casualtry and Medical Statistics of the Great War, HMSO (1931)

Mollo, B., *The Sharpshooters: 3rd County of London Yeomanry, 1900–1961, Kent and County of London Yeomanry, 1961–1970*, Historical Research Unit (1969)

Moore, Lieutenant A.B., *The Mounted Rifleman in Sinai and Palestine*, Whitcombe & Tombs Ltd, Auckland (1920)

Murray, General Sir A., *Sir Archibald Murray's Despatches*, HMSO (1920)

Myres, J.N.L., *Commander J. L. Myres RNVR: The Blackbeard of the Aegean*, Leopard's Head Press Ltd, London (1980)

Orange, Dr V. & Stapleton, A.V.M., DC, *Winged Promises: a History of No. 14 Squadron RAF, 1915–45*, RAF Benevolent Find Enterprises, Fairford (1996)

Powell, A., *Women in the War Zone: Hospital Service in the First World War*, The History Press, Stroud (2009)

Powles, Colonel C.G., CMG DSO (ed.), *The history of the Canterbury Mounted Rifles, 1914–19*, Whitcombe & Tombs Ltd, Auckland (1928)

Pugh, R., *Wingate Pasha: The Life of General Sir Francis Reginald Wingate, 1861–1953*, Pen & Sword Military, Barnsley (2011)

Richmond, J.C.B., *Egypt 1798–1952*, Mathuen & Co. Ltd, London (1977)

Robertson, J., *With the Cameliers in Palestine*, Leonaur Ltd (2009)

Rolls, S.C., *Steel Chariots in the Desert*, Leonaur Ltd (2005)

Roskill, Captain S.W., DSC (ed.), *Documents Relating to the Naval Air Service Vol. 1: 1908–1918*, The Navy Records Society (1969)

Samson, Air Cdre C.R., CMG DSO AFC, *Fights and Flights*, Ernest Benn Ltd, London (1930)

Sanders, General L. von, *Five Years in Turkey*, US Naval Institute, Annapolis (1928)

Schonfield, H.J., *The Suez Canal*, Penguin, London (1939)

Schonfield, H.J., *The Suez Canal in World Affairs*, Constellation Books, London (1952)

Seward, D., *Wings Over the Desert: In Action with an RFC Pilot in Palestine, 1916–18*, Haynes Publishing, Yeovil (2009)

Sheffy, Y., *British Military Intelligence in the Palestine Campaign, 1914–1918*, Frank Cass, London (1998)

Storrs, R., *Orientations*, Nicholson & Watson, London (1943)

Teichman, Captain O., DSO MC, *The Diary of a Yeomanry M.O.*, T. Fisher Unwin Ltd, London (1921)

Terraine, J., *Business in Great Waters*, Leo Cooper, London (1989)

Terraine, J., *The U-Boat Wars, 1916–1945*, Owl Books, New York (1989)

Thornton, G., *With the ANZACs in Cairo*, H.R. Allenson Ltd, London (1918)

Van der Vat, D., *The Ship that Changed the World: The Escape of the Goeben to the Dardanelles in 1914*, Birlinn Ltd, Edinburgh (2000)

Vatikiotis, P.J., *The History of Modern Egypt*, Weidenfeld & Nicolson, London (1991)

Wakefield, A. & Moody, S., *Under the Devil's Eye: Britain's Forgotten Army at Salonika, 1915–18*, Sutton Publishing, Stroud (2004)

Wavell, Colonel A.P., *The Palestine Campaign*, Constable and Co. Ltd, London (1928)

Weldon, Captain L.B., MC, *'Hard Lying': Eastern Mediterranean 1914–19*, Herbert Jenkins Ltd, London (1925)

Wilson, R., *Palestine 1917*, D.J. Costello (Publishers) Ltd, Tunbridge Wells (1987)

Winstone, H.V.F. (ed.), *The Diaries of Parker Pasha*, Quartet Books, London (1983)

Wragg, D., *Royal Navy Handbook 1914–18*, Sutton Publishing Ltd, Stroud (2006)

Woodward, D.R., *Forgotten Soldiers of the First World War*, Tempus Publishing Ltd, Stroud (2007)

Articles & Papers

Askakal, M., 'Holy War Made in Germany? Ottoman origins of the 1914 Jihad' in *War in History*, Vol. 2, No. 18, 2011

Clode, G., 'The Model of What a War Hospital under Canvas Should Be' in *Military Times*, September 2012

Erickson, Lieutenant Colonel E.J. (Retd.), 'Bayonets on Musa Dagh: Ottoman Counterinsurgency Operations, 1915' in *Journal of Strategic Studies*, Vol. 3, No. 28, 2005

Erickson, Lieutenant Colonel E.J. (Retd.), 'Captain Larkin [sic] and the Turks: The Strategic Impact of the Operations of HMS *Doris* in Early 1915' in *Middle Eastern Studies*, Vol. 1, No. 46, 2010

Flanagan, Dr B.P. (ed.), 'The History of the Ottoman Air Force in the Great War' in *Cross and Cockade Journal*, Vol. 11, No. 2, Summer 1970; Vol. 11, No. 3, Autumn 1970; Vol. 11, No. 4, Winter 1970; Vol. 13, No. 2, Summer 1972

Gill, D.W.J., 'Harry Pirie-Gordon: Historical Research, Journalism and Intelligence

Gathering in the Eastern Mediterranean 1908–18' in *Intelligence and National Security*, Vol. 6, No. 21, 2006

Gröschel, D.H.M. & Ladek, J., 'Wings over Sinai and Palestine: The Adventures of Flieger Abteilung 300 "Pascha" in the Fight Against the Egyptian Expeditionary Corps, from April 1916 until the Third Battle of Gaza in November 1917' in *Over the Front*, Vol. 13, No. 1, Spring 1998

Kitchen, J.E., 'Khaki Crusaders: Crusading Rhetoric and the British Imperial Soldier during the Egypt and Palestine Campaigns, 1916–18' in *First World War Studies*, Vol. 1, No. 2, 2010

Kress von Kressenstein, Colonel Baron, 'The Campaign in Palestine from the Enemy's Side' in *Journal of the Royal United Services Institution*, Vol. 62, 1922

Langenberg, W.H., 'U-Boat Ace of Aces' in *The Sea Classics*, May 2004

McClenaghan, T., 'The Imperial Service Troop Scheme in the 19th and 20th Centuries' in *Mars & Clio*, No. 35, Autumn 2012

Özbeck, N., 'Defining the Public Sphere During the Late Ottoman Empire: War, Mass Mobilisation and the Young Turk Regime, 1908–18' in *Middle Eastern Studies*, Vol. 5, No. 43, 2007

Sheffy, Y., 'British intelligence and the Middle East, 1900–1918: How Much Do We Know?' in *Intelligence and National Security*, Vol. 1, No. 17, 2002

Sheffy, Y., 'The Spy Who Never Was: An Intelligence Myth in Palestine, 1914–18' in *Intelligence and National Security*, Vol. 3, No. 14, 1999

Stoker, D., 'Before the Sound of Music' in *Military History Quarterly*, Vol. 20, No. 3, Spring 2008

Websites

War Diary of 605th German Machine Gun Company: http://alh-research.tripod.com/Light_Horse

Diary of Lieutenant E.T. Cripps, Royal Gloucestershire Hussars: http://freepages.genealogy.rootsweb.ancestry.com/~terryw/gloucest/gloucest.htm#Diary_of_ET_Cripps

There are regrettably few websites dedicated to the campaigns in Egypt and Palestine during the First World War. However, I can recommend the excellent and comprehensive Australian Light Horse Studies Centre (alh-research.tripod.com) and the Australian War Memorial. The latter includes online pdf copies of the Australian Official Histories.

There are many general First World War forums that include areas on Egypt and Palestine, such as: Desert Column (desert-column.phpbb3now.com) for all Australian military 1899–1920; The Great War Forum (1914–1918.invasionzone.com); and New Zealand Mounted Rifles Forum (www.nzmr.org).

NOTES

Prologue

1.   QOWH(Y)M, Arthur Dabbs.
2.   'C', pp.49–50.
3.   'C', pp.50–1.
4.   Jones, Vol. 5, p.182.
5.   'C', p.51; MacMunn and Falls, Vol. 1, p.162.
6.   Jones, Vol. 5, pp.180–1.
7.   MacMunn and Falls, Vol. 1, p.163.
8.   'C', p.55; MacMunn and Falls, Vol. 1, p.168.
9.   'C', p.54.
10. QOWH(Y)M, Horace Mantle.
11. 'C', 53.
12. *Berrow's Worcester Journal*, 4 November, 1916.
13. MacMunn and Falls, Vol. 1, p.164.
14. QOWH(Y)M, Arthur Dabbs.
15. QOWH(Y)M, Arthur Dabbs.
16. MacMunn and Falls, Vol. 1, p.166.
17. Clifford, p.9.
18. 'C', p.57.
19. *Fifth Battalion Highland Light Infantry*, pp.77–8.
20. Fayle, Vol. 1, p.32.
21. Schinfield, *The Suez Canal in World Affairs*, p.168.

Chapter 1

22. TNA CAB38/24/23.
23. McMeekin, chapter 3, *passim*.
24. Richmond, p.156.
25. Alexander, p.60.
26. Elgood, pp.34–5 and Richmond, pp.167–9.
27. TNA CAB38/24/23.

28. Storrs, p.123.
29. McGuirk, p.51.
30. Elgood, p.42.
31. Elgood, p.42.
32. Elgood, p.47.
33. Elgood, pp.46–7.
34. *See*, for example, Storrs, chapter 7, *passim*.
35. Elgood, p.51.
36. Elgood, pp.48–50.
37. Elgood, pp.52–5.

Chapter 2

38. McMeekin, p.112.
39. Van der Vat, p.40.
40. McMeekin, p.106.
41. McMeekin, pp.107–8.
42. For an entertaining biography of this colourful character, *see* McMeekin's *The Berlin–Bagdad Express* (which is also essential reading on the growth of the Ottoman-German relationship).
43. Hopkirk, p.4.
44. TNA FO141/636/2.
45. For a full account, *see* Hopkirk's excellent book, *On Secret Service East of Constantinople*, or John Buchanan's semi-fictional 1916 account, *Greenmantle*.
46. *See* Aksakal, 'Holy War Made in Germany? Ottoman Origins of the 1914 jihad'.
47. *See* Aksakal, 'Holy War Made in Germany?' Ottoman Origins of the 1914 jihad'.
48. Corbett, Vol. 1, pp.7–9.
49. Corbett, Vol. 1, p.7.
50. IWM P389, Captain G.H. Warner RN.
51. Corbett, Vol. 1, p.25.
52. Albania had declared itself independent from the Ottoman Empire in 1912, and had been recognised by the international community in July 1913. A series of invasions had been made by Albania's Balkan neighbours, and forces from the Great Powers were deployed to guarantee its borders.
53. The light cruiser HMS *Doris*, for example, carried just over 1,000 tons of coal. Her normal cruising speed, 11mph, consumed 2.5 tons of coal per hour, or achieved 4.4 miles per ton. At full speed, 18mph, this went up to 7.5 tons per hour, or 2.4 miles per ton.
54. IWM P389, Captain G.H. Warner R.
55. Corbett, Vol. 1, p.34.
56. Corbett, Vol. 1, p.35.
57. Corbett, Vol. 1, p.55.
58. Van der Vat, pp.95–6.
59. Van der Vat, chapter 3, *passim*.
60. Corbett, Vol. 1, p.55.
61. Van der Vat, pp.96–7.
62. Van der Vat, p.97.
63. Corbett, Vol. 1, p.56.

64. Quoted in Van der Vat, p.99.
65. For full accounts of this encounters, *see* Corbett, Vol. 1, p.57 and Van der Vat, pp.71–6 and 98–9.
66. Van der Vat, p.76.
67. Corbett, Vol. 1, p.63.
68. Corbett, Vol. 1, p.65; TNA ADM137/899.
69. Van der Vat, p.85.
70. Van der Vat, p.87.
71. Corbett, Vol. 1, p.66 & Van der Vat, pp.89–90.
72. Corbett, Vol. 1, pp.66–7.
73. Van der Vat, pp.116–7.
74. Corbett, Vol. 1, pp.84–7.
75. Corbett, Vol. 1, p.280.
76. TNA FO891/14.
77. Elgood, pp.90–98; MacMunn and Falls, Vol. 1, p.17.
78. MacMunn and Falls, Vol., 1 p.17.
79. Britain had initially abstained from this convention, and had only signed it in 1904. Elgood, p.78.
80. Schonfield, *The Suez Canal*, p.71.
81. MacMunn and Falls, Vol. 1, p.12.
82. Fayle, Vol. 1, p.128.
83. Corbett, Vol. 1, p.88.
84. Elgood, pp.80–1.
85. Corbett, Vol. 1, pp.374–5 and pp.383–5.
86. Corbett, Vol. 1, p.364.
87. Corbett, Vol. 2, p.74.
88. Corbett, Vol. 1, p.363.
89. Corbett, Vol. 2, pp.73–4.
90. Corbett, Vol. 2, p.77.
91. TNA CAB37/124/13.
92. IWM 13271, Anonymous.
93. TNA CAB37/124/13.
94. IWM 13271, Anon.
95. *See* for example, IWM P354, Captain Alan Twigg.
96. For a full account of this episode, *see* Corbett, Vol. 2, pp.74–7, and Larken's report in TNA CAB37/124/13.
97. Corbett, Vol. 2, p.77.
98. Erickson, *HMS Doris*.
99. Sheffy, *British Military Intelligence*, pp.44–5.
100. TNA WO33/796, p.2; McGuirk, pp.66–8.

Chapter 3

101. 3rd Dragoon Guards, 'T' Battery Royal Horse Artillery, 7th Mountain Battery Royal Garrison Artillery, 2nd Field Company Royal Engineers, 2nd Battalion Devonshire Regiment, 1st Battalion Worcestershire Regiment, 2nd Battalion Northamptonshire Regiment, and 2nd Battalion Gordon Highlanders.

102. MacMunn and Falls, Vol. 1, p.13.
103. Ellingwood, p.361.
104. MacMunn and Falls, Vol. 1, p.13.
105. MacMunn and Falls, Vol. 1, p.14.
106. MacMunn and Falls, Vol. 1, p.15.
107. MacMunn and Falls, Vol. 1, p.19.
108. Bean, Vol. 1, p.116.
109. TNA WO33/714.
110. All kinds of factors, from the ship to the weather, could affect travel times. Later, the need to move in convoys or zig-zag to confuse enemy submarines also caused delays, although from 1915 it became more common to travel by ship to France, then by train to the Mediterranean coast, followed by a much shorter dash by troopship across to Egypt.
111. Bluett, p.11.
112. IWM 11765, Pte William Lindsay. Letter home, May 1915.
113. Hatton, pp.45–6.
114. TNA MT/327.
115. Hatton, p.48.
116. IWM 11665, Pte H. Henfrey. Letter home, 7 October, 1914.
117. IWM 16631, Pte John Taberner. Letter home, 29 September, 1914.
118. IWM 16631, Pte John Taberner. Letter home, 29 September, 1914.
119. Wahlert. Problems in Australia, p.20; on the troopships, p.25.
120. Bean, Vol. 1, pp.128–9.
121. Wahlert, p.22.
122. *See*, for example, comments on how Australians drove up prices in IWM 17767, Pte Thomas Burleigh.
123. Wahlert, p.27.
124. Thornton, pp.62–5.
125. Elgood, pp.198–9.
126. Hatton, p.61.
127. Bean, Vol. 1, pp.120–3.
128. Quoted in Wahlert, p.26.
129. Wahlert, p.27.
130. McMullin, pp.103–4.
131. *Medical History*, Mitchell and Smith, p.73.
132. Thornton, p.125.
133. Bean, Vol. 1, p.130; Wahlert, p.28 and p.36.
134. Wahlert, p.40.
135. Hatton, p.60.
136. Godrich, p.41.
137. Godrich, p.45.
138. Godrich, p.45.
139. 5th Highland Light Infantry, p.82.
140. Moore, p.27.
141. Moore, p.25.
142. Medical History, p.215.
143. Medical History, p.213. An average of 724,27 men per 1,000.

144. Medical History, p.213.
145. Hatton, p.74.

Chapter 4

146. Erickson, *Ordered to Die*, p.10. Most of the information in this chapter about the Ottoman forces comes from the writing of Colonel Edward Erickson (Retd) of the US Army, who has been given (for a Westerner) unprecedented access to Turkish Army records. However, some concerns have been raised about this process: the Turks have been very selective about what records they have released, while of course anything he writes naturally cannot be corroborated. The author has done his best to check against other sources where they are available, and in particular can recommend the British General Staff's *Handbook of the Turkish Army*.
147. Erickson, *Effectiveness*, p.9.
148. Erickson, *Effectiveness*, p.9.
149. Zürcher, p.239.
150. Erickson, *Effectiveness*, pp.10–11.
151. Erickson, *Effectiveness*, p.9.
152. Erickson, *Ordered to Die*, p.6.
153. Erickson, *Effectiveness*, p.12.
154. Erickson, *Effectiveness*, p.12.
155. Aaronsohn, chapter 2.
156. IWM 13271, Anon.
157. Erickson, *Ordered to Die*, pp.7–8; Erickson, *Effectiveness*, p.14; Zürcher, p.245.
158. Erickson, *Ordered to Die*, p.5.
159. Zürcher, p.240.
160. Aaronsohn, chapter 6.
161. Aaronsohn, chapter 4.
162. Zürcher, p.240.
163. Zürcher, p.241.
164. Aaronsohn, chapter 2.
165. Zürcher, p.247.
166. Zürcher, pp.248–9.
167. In his memoirs, Djemal claims otherwise. However, as a still-active politician with a clear agenda of his own, not all of Djemal's writings can be taken as an honest account of events.
168. Erickson, *Ordered to Die*, pp.68–9.
169. Erickson, *Ordered to Die*, p.41.
170. Djemal, pp.148–9.
171. Djemal, p.149.
172. Djemal, pp.149–50.
173. Aaronsohn, Chapter 6.
174. Erickson, *Ordered to Die*, p.69.
175. Djemal, pp.152–3; Erickson, *Ordered to Die*, p.70.
176. Kress, quoted in MacMunn and Falls, Vol. 1, p.35.
177. Djemal, pp.154–5.
178. Kress, quoted in MacMunn and Falls, Vol. 1, p.35.

179. Aaronsohn, chapter 6.
180. Jones, Vol. 5, p.160; Weldon, *Hard lying*, Chapters 1 and 2. The *Aenne Rickmers* was also employed to land agents.
181. Jones, Vol. 5, p.160; The aircraft from the UK were two S.7 Longhorns bought from the Aircraft Manufacturing Company at Hendon, and one S.11 Shorthorn. They also had two Crossley tenders, one Leyland repair lorry, two canvas hangars and fuel for six months. Hamlin, p.11.
182. Hamlin, p.11.
183. Hamlin, p.11.
184. Jones, Vol. 5, pp.160–1.
185. Jones, Vol. 5, pp.161–3; MacMunn and Falls, Vol. 1, pp.28–31.
186. MacMunn and Falls, Vol. 1, p 24. The Great and Small Bitter Lakes were 22 miles in length, and Lake Timsah 7 miles.
187. MacMunn and Falls, Vol. 1, p.25.
188. MacMunn and Falls, Vol. 1, p.19.
189. Bruce, pp.15–16.
190. TNA WO33/796, pp.2–3.
191. MacMunn and Falls, Vol. 1, pp.33–4.
192. MacMunn and Falls, Vol. 1, p.29.
193. TNA WO33/796, p.3.
194. TNA WO33/796, p.3; MacMunn and Falls, Vol. 1, p.29.
195. TNA WO33/796, p.3.
196. Corbett, Vol. 2, p.111.
197. Corbett, Vol. 2, p.113.
198. Corbett, Vol. 2, p.113; TNA WO33/796, p.6.
199. MacMunn and Falls, Vol. 1, p.37.
200. Erickson, *Ordered to Die*, p.71.
201. TNA WO33/796, p.8.
202. MacMunn and Falls, Vol. 1, p.39; TNA WO33/796, p.3.
203. MacMunn and Falls, Vol. 1, pp.40–1; TNA WO33/796, pp.3–7.
204. MacMunn and Falls, Vol. 1, p.41; TNA WO33/796, p.6.
205. MacMunn and Falls, Vol. 1, pp.41–4; TNA WO33/796, pp.6–10.
206. Djemal, p.156.
207. MacMunn and Falls, Vol. 1, pp.43–4; TNA WO33/796, p.4.
208. MacMunn and Falls, Vol. 1, pp.45–6; TNA WO33/796, pp.4–5.
209. Djemal, pp.156–7.
210. MacMunn and Falls, Vol. 1, pp.46–9; TNA WO33/796, pp.4–5.
211. Sheffy, *British Military Intelligence*, pp.51–9.
212. MacMunn and Falls, Vol. 1, p.49.
213. Djemal, p.159; Kress, quoted in MacMunn and Falls, Vol. 1, p.50.
214. MacMunn and Falls, Vol. 1, p.50.
215. Djemal, p.164.
216. Aaronsohn, chapter 6.
217. TNA PRO30/57/47, Storrs to FitzGerald 15/2/15.
218. Fayle, Vol. 2, p.33.
219. Fayle, Vol. 2, p.33.

Chapter 5

220. Erickson, *Gallipoli and the Middle East*, p.54.
221. Erickson, *Gallipoli and the Middle East*, p.55.
222. Erickson, *Gallipoli and the Middle East*, p.55.
223. Erickson, *Gallipoli and the Middle East*, p.55.
224. MacMunn and Falls, Vol. 1, p.55.
225. MacMunn and Falls, Vol. 1, pp.55–6.
226. Erickson, *Gallipoli and the Middle East*, pp.62–3; MacMunn and Falls, Vol. 1, p.55.
227. MacMunn and Falls, Vol. 1, p.56.
228. MacMunn and Falls, Vol. 1, p.56.
229. MacMunn and Falls, Vol. 1, p.57.
230. MacMunn and Falls, Vol. 1, pp.57–8.
231. MacMunn and Falls, Vol. 1, p.58, and Bean Vol. 2 pp.422–3.
232. 9th Bhopal Infantry and 125th Napier's Rifles.
233. MacMunn and Falls, Vol. 1, pp.58–9.
234. MacMunn and Falls, Vol. 1, p.59.
235. MacMunn and Falls, Vol. 1, pp.59 & 68.
236. MacMunn and Falls, Vol. 1, p.60.
237. Bean, Vol. 2, pp.806–7.
238. Storrs, p.200.
239. McGreal, p.64.
240. McGreal, p.64.
241. Quoted in Powell, p.214.
242. McGreal, p.66.
243. TNA MT23/403.
244. Elgood, p.170.
245. Elgood, p.170–2, & Clode, 'A Model of What a War Hospital Should Be'.
246. TNA MT23/465. There were also 10,000 beds on Mudros, 5,000 in Gallipoli, and 3,000 in Salonika.
247. Elgood, p.207.
248. Storrs, pp.200–1.
249. Mary Herbert, wife of Aubrey Herbert, ex-Irish Guards, who had been wounded and nearly blinded at Mons, but was now on Maxwell's staff. He was the second son of the Earl of Carnarvon and had been an MP pre-war, and had played an important role in Albania gaining independence. Later he would work in intelligence, including in Arabia.
250. Lady Margherita Howard de Walden, quoted in Powell, p.209.
251. *See* Powell, p.207.
252. IWM 11765, Pte William Lindsay. Letter home, August 1915.
253. Elgood, pp.198–9.
254. Elgood, p.200.
255. Walhert, p.34.
256. TNA PRO 30/57/46.
257. IWM 10440 King Edward VIII, Letter, 21 March 1916.
258. TNA PRO30/57/64.
259. Walhert, p.34.

260. Elgood, pp.216–21 and Vatikiotis, p.254.
261. IWM 9879 C.H. Rastall, Letter home, 24 July 1915.
262. Clifford, p.52.
263. IWM 87/17/1, R. Loudon.
264. TNA FO141/825/1132.
265. Elgood, p.208.
266. Vatikiotis, p.255.
267. Mitchell and Smith, p.81.
268. Mitchell and Smith, pp.202–3.
269. TNA MT23/611.
270. Holland, pp.158–9.
271. For more information, *see* Wakefield and Moody, *Under the Devil's Eye.*
272. MacMunn and Falls, Vol. 1, p.75.
273. MacMunn and Falls, Vol. 1, p.75.
274. *See*, for example, Elgood, p.227 fn. 2.
275. Elgood, p.227 fn. 1.
276. IWM 4684, F.S. Hook, Diary, 28 April 1916.
277. IWM 87/17/1 R. Loudon.
278. IWM 13222, W.R. Bowden, Letter, 30 November 1916.
279. IWM 13222, W.R. Bowden, Letter, 4 December 1916.

Chapter 6

280. Inchbald, pp.55–6.
281. Winstone, p.58.
282. Asher, p.127.
283. Winstone, pp.33–4.
284. Winstone, pp.61–3.
285. MacMunn and Falls, Vol. 1, p.53; Winstone, pp.76–6.
286. Mackay, p.28.
287. Winstone, p.78.
288. Winstone, p.78.
289. MacMunn and Falls, Vol. 1, p.53, 60 killed, 102 captured; Mackay, p.28, 86 killed, 108 captured; Winstone p.79, 70 killed, 100 captured.
290. MacMunn and Falls, Vol. 1, p.53.
291. MacMunn and Falls, Vol. 1, p.222; MacMunn, p.476.
292. MacMunn, p.476.
293. MacMunn and Falls, p.222; MacMunn, p.476.
294. MacMunn, p.477.
295. MacMunn, pp.478–9.
296. MacMunn and Falls, p.223.
297. MacMunn, p.480.
298. MacMunn and Falls, p.223.
299. MacMunn and Falls, p.223.
300. MacMunn and Falls, p.224.
301. Haythornthwaite p.123.
302. Jones, Vol. 5, p.381.

303. Jones, Vol. 5, p.382.
304. FO Handbook No. 107, p.36.
305. TNA PRO30/57/47, Wingate to FitzGerald, 18 January 1915, 24 February 1915.
306. TNA PRO30/57/47, Wingate to FitzGerald, 28 July 1915.
307. MacMunn and Falls, p.148.
308. Wingate's Despatch, *London Gazette*, 25 October 1916.
309. MacMunn and Falls, p.149.
310. MacMunn and Falls, p.149.
311. Jones, Vol. 5, pp.172–3.
312. Slessor, p.18.
313. Jones, Vol. 5, p.174.
314. Jones, Vol. 5, p.175.
315. Slessor, p.646.
316. MacMunn and Falls, p.150.
317. Slessor, p.650.
318. Jones, Vol. 5, p.176.
319. MacMunn and Falls, p.152.
320. For more information on the causes of the Arab Revolt, *see* Barr, *Setting the Desert on Fire*, and a useful summary in MacMunn and Falls, Vol. 1.
321. This meeting was handled by Ronald Storrs, and his account can be found in Storrs, pp.124–5.
322. TNA CAB42/15/15.
323. MacMunn and Falls, Vol. 1, pp.228–30.
324. Jones, Vol. 5, p.219.
325. *See*, for example, TNA WO158/625.
326. TNA CAB23/1; MacMunn and Falls, Vol. 1, pp.232–3.
327. TNA WO158/626; Jones, Vol. 5, pp.220–1.
328. MacMunn and Falls, Vol. 1, p.235.
329. Barr, *Setting the Desert on Fire*, pp.58–73.
330. Barr, *Setting the Desert on Fire*, pp.80–100; Asher, pp.196–203; MacMunn and Falls, Vol. 1, p.236; Bruce, pp.66–9.

Chapter 7

331. Hatton, p.93.
332. MacMunn and Falls, Vol. 1, pp.60–2.
333. MacMunn and Falls, Vol. 1, p.63 & pp.71–2.
334. MacMunn and Falls, Vol. 1, p.61.
335. MacMunn and Falls, Vol. 1, p.61.
336. MacMunn and Falls, Vol. 1, pp.63–4.
337. MacMunn and Falls, Vol. 1, p.71.
338. Hamlin, pp.13–4.
339. Jones, Vol. 5, p.165.
340. No. 1 AFC arrived at Tel-el-Kebir in April 1916, but due to shortages of aircraft and engines in Australia, the level of training among both air- and ground-crews was found to be insufficient and further instruction was necessary. Of thirteen pilots, eight were kept in Egypt for advanced training, and five sent to training schools in the UK. The

seven observers were also sent back to Australia, to be retrained as pilots. The 200 or so ground crew were split among the existing RFC units for six weeks intensive on-the-job training (TNA AIR1/2283/209/75/4). The squadron did not become fully active until June 1916 (Cutlack, *Australian Flying Corps*, p.35).

341. Jones, Vol. 5, pp.186–7.
342. Jones, Vol. 5, p.178.
343. Hill, p.40.
344. Orange and Stapleton, pp.5–6; Hill, pp.36–40.
345. *See* Gröschel & Ladek, 'Wings Over Sinai and Palestine'.
346. Gröschel and Ladek, 'Wings Over Sinai and Palestine'; Jones, Vol. 5, p.184.
347. Jones, Vol. 5, p.186.
348. Jones, Vol. 5, pp.185–6.
349. Bluett, p.31.
350. Bluett, p.27.
351. Bluett, p.28.
352. Wright letters, QOWH Museum.
353. *Fifth Battalion Highland Light Infantry*, p.102.
354. *Fifth Battalion Highland Light Infantry*, p.98.
355. Bluett, p.29.
356. Frederick Barter, QOWH Museum.
357. Hatton, p.95.
358. Hatton, p.95.
359. Teichman, p.47.
360. Hatton, p.96.
361. *Fifth Battalion Highland Light Infantry*, pp.113–14.
362. *Fifth Battalion Highland Light Infantry*, pp.84–5.
363. Bluett, p.53.
364. *See* Murray's Despatch of 1 June 1916, Section 3; Murray's Despatch of 28 June 1917, Appendix E; MacMunn & Falls, Vol. 1, p.93.
365. *See* Murray's Despatch of 1 March 1917, Section 4; MacMunn and Falls, Vol. 1, pp.91–2.
366. *See* Murray's Despatch of 28 June 1917, Appendix E; MacMunn and Falls, Vol. 1, p.93.
367. Elgood, p.236.
368. *See* Murray's Despatch of 28 June 1917, Appendix D.
369. Murray's Despatch of 1 June 1916, Section 3.
370. MacMunn and Falls, Vol. 1, p.96.
371. MacMunn and Falls, Vol. 1, pp.242–3.

Chapter 8

372. Most of the details on the history of the Senussi are drawn from the excellent book by McGuirk, with cross-referencing with MacMunn and Falls.
373. TNA CAB42/5/3.
374. Rolls, p.26.
375. McGuirk, pp.113–14.
376. TNA FO371/2354.
377. McGuirk, pp.131–2.
378. For more details on the captivity of the survivors from HMS *Tara*, McGuirk gives

a potted account of their activity. Captain Gwatkin-William published a vivid and moving memoir, *Prisoners of the Red Desert*.

379. McGuirk, pp.8–9 and pp.132–3.
380. TNA CAB42/5/3.
381. TNA WO95/4437.
382. MacMunn and Falls, Vol. 1, p.108.
383. McGuirk, p.148.
384. McGuirk, pp.152–3.
385. MacMunn and Falls, Vol. 1, p.107.
386. MacMunn and Falls, Vol. 1, p.108.
387. McGuirk, p.163.
388. MacMunn and Falls, Vol. 1, pp.110–1; McGuirk, pp.163–5; Maxwell's Despatch, 21 June 1916.
389. MacMunn and Falls, Vol. 1, p.113 fn. 1; McGuirk, p.171.
390. MacMunn and Falls, Vol. 1, pp.112–3; McGuirk, pp.167–72; Maxwell's Despatch, 21 June 1916.
391. MacMunn and Falls, Vol. 1, pp.113–8; McGuirk, pp.186–98; Maxwell's Despatch, 21 June 1916.
392. Bluett, p.16.
393. TNA WO95/4428.
394. Bluett, pp.17–18.
395. Maxwell's Despatch, 21 June 1916.
396. MacMunn and Falls, Vol. 1, pp.119–23; McGuirk, pp.205–12; Maxwell's Despatch, 21 June 1916.

Chapter 9

397. Maxwell's Despatch, 21 June 1916.
398. MacMunn and Falls, Vol. 1, p.124.
399. McGuirk, pp.213–8.
400. *See* Blaksley, quoted in Anglesey, Vol. 5, p.31.
401. MacMunn and Falls, Vol. 1, pp.125–9; McGuirk, pp.213–27; Maxwell's Despatch, 21 June 1916.
402. Quoted in Anglesey, Vol. 5, p.31.
403. Quoted in Maxwell's Despatch, 21 June 1916.
404. Quoted in Anglesey, Vol. 5, p.31.
405. Quoted in Maxwell's Despatch, 21 June 1916.
406. MacMunn and Falls, Vol. 1, pp.129–31.
407. Rolls, p.31.
408. MacMunn and Falls, Vol. 1, pp.131–2.
409. Rolls, p.34.
410. MacMunn and Falls, Vol. 1, pp.125–9; McGuirk, pp.213–27; Maxwell's Despatch, 21 June 1916.
411. Gwatkin-Williams, p.294.
412. Rolls, pp.47–8.
413. Gwatkin-Williams, p.297.
414. MacMunn and Falls, Vol. 1, pp.133–4; McGuirk, pp.250–8; Maxwell's Despatch, 21 June 1916.

415. MacMunn and Falls, Vol. 1, pp. 140–1.

416. Inchbald, p. 73.

417. McGuirk, p. 262.

418. TNA CAB44/14.

419. Robertson, p. 35.

420. Murray, Appendix G.

421. MacMunn and Falls, Vol. 1, Appendix 4.

422. *See* Woodward, pp. 52–63, for a very good summation of the uses and treatment of the CTC.

423. Hogue, p. 15.

Chapter 10

424. Holland, pp. 166–7.

425. TNA CAB24/2.

426. Fayle, Vol. 1, pp. 119–20.

427. TNA CAB24/2.

428. TNA MT23/498 .

429. Fayle, Vol. 2, p. 369. The rest of the meat came from: 21,000 tons from the UK, 12,700 tons from Australia, 13,000 tons from other sources.

430. TNA MT23/664.

431. TNA CAB24/15/4.

432. Fayle, Vol. 2, p. 369.

433. TNA CAB24/2.

434. Fayle, Vol. 2, p. 368.

435. In 1914 Allenby had been unable to find an appointment with the RN and so in early 1915 had retired and joined the army as a lieutenant colonel instead. He was recalled to the RN to take up this post.

436. TNA MT23/671.

437. Stoker, 'Before the Sound of Music'.

438. Halpern, *British Naval Records*, p. 5 and p. 163.

439. Terraine, *U-Boat Wars*, pp. 5–8.

440. Compton-Hall, p. 208.

441. Halpern, *Otranto Barrage*, p. 11.

442. Terraine, *U-Boat Wars*, p. 19.

443. Compton-Hall, p. 209.

444. Halpern, *Otranto Barrage*, p. 11.

445. Langenberg, 'U-Boat Ace of Aces'.

446. Compton-Hall, pp. 209–10.

447. Quoted in Hurd, Vol. 2, p. 220.

448. Edwards, *War Under the Red Ensign*, chapter 7; Hurd, Vol. II, chapter 9.

449. *See* Halpern, *Otranto Barrage*.

450. Halpern, *Royal Navy*, p. 9.

451. Halpern, *Royal Navy*, p. 66.

452. *See* Elgood, Chapter 8.

453. Burns, *Ben-My-Chree*, pp. 122–5.

454. Burns, *Ben-My-Chree*, pp. 123.

455. Quoted in Burns, *Ben-My-Chree*, p. 127.

456. Dorling, p.95.

457. Dorling, p.97. This officer was probably Captain Cunningham, who voices similar opinions and gives further details in his memoirs, *A Sailor's Odyssey*, pp.80–2.

458. Dorling, p.98.

459. Cunningham, *A Sailor's Odyssey*, p.82.

460. Halpern, *Royal Navy*, p.71.

461. Halpern, *Royal Navy*, p.72.

Chapter 11

462. *See*, for example, WO106/1570.

463. *See* TNA CAB42/5 and CAB42/6 *passim*.

464. TNA CAB42/5/12.

465. *See* for example, TNA CAB42/5/20.

466. TNA CAB42/5/3 & WO106/713.

467. TNA CAB42/6/14 & CAB42/5/20.

468. Of the others, 20,000 were in hospital, 13,000 were still being trained at the ANZAC Depot, 26,300 were attached to the Base of the MEF, and 5,000 were in 'second line' garrison battalions, unsuitable for front line duties. TNA CAB42/5/8

469. MacMunn and Falls, Vol. 1, p.98.

470. TNA CAB42/5/10 & CAB37/138/6.

471. TNA CAB42/6/8.

472. MacMunn and Falls, Vol. 1, pp.94–5.

473. TNA CAB42/5/20.

474. Some of these criticisms were based on ignorance or arrogance, and unsettling to see in one so senior. The Egyptian intelligence system, he felt, was based on 'bazaar gossip', and boasted in January that after only a few weeks in Egypt that his own intelligence staff had a better grasp of the situation than Maxwell's men did (IWM 90/1/1 ALB1/1/6 16 January 1916) Six weeks later, he was confidently dismissing local fears of an impending Ottoman attack on the Canal, stating that no attack was likely that summer (IWM 90/1/1 ALB1/1/6 28 February 1916). Eight weeks later, Kress von Kressenstein swept down on Katia and was narrowly turned back from the Canal, and twelve weeks after that he renewed the attack with a full Ottoman division. A few weeks earlier, Lynden-Bell complained that 'Maxwell is making rather an ass of himself again about this threatened invasion of Baharia', which Lyden-Bell dismissed as a force of raiders (IWM 90/1/1 ALB1/1/6 14 February 1916). This force was in fact a Senussi army, opening a new front in the Western Desert campaign to threaten the Nile Delta, and which would take over a year's campaigning to subdue.

475. IWM 90/1/1 ALB1/1/6, 16 January 1916.

476. Storrs, p.145.

477. MacMunn and Falls, Vol. 1, p.96.

478. IWM 90/1/1 ALB1/1/6, 15 March 1916.

479. Storrs, p.145 fn.

480. *Dictionary of National Biography*.

481. Murray's Despatch of 1 October 1916, Section 4.

482. Murray's Despatch of 1 October 1916, Section 4. Murray used the term 'weak' to denote that they were, in his opinion, of poor quality as fighting troops.

483. MacMunn and Falls, Vol. 1, pp.97–8.

484. MacMunn and Falls, Vol. 1, p.161.

485. MacMunn and Falls, Vol. 1, p.160.

486. MacMunn and Falls, Vol. 1, p.178.

487. Sanders, p.140.

488. *See* 605th German Machine Gun Company war diary, held by AWM but used here from the translation on the Australian Light Horse Studies Centre website.

489. Kress von Kressenstein, p.505.

490. MacMunn and Falls, Vol., 1 p.175.

491. *See*, for example, 'C', p.47; Sanders, p.140; 5th HLI, p.113.

492. As well as above, *see* Gullett, Vol. 7, pp.102–3.

493. Gullett, Vol. 7, p.110; Powles, p.98.

494. Bourne, p.30.

495. Gullett, Vol. 7, pp.104–5; MacMunn and Falls, Vol. 1, p.176 fn.

496. 605th MGC (*see* note above), entry 3 June 1916.

497. 605th MGC, entries 5 June & 1 July 1916.

498. 605th MGC, entries 10 July 1916.

499. Sanders, p.142.

500. *See* Kress von Kressenstein, pp.505–6; Djemal Pasha, p.171; Sanders, p.143.

501. Sanders, p.141.

502. Erickson, *Ordered to Die*, p.155.

503. Gullett, Vol. VII, p.141.

504. Erickson, *Ordered to Die*, p.155; MacMunn and Falls, Vol. 1, p.202.

505. Sheffy, *British Military Intelligence*, p.204.

506. MacMunn and Falls, Vol. 1, p.179.

507. MacMunn and Falls, Vol. 1, pp.180–1.

508. MacMunn and Falls, Vol. 1, p.184.

509. Gullett, Vol. 7, pp.131–2.

510. Gullett, Vol. 7, p.127.

511. MacMunn and Falls, Vol. 1, pp.181–2.

512. The permanent commander, Lieutenant Colonel Charles Cox, was on sick leave.

513. The permanent commander, Brigadier General Granville Ryrie, was an Australian MP, and had gone to London to attend the Empire Parliamentary Conference.

514. MacMunn and Falls, Vol. 1, p.183.

Chapter 12

515. AWM4/1/60/6, GHQ A&NZ Mounted Division; Bourne, p.33.

516. Bourne, p.34.

517. AWM4/1/60/6, GHQ A&NZ Mounted Division; Bourne, p.34; Gullett, Vol. VII, p.145.

518. Bourne, p.34; Gullett, Vol. VII, pp.145–7; MacMunn and Falls, Vol. 1, p.185.

519. Bourne, p.34.

520. AWM4/1/60/6, GHQ A&NZ Mounted Division; Gullett, Vol. VII, p.148.

521. AWM4/1/60/6, GHQ A&NZ Mounted Division; Gullett, Vol. VII, p.149; MacMunn and Falls, Vol. 1, p.186.

522. MacMunn and Falls, Vol. 1, p.188.

523. *Fifth Battalion Highland Light Infantry*, p.97.

524. MacMunn and Falls, Vol. 1, p.188.

525. Gullett, Vol. VII, p.150.

526. Hogue, p.42.

527. Gullet, Vol. 7, p.152.

528. MacMunn and Falls, Vol. 1, p.187.

529. MacMunn and Falls, Vol. 1, pp.186–7; AWM4/1/60/6, GHQ A&NZ Mounted Division.

530. MacMunn and Falls, Vol. 1, pp.188–9; AWM4/1/60/6, GHQ A&NZ Mounted Division; Gullett, Vol. VII, p.158.

531. Cripps, letter, 5 August 1916.

532. Gullett, Vol. VII, p.158; MacMunn and Falls, Vol. 1, p.189; Ward, *Royal Welch Fusiliers*, pp.116–17.

533. Gullett, Vol. 7, p.157.

534. Gullett, Vol. 7, p.158.

535. Anglesey, Vol. 5, p.67 fn.

536. Gullett, Vol. 7, p.157.

537. Gullett, Vol. 7, p.162.

538. Teichman, pp.78–9.

539. Gullett, Vol. 7, p.159.

540. Gullett, Vol. 7, p.161.

541. Trooper Byron Baly, quoted in Baly, p.28.

542. MacMunn and Falls, Vol. 1, pp.190–1.

543. Gullett Vol., 7, p.164.

544. Gullett Vol., 7, p.165.

545. MacMunn and Falls, Vol. 1, pp.191–2; Gullett, Vol. 7, p.175.

546. *Fifth Battalion Highland Light Infantry*, p.99.

547. *Fifth Battalion Highland Light Infantry*, p.100.

548. Gullett, Vol. 7, p.173.

549. Quoted in Baly, p.29.

550. MacMunn and Falls, Vol. 1, p.193.

551. MacMunn and Falls, Vol. 1, p.194.

552. MacMunn and Falls, Vol. 1, p.245.

553. MacMunn and Falls, Vol. 1, pp.194–8.

554. MacMunn and Falls, Vol. 1, p.245; Murray's Despatch of 1 October 1916

555. Murray's Despatch of 1 October 1916; MacMunn and Falls, Vol. 1, pp.245–6.

556. Gröschel & Ladek, 'Wings Over Sinai and Palestine', p.25.

557. Jones, Vol. 5, pp.196–8; one of the pilots, Lieutenant J.L. Bankes-Price RNAS, was killed. Gröschel and Ladek, 'Wings Over Sinai and Palestine', p.26.

558. MacMunn and Falls, Vol. 1, p.178 and pp.250–1.

559. Murray's Despatch of 1 October 1916.

560. Murray's Despatch of 1 October 1916; MacMunn and Falls, Vol. 1, pp.243–4.

561. Murray's Despatch of 1 October 1916; MacMunn and Falls, Vol. 1, pp.243–4.

562. Murray's Despatch of 1 October 1916.

Chapter 13

563. Briscoe Moore, pp.45–7.

564. Bluett, p.69.

565. *Fifth Battalion Highland Light Infantry*, p.122.

566. *Fifth Battalion Highland Light Infantry*, pp.125–6.

567. Bluett, pp.72–5.

568. Godrich, p.83.

569. *Fifth Battalion Highland Light Infantry*, p.124.

570. Gullett, Vol. 7, p.208.

571. MacMunn and Falls, Vol. 1, p.251; Ottoman troop numbers from Sheffy, *British Military Intelligence*, p.205.

572. Sheffy, *British Military Intelligence*, p.206.

573. Quoted in Gullett, Vol. 7, p.209.

574. Orange & Stapleton, p.13; Gröschel & Ladek, 'Wings Over Sinai and Palestine', p.29.

575. Gullett, Vol. 7, p.216.

576. In the Australian *Official History*, Gullett numbers these redoubts on the northern bank No. 2 (on the western flank) and No. 3 (on the eastern flank), and those on the southern bank No. 1 (in the west), No. 5 (in the centre) and No. 4 (in the east). In the British *Official History*, MacMunn and Falls number the redoubts on the northern bank No. 1 (on the western flank) and No. 5 (on the eastern flank) and those on the southern bank No. 2 (in the west), No. 3 (in the centre) and No. 4 (in the east). I have used the British designations, mainly because the map in MacMunn and Falls is much clearer and is the one that I have been using.

577. MacMunn and Falls, Vol. 1, pp.253–4; Gullett, Vol. 7, p.217.

578. MacMunn and Falls, Vol. 1, pp.253–4; Gullett, Vol. 7, pp.218–9.

579. MacMunn and Falls, Vol. 1, pp.254–5; Gullett, Vol. 7, p.219.

580. Powles, p.125; MacMunn and Falls, Vol. 1, pp.255–6.

581. Gullett, Vol. 7, p.221.

582. MacMunn and Falls, Vol. 1, p.256; Gullett, Vol. 7, pp.220–1.

583. MacMunn and Falls, Vol. 1, pp.256–7; Gullett, Vol. 7, pp.221–6.

584. Gullett, Vol. 7, p.226.

585. Hamilton, *Riders of Destiny*, p.14.

586. Powles, p.127.

587. Anglesey, Vol. 5, p.85.

588. Gullett, Vol. 7, p.227.

589. Gullett, Vol. 7, p.230.

590. MacMunn and Falls, Vol. 1, pp.262–3; Gullett Vol. 7 p.230.

591. MacMunn and Falls, Vol. 1, p.263.

592. MacMunn and Falls, Vol. 1, p.264.

593. MacMunn and Falls, Vol. 1, p.264.

594. MacMunn and Falls, Vol. 1, pp.264–5; Gullett, Vol. 7, p.232.

595. Powles, p.132.

596. Gullett, Vol. 7, p.232.

597. Powles, p.132.

598. MacMunn and Falls, Vol. 1, p.265.

599. Jones, Vol. 5, p.203.

600. Powles, p.136.

601. MacMunn and Falls, Vol. 1, p.271.

602. MacMunn and Falls, Vol. 1, p.267; Gullett, Vol. 7, pp.235–6.

603. MacMunn and Falls, Vol. 1, p.267.

604. Gullett, Vol. 7, p.239.

605. Cripps, letter 9 January 1917.

606. 'C', pp.79–80.

607. MacMunn and Falls, Vol. 1, p.269.

608. Teichman, pp.103–4.

609. Hamilton, *Riders of Destiny*, p.18.

Epilogue

610. From 11,656,038 tons (2,736 ships) in 1915 to 6,164,201 tons (1,647 ships) in 1917. In 1918 it would rise again to 7,356,371 tons (1,862 ships). Including non-British shipping, the wartime totals were:

  1913: 20,033,884 tons, 5,085 ships
  1914: 19,409,495 tons, 4,802 ships
  1915: 15,266,155 tons, 3,708 ships
  1916: 12,325,347 tons, 3,110 ships
  1917: 8,368,918 tons, 2,353 ships
  1918: 9,251,601 tons, 1,862 ships
  1919: 16,013,802 tons, 3,986 ships
  Schonfield, *The Suez Canal*, p.168.

Appendix B

611. For more on this issue, see Mason, chapters 15–17.

Appendix E

612. de Robeck's Chief of Staff at the time of the establishment of these raiding parties was Commander Roger Keyes. In 1940–41, as Admiral of the Fleet Sir Roger Keyes, he would be the Director of Combined Operations, in charge of raising and deploying commandoes in raids against the coast of occupied Europe.

613. TNA ADM137/1199.

614. Terraine, *Business in Great Waters*, p.290.

615. The Italians carried out similar raids on the Anatolian coast. Terraine, *Business in Great Waters*, p.292.

616. Halpern, *Royal Navy in the Mediterranean*, Document 76.

617. Halpern, *Royal Navy in the Mediterranean*, Document 76.

618. TNA ADM137/364, and Terraine, *Business in Great Waters*, p.290.

619. TNA ADM137/545.

620. Later Sir John Linton Myres OBE.

621. Myres, *Blackbeard of the Aegean*, pp.14–16.

622. Myres, *Blackbeard of the Aegean*, pp.15–16.

623. TNA ADM137/364.

624. Myres, *Blackbeard of the Aegean*, Appendix 3.

625. TNA ADM137/365.

626. Myres, *Blackbeard of the Aegean*, p.21.

627. Myres, *Blackbeard of the Aegean*, Appendix 2.

628. TNA ADM137/366.

629. Halpern, *Royal Navy in the Mediterranean*, Document 76.

630. Myres, *Blackbeard of the Aegean*, Appendix 6.

631. Myres, *Blackbeard of the Aegean*, Appendix 6.

632. Myres, *Blackbeard of the Aegean*, p.20.

633. Myres, *Blackbeard of the Aegean*, Appendix 6.

634. Myres, *Blackbeard of the Aegean*, Appendix 5.

635. TNA AD137/366.

636. TNA 137/366. Also *see* Terraine, *Business in Great Waters*, pp.292–3.

637. Dorling, p.96.

638. TNA ADM137/365.

639. Myres, *Blackbeard of the Aegean*, p.22.

640. von Sanders, *Five Years*, p.123.

641. von Sanders, *Five Years*, pp.117–20.

642. von Sanders, *Five Years*, p.148.

643. Terraine, *Business in Great Waters*, pp.291–3.

644. Terraine, *Business in Great Waters*, p.293.

645. TNA ADM137/357. As Terraine points out (*Business in Great Waters*, p.293) it is quite disturbing to speculate on what that particular 'etc' encompassed.

646. Halpern, *Royal Navy in the Mediterranean*, Document 145.

Appendix J

647. Elgood, p.181 fn.

648. Jones, *The Road to En-Dor*.

649. Also *see* Hill, *The Spook and the Commandant*.

650. QOWH(Y)M, Letters of Lieutenant George Wright.

651. Letter in *Kedos Gazette*, April 1918.

652. QOWH(Y)M, Diary of Lieutenant Arthur Holyoake.

653. Bishop, *A Kut Prisoner*.

654. Elgood, p.181 fn.

INDEX